MW00651910

OUTDOOR LIFE

TIM MACWELCH
AND THE EDITORS OF OUTDOOR LIFE

ULTIMATE SURVIVAL HACKS

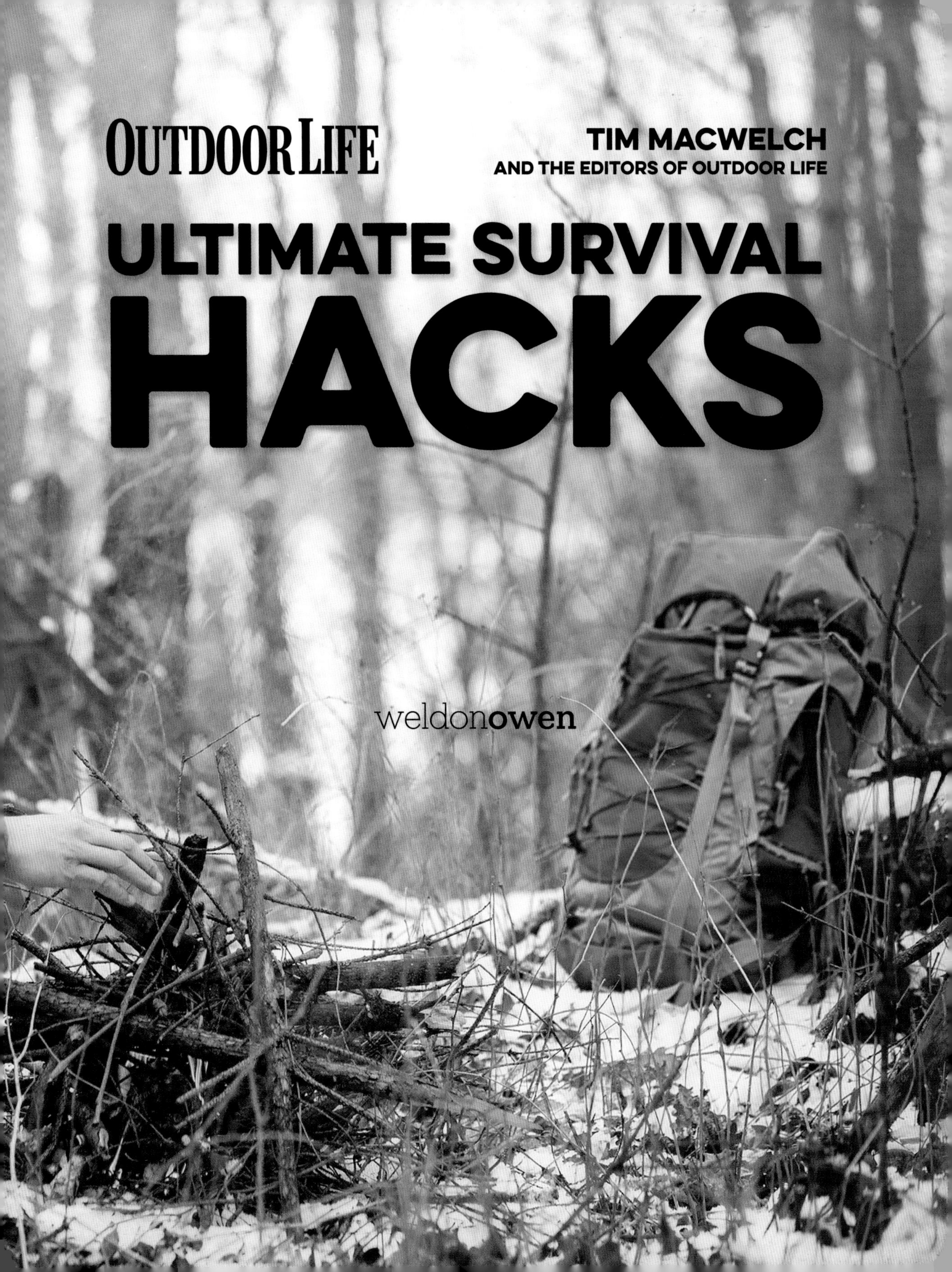

OUTDOOR LIFE

TIM MACWELCH
AND THE EDITORS OF OUTDOOR LIFE

ULTIMATE SURVIVAL HACKS

weldonowen

CONTENTS

DISASTER

CONTENTS

CONTENTS

OUTDOOR LIFE
HOW TO SURVIVE ANYTHING
FROM ANIMAL ATTACKS TO THE END OF THE WORLD
TIM MACWELCH

THE WORD "HACK" CAN HAVE MANY MEANINGS IN OUR MODERN LANGUAGE.

You might hack your way through a thicket—intellectual or vegetative. You might cry out "I've been hacked!" when someone gains unauthorized access to your computer and makes unwelcome changes to your online property. Or you might perform a "life hack," accomplishing a task with an unexpected tool or technique. As you've already guessed, it's the latter meaning we have used as the inspiration for this book.

A survival hack, as we're defining it, is a creative way to accomplish an emergency task or self-reliance chore by turning the things you have into the things you need. And if there ever was an arena when hacks really mattered, it is the realm of survival and self-reliance.

In this book, we'll look at three settings where these improvisations would be particularly valuable. First, we'll take a look at hacks you'd use in some all-too-common disaster scenarios. Natural disasters are the most likely threats that the average person would face, and these events frequently cut off supplies, causing us to fend for ourselves for a time. Our second arena is the wilderness. Getting lost or hurt in the great outdoors can plunge a person into a wilderness survival scenario, forcing you to make what you need from the land. And for the final section of this manual, anything goes! From daily dilemmas to rare and bizarre situations, this section will prepare you for events outside the scope of wilderness survival and disaster preparedness (in fact, we've nicknamed it the Mad Max chapter). So, embrace that hallmark of humanity—your natural creativity—and enjoy this book!

DISASTER

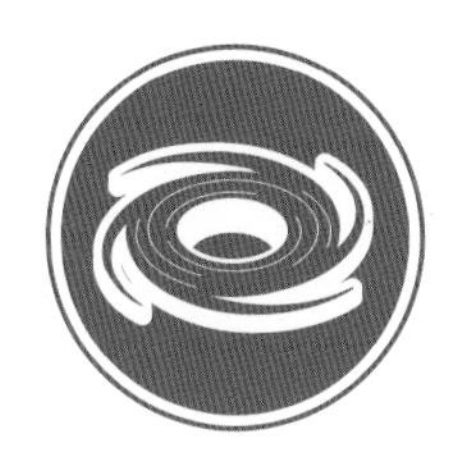

HURRICANES, VOLCANOES, EARTHQUAKES, FIRES, AND FLOODS HAVE BEEN THE STUFF OF NIGHTMARES THROUGHOUT HUMAN HISTORY. THEY STILL ARE.

And now, in addition to the host of natural disasters, we have to face the possibility of human-made disasters (like acts of terrorism and nuclear-power plant meltdowns). A disaster can be defined as any accident, event, or catastrophe that happens quickly and causes great damage or loss of life. And it's far more likely that you'll be caught in a disaster at some point in your lifetime than that you'll have to face any other situation in this book. But don't let that freak you out.

Disasters happen, and preparedness is the key to surviving them. When you become an active participant in your own survival, your attitude improves—and so do your chances! So stock up on supplies, develop a plan, and learn at least a few of the of the following hacks. And while we hope you never need them, we do also hope that you will add them to your survival "toolkit."

01 PRIORITIZE PROBLEMS

When any kind of emergency situation arises, how do you decide what to do first? Survival instructors around the globe have illustrated our vulnerabilities through something called the "Rule of Threes." This is a basic framework for understanding the necessities of survival. The rule states that you have:

3 MINUTES TO LIVE WITHOUT AIR
3 HOURS TO LIVE WITHOUT SHELTER*
3 DAYS TO LIVE WITHOUT WATER
3 WEEKS TO LIVE WITHOUT FOOD

**in extreme environments*

This simple and memorable list can be an effective tool to help you focus and prioritize during many of the scary situations you might find yourself having to deal with. But unfortunately, this "rule" doesn't cover absolutely everything. Where does heat stroke fall in this sequence? How about being attacked by a wild animal—or even a homicidal human being? A nice, simple rule rarely addresses every scenario, only the very basics.

There's a simpler way to keep your priorities in order: Tackle the worst problems first. Determine the greatest threat you face, and deal with it. Then turn to handle the next most threatening element, and so on. Soon, you'll have all of the threats in check, and you'll be able to move onto the other aspects of survival (such as signaling for help or getting to a safer area). Be rigorous in ranking those threats. Even though you might be hungry, shelter and water are more important than food.

02 MAKE FIRST AID YOUR FIRST PRIORITY

If you're in a tough situation with no injured parties, you should count yourself lucky. When something bad happens, medical skills and supplies may be the very first things you need (rather than shelter). Sure, the cold air could kill you in a few hours, but someone with a severe wound can bleed out in a matter of minutes without effective medical care. In a case like this, you'll need to deal with major injuries right away, with all the first-aid skills and supplies you can muster. Get some hands-on first aid training and carry a med kit. You'll almost certainly use any medical skills you learn at some point in your lifetime.

03 SEEK SHELTER RIGHT AWAY

Since the deep cold can kill in hours and intense heat can kill in a day, shelter is your first survival priority when no one has life threatening injuries or illnesses. Throughout this book you'll see many methods to enhance a shelter you may already have (like your home or vehicle) , and even a few ways to create your own shelter from available materials. Just make sure you have a backup plan for shelter, where ever you go. A small lightweight poncho and a space blanket can fit in your purse, pack, or pocket—and provide you with lifesaving shelter, wherever you may roam.

04 GET WATER AND FOOD

Normally, we say "food and water," assigning an unreasonably high importance to eating. But let's face facts: Even though most people are used to three square meals a day and plenty of snacks, we need water a lot more than we need food. In particularly hot dry and windy conditions, the desiccating breeze can cause death from dehydration in less than three days if no water is available. But as soon as you secure both shelter and a water source, the pressure for survival shifts to food. This is the long game. In extended emergencies, the daily quest for food can quickly become your all-consuming task. Hope you're not picky!

05 DEFEND LIKE YOUR LIFE DEPENDS ON IT

Let's go back to our "Rule of Threes" for a moment. What if I suggested that there's another "three" you could add to the list, one that may only give you three seconds to live? It's a self-defense situation. For many of us, it's a lot more disturbing to consider fighting off an attacker than it is to imagine dealing with an injury or a hostile environment. But unfortunately, any one of us may find ourselves facing an adversary, with only seconds to react correctly. And whether you are facing man or beast, your quick response could mean survival. Being able to defend yourself from the most likely adversaries and being able to act quickly (rather than being frozen in fear) are critical parts of preparedness.

MENTAL HACK // **THE OODA LOOP**

This concept was developed U.S. Air Force Colonel John Boyd, a military strategist in the 1960s. The Colonel built this tool to assist in the planning and thought processes behind certain military operations and to create more intelligent reactions during changing situations. Here's where it gets really interesting: You've already been using this decision making cycle your whole life. OODA stands for: Observe, Orient, Decide, and Act.

Of course, there's much more to OODA than that. There are cycles within cycles and repeating loops with feedback opportunities. But this basic concept of a simplified and rapid OODA loop can help us to survive. Here's an example in a wilderness setting. You stop to observe that your hands are turning blue and you're shivering. Now, you can orient yourself using your experience and knowledge. This lets you decide whether it makes more sense to build a shelter or a fire (shelter is usually the better answer). Then, act on that decision. By taking the time to understand what we are doing and why we are doing it, we can make smarter choices, in survival and in life.

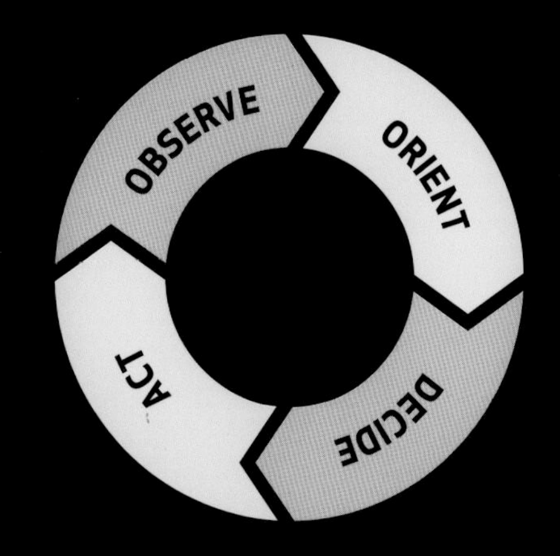

06 PREPARE FOR DISASTER

If you live in an area that is prone to natural disasters, then I don't have to convince you how important it is to be prepared. You already know that disasters come in all sizes and types, with and without warning, and you know what it's like to have your normal way of life disrupted by conditions that are completely out of your control. And whether you're exposed to hurricanes and tornadoes or endangered by earthquakes and flooding, you know that there are numerous conditions that can cut off your utilities, limit mobility, close schools, and prevent your local stores from restocking their shelves. In the modern world, disasters may also be man-made. Acts of war and terrorism, industrial accidents, train car derailments, arson-sparked wildfires, and nuclear power plant meltdowns are just a few of the threats we may find ourselves facing. So, what does all this mean to you and your loved ones? It means that you might be on your own for a while. Maybe a good long while, if the disaster is particularly severe. And in that setting, you'll have to be able to provide for yourself and your family. You'll need to have your own "store" that you can visit for sustenance. That's why we build disaster readiness kits.

07 GRAB THE GEAR

A great model for disaster planning is to emulate the provisions in an old-fashioned general store; these places carried a little bit of everything. Create a diversified kit in one or several waterproof bins, filled with the things you'd absolutely need (and a few things you'd just want).

CANNED GOODS Choose high calorie foods, preferably those than can be eaten straight from the can. Meaty stews, hearty soups, chili, and pasta dishes are all good choices. Don't forget to add a hand-cranked can opener!

DRY GOODS If you have a way to cook when the power's out (like a camp stove), dry goods are cheap and they last a long time. Dry pasta is the highest calorie dry staple, and you only need boiling water to prepare it. Rice, beans, oats, powdered milk, flour, sugar, corn meal, and hard candy are also additions to the "dry goods" department. A small, lightweight metal pot could be added to the kit, just in case you have to grab your supplies and leave home in a hurry.

DRINKS Hot cocoa, tea, coffee, and various instant beverages (like lemonade mix) are an important source of calories, hydration, and morale.

WATER Most relief agencies recommend having 3 gallons (11.5 L) of water per person in your emergency supplies in case your water supply is cut off. I would also recommend a water filter or at least some disinfection tablets, as your budget allows.

LIGHTING Fresh batteries and flashlights will be needed during power outages. Some candles wouldn't hurt as a backup either, but non-flame lighting is a much safer choice. You don't need to add a house fire to your list of problems during a crisis.

FIRST AID SUPPLIES Cuts and burns are common injuries in the best of times. Keep burn cream and trauma dressings on hand (as well as band aids and other supplies) in case you can't get to a doctor, and help cannot make it to your location.

HYGIENE ITEMS Your emergency shelter can get pretty smelly. Keep abundant supplies of bathroom products handy, along with disinfectants and an emergency bucket "toilet" with a tight-fitting lid.

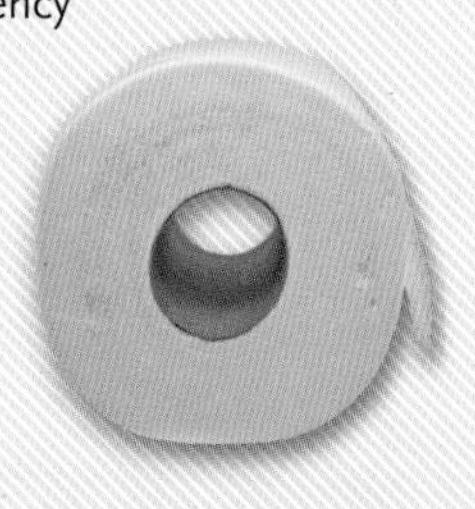

08 ADD THE UNEXPECTED

You can't really expect the unexpected – that violates the definition of unexpected. But you can add the unexpected to your disaster readiness kit. Here are a few off-the-wall items that could prove invaluable in a crisis.

- □ A battery-powered or hand-cranked radio, with NOAA weather bands. This will keep you in the loop of the events and possible dangers around you.
- □ A utility shut-off wrench, if you have gas or municipal water.
- □ Mobile phone chargers, either solar or battery-powered.
- □ Morale boosters. Chocolate, cookies, and similar treats are good calorie sources, and good at lifting spirits. Activity books, crayons and coloring books, or a new board game can be a sanity saver for the parents of active children.
- □ Dust masks can help filter contaminated air. Plastic sheeting and duct tape can seal off doors and windows if you must shelter in place.
- □ Local and regional maps can be crucial should you need to evacuate using alternative routes without GPS access or working phone.
- □ Copies of vital documents (like deeds, identification, insurance and certificates) on a thumb drive or some other discrete storage. These can help you get your life back on track when it's all over.
- □ An inventory of home possessions can be very handy for insurance purposes. Include photos (or even a video) of the interior and exterior of your home, including all personal belongings.
- □ Cash money will allow you to make purchases when cards aren't working due to communication breakdowns.
- □ Baby formula, diapers, wipes, and medicine are a big deal for families with little ones.

HACK HAZARDS

IMPROPER STORAGE

I'll never forget how nasty the "black bin" looked and smelled. I had filled a plastic bin with dry goods like oatmeal and pasta, plus a few plastic jugs of water. I put it in an out-of-the-way spot and largely forgot about it. A few months later, I was checking our emergency supplies and remembered the bin. I cracked open the lid and looked inside. My reaction was one of puzzlement, since I couldn't recall filling a bin with black fur. Then the moldy smell hit me, and I made out the vague shapes of food packages under the blanket of ebony hairs. The friendly Quaker Oats guy looked more like an angry Blackbeard the pirate. It turned out that one of the water jugs had leaked, turning my bin of supplies into a mold farm. Lesson learned. After that, I never again stored any wet and dry goods together. Improper storage practices like this can ruin your supplies, wasting time and money. Make sure you store each item under the best available conditions. Keep wet and dry separate. Keep foods cool, dry and dark. Set traps for rodents. Don't dump loose batteries in to a bag or box (the terminals can touch and discharge). Store it right, and your supplies will survive —and hopefully you will too.

09 CREATE AN EMERGENCY PLAN

Now that you've built a disaster readiness kit, you need an emergency plan. In the event of a crisis, a well-thought-out family emergency plan can eliminate stress, limit confusion, and save a great deal of time. Instead of wasting precious minutes wondering what to do or when to do it, you can put your emergency plan to work right away, bringing sanity and safety to dangerous situations. Your family's emergency plan should encompass the following.

- ☐ Maintaining up-to-date contact information cards or sheets for each family member
- ☐ Communication strategies for keeping in touch, with options in case the phones are out
- ☐ Ways to assist or care for anyone with mobility or medical issues, communication difficulties, or special needs.
- ☐ The maintenance, inspection, and rotation of emergency supplies, such as non-perishable food, water, first aid, lighting, and communication equipment
- ☐ The maintenance of specialized supplies for any infants, young children, or elderly in your family
- ☐ A plan and supplies for the care of pets and livestock
- ☐ The knowledge and tools to shut off your utilities
- ☐ Self-sufficiency skills and supplies, should you have to shelter in place without utilities
- ☐ Evacuation plans and routes, should you have to leave your home
- ☐ Learning and practicing safety skills, such as first aid, CPR, and fire prevention

10 PLAN WISELY

One important part of planning for emergencies is determining which disasters are most likely to affect your household. The most common group is natural disasters, which affect hundreds of thousands of people every year worldwide. You probably don't have to worry much about hurricanes in the Midwest or blizzards in the Caribbean. Many disasters are predictable events, but others, unfortunately, can hit us by complete surprise.

Common natural disasters can include tornadoes, hurricanes, severe thunderstorms, wild fires, winter storms, earthquakes, and extreme heat. Extreme heat and drought have killed more people in the U.S. since 1970 than any other natural disaster, though they were followed closely by fatalities from flooding and severe thunderstorms. The threat of technological disasters (such as nuclear power plant meltdowns and toxic chemical spills) has increased as well. And finally, the threat of a disaster spawned from terrorism has caused many people to take emergency preparedness into their own hands.

11 PUT ACTION IN YOUR PLAN

Counting water bottles and inspecting batteries aren't the only things you'll want to do for emergency planning. You and your family will need to be prepared to act—especially on short notice. Get every family member involved!

GET THE LAY OF THE LAND Draw a map of your home and every potential escape route.

PLAN A MEETING PLACE Determine a meeting place near your home, if your family needs to rally outside of the house.

GO FURTHER ABROAD Pick a meeting place outside of your neighborhood, to be used if you cannot return home or are told to evacuate.

LOOK AT THE ROUTES Decide which route you'd take to get to meeting places, plus an alternate route in case the first is unusable.

CHOOSE A CONTACT Pick a contact person outside of your immediate area who could relay messages if your household is separated or unable to communicate with each other.

12 MARK YOUR CALENDAR

Even though many foods and supplies in your disaster kit will remain usable well after the expiration date printed on the label, it's still smart to set up calendar dates to restock and review your kit. Twice each year, or better yet, once each season, mark a date on your calendar to open up your kits and supplies to inspect the contents. Ideally, you should remove short-lived items and replace them with fresh ones. These supplies don't have to be wasted. Your disaster kit should be full of things you normally use. This gear check is an opportunity to check for leaks, pests, and other problems. It's also a chance to reassess the supplies you have chosen and the amounts you have procured. Maybe you need something different, or you simply need more.

13 DRILL FOR SUCCESS

Mark some dates on your calendar to perform emergency drills with your family. They may not want to participate, but find a way to get them involved nevertheless. Here are some emergency drills that can keep a family's skills sharp.

DISTANT CONTACT ▼ Have each family member contact a friend or relative who lives outside your area, without using a cell phone or landline phone. This could be done through email, social media, satellite phone, ham radio or even a carrier pigeon. Get creative!

SUPPLY SHAKEDOWN ▶ Pull out all of your emergency supplies, take inventory, check expiration dates, use up older items, replace them with new supplies, and make sure you end up with a few more items stashed away each time you do this.

FIRE DRILL ▲ Start with a classic fire drill, in which you practice evacuating the home on short notice. Make sure you have a planned meeting place outside the home, and have everyone low crawl out of the house when you sound the alarm. For more advanced drills, eliminate the easy exits and add some obstacles. Also, round out the exercise with some stop, drop and roll, every time you have a fire drill.

EVAC DRILL ▼ Take the fire drill one step further with a mock evacuation. Announce that everyone has 2 minutes to grab some clothes and supplies and get to the family vehicle.

14 PREPARE FOR A HURRICANE

Hurricanes are a major force for destruction. Knowing when and how to prepare is crucial everywhere in hurricane country.

BE AWARE Hurricanes start out as tropical thunderstorms; when they build until they form an area of low pressure with rotation, they are far more powerful than any local summer squall. These massive tropical storms officially become hurricanes when the sustained winds reach a speed of 74 mph (119 kph), and that's just the beginning. During hurricane (or cyclone) season, it's important for you to stay alert to the watches, warnings and advisories in your region.

BE PREPARED You'll want to have supplies and resources ready to go. Prep your vehicles by keeping a full tank of gas and basic emergency supplies (like a first aid kit, food, water, tools, jumper cables, and such). Stash flashlights in practical places throughout the house, in case of a nighttime power failure. Make sure you have propane to use your grill for cooking (outside only, and after the storm, please). Get everything in place to hunker down for a few days, and be prepared to flee with your family and pets if evacuation orders are given.

15 DRAW A BATH

When a hurricane is predicted to make landfall in your area, your water supply may be affected. Prepare by filling up the bathtub with cold water. Plug the drain with a stopper and cover it with several pieces of duct tape, whether it tends to leak or not. Then fill the tub until the water reaches the overflow (that metallic disc near the top of the tub). Regardless of whether you have your own well in a rural area or if you are on a municipal supply, there's no guarantee that the water will keep flowing during and after a hurricane. But with a bathtub full of water, you now have a backup for toilet flushing, cleaning, cooking (if it will reach boiling temperatures during food prep), and even for drinking (after disinfecting it, of course). Sure, bathtub water is less than appetizing, particularly from a nasty-looking tub. But it's far more pure than the flood waters out there after a storm, which may be your only alternative without a glorious bath basin filled with H_2O.

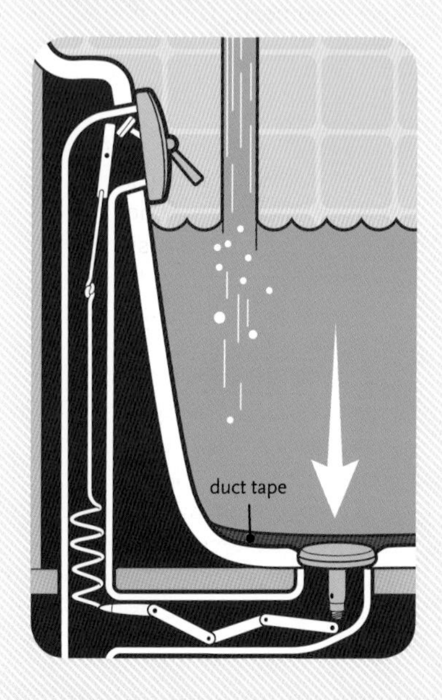

16 BOARD IT UP

If you live in an area prone to massive storms, and shutters aren't an option, you can pre-cut pieces of sturdy plywood to cover your windows and doors. Your windows may not all be exactly the same shape, so cut each piece to fit a specific window and use a system of numbers and letters to make installation easier. For example, the front three windows of your home could be F1, F2 and F3, going from left to right. The left side could be "L", the back of the home could be "B," and so on. Use long wood screws to affix the plywood to the wall framing around doors and windows—don't just screw the plywood to the decorative trim on the surface (which can tear off).

17 PROTECT YOUR STUFF

Paper documents, family photos, your giant flat screen TV—these are just a few of the precious items you'll want to protect from the storm. If you must ride out the storm where you are, consider these two strategies.

BACK IT UP First, keep a backup copy of everything important at a secure location in another area (except for the electronics, naturally), such as a trusted family member or a safe deposit box at a bank. If this isn't practical or you don't feel comfortable with sensitive information in two places, then your second choice is to use some part of your home as a "storm vault," If your home has an attic, you already have a high and dry spot.

BE CREATIVE If you don't have an attic, a high shelf in a closet on an upper level may do the trick. For a storm that could tear your roof off, make your "safe spot" on a middle floor of a multi-level home. Bag your papers, photos, discs, and thumb drives inside multiple layers of plastic bags, add a weighty item to each bag, and squeeze out the air before sealing, so the bags are less likely to float away should the water rise above your safe spot.

Worth Every Penny

STORM SHUTTERS

It's common before a hurricane to see people covering their windows with large "X"s made of tape in the hope of stopping the window from shattering. Thing is, debris thrown by hurricane force winds can still penetrate the window and cause the glass pane to explode. So, if you're looking for a better way to protect a home or business, take a page out of the past and have functional shutters installed on the windows. These wooden or metal barriers are a long-lasting investment in the safety of your property (metal shutters also offer greater home security). It also doesn't hurt to move prospective projectiles out of the storm's reach. Store all yard items (like furniture, toys, garbage cans, bird feeders, and other stuff that could become storm-thrown missiles) in a garage or shed for safety.

Quick Tip

Remember that Category 5 hurricane that's supposed to tear the roof off your house? It's no joke. Most people love their homes and all of the things inside, especially if they've lived there for many years. But that house shouldn't become a tomb. Evacuate when the authorities direct you. The lives you save may be your own or those of the first responders trying to rescue stubborn holdouts.

18 SOAK UP THE SUN

A power outage during cold weather can leave a modern residence very cold; hypothermia is a real threat to your safety, especially in subfreezing outdoor temperatures. Once the storm clouds have passed you can take advantage of sunlight for partial home heating. An off-grid home-heating solar array on your roof would be a great idea, but you can still get a warming effect with smart use of the assets that you already have. Take advantage of passive solar heat during daylight hours by staying in a room with south-facing windows, or better yet, a southern room with lots of windows in the Northern Hemisphere (pick a northern room if you're below the equator). Lay out dark-colored blankets and rugs to absorb the heat from the sunlight. The more light you have pouring through the windows, and the more dark colors you place in the light, the more heat you will have. Stay in that sunny room for warmth, and then take steps to keep some of the heat inside the room when night falls.

19 HANG UP BLANKETS

The sun can warm up a room on a bright day, and you can use appropriate heaters (such as kerosene and propane heaters designed for indoor use) at night or when it's cloudy. But even with excellent insulation, your warmed-up room will still lose heat at night. Windows are the greatest source of heat loss, but a home's walls, ceiling, and floor also shed heat. Thankfully, spare blankets or thick drapes (or other improvised insulation) can be hung over your windows to insulate you and block the chill after sundown. You can also hang blankets over openings that don't have a door, to better hold in heat. You can even hang blankets from low ceilings to reduce the size of a room, thereby reducing the size of the space you need to heat. And whether your heat comes primarily from sunlight or some other method, your blankets and drapes will keep out the cold—just what you need when an emergency leaves you chilled.

20 CAMP IN THE CAR

A vehicle can certainly provide you with basic shelter, if you find yourself stuck somewhere without better accommodations—but camping out like this can be dangerous. For starters, it's common for folks to run the engine for heat in cold weather. That can help you (while the fuel holds out), but it can also kill you. If the tailpipe happens to be blocked by snow, mud, dirt, sand, or any other obstruction, carbon monoxide can back up into the vehicle cabin.

Another hazard when sheltering in vehicles is the cold. Few cars or trucks offer any serious insulation, and the metal body and frame make it feel even colder inside than it should be, conducting away what little body heat passengers are generating.

And then in summer, cars can get dangerously hot. So what's the solution? Stuff your car with insulation for warmth in cold climates and relax in the shade under the car in hot ones. Your insulation could be almost anything, as long as it provides dead air space. Leaves, grass, and pine needles, along with crumpled paper and bubble wrap, will all do their part to keep you warm (or you could just carry some sleeping bags in the car).

21 LIMIT YOUR RISKS

Dangers increase when the power goes out. Follow these tips to stay safe in an outage.

PICK ONE ROOM Use a smaller room with a low ceiling to be your main living area during the power outage. Don't try to make every room warm and comfortable again.

STAY VENTILATED You risk carbon monoxide poisoning if you use an outdoor propane cooker, a gas grill, or your gas kitchen stove for heat. Even a kerosene heater needs to have some fresh air to operate safely.

AVOID CANDLES If you use enough candles to warm up a room, you have a serious fire hazard. After all, candles start house fires all the time. If you must use candles, limit when and how many, and make sure you have a working smoke alarm.

22 TRY STICKS AND STONES

It is possible to heat your dwelling with fire without risking carbon monoxide poisoning. The trick? Keep the fire outside, and only bring the heat in. Burn sticks, wood, or ugly furniture to heat up bricks or rocks, which can be used as portable radiant heaters.

STEP 1 Set up a heatproof platform in the room you intend to warm up. A 2-foot (0.4-m) square of bricks placed on the floor will work fine. Then, get some rocks to heat up, or a few bricks. Either way, be sure they're dry.

STEP 2 Light up the grill or build a fire outside, and throw the rocks or bricks into the coals to heat up. Let them soak up heat for about 45 minutes, then scoop them out with a shovel. Use the shovel to scrape off any and all coals and sparks.

STEP 3 Drop your rocks or bricks into a stainless steel cooking pot (other types of metal pots may be damaged by the heat, and galvanized metal containers can release some toxic vapors at these high temperatures).

STEP 4 Carefully bring the pot inside and set it on your fireproof, heatproof platform. Let the heat warm the area, and repeat as needed every few hours.

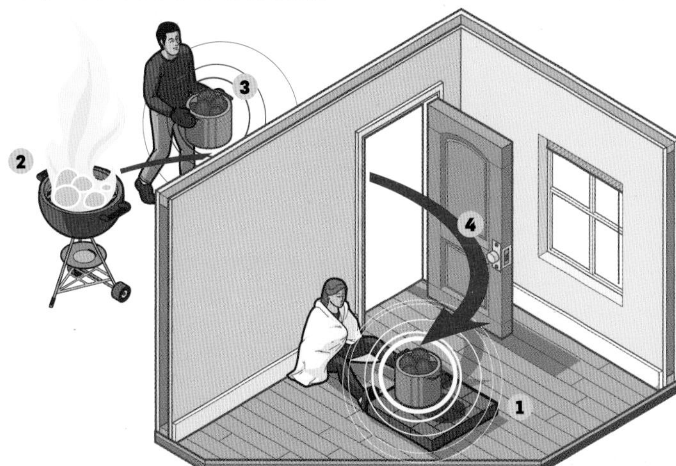

HACK HAZARDS

CARBON MONOXIDE

Every winter, inventive but unwise people kill themselves by accident, along with their families, during power outages in cold weather. They drag the family's barbecue grill into the living room and fire it up to provide heat. Everything works out great, for a while. But as the fire dies down, the lower flames start to produce carbon monoxide. This deadly gas can take the place of oxygen in your blood—in fact, the hemoglobin in your red blood cells can absorb it more than 200 times more readily and rapidly than oxygen—making you sleepy, and then suffocating you and your loved ones while you snooze. To avoid such a tragedy, only use heating products indoors if they are designed for indoor use. Ideally, the device should have some kind of low oxygen shutoff mechanism. And either way, you'll need to crack a window somewhere to allow air flow (you won't want to, because you're already cold, but you must.) Never use combustion for heat without adequate ventilation; carbon monoxide is colorless, odorless, and deadly. When buying smoke alarms for your home, make sure you buy at least one that also has a carbon monoxide detector, and replace its batteries regularly.

23 DELIVER A BABY

Expectant mothers may go into labor at the most inopportune moment, like in the middle of a disaster. When this happens, and EMS can't reach you, those moms-to-be may need your help.

STEP 1 Stay calm and assess the situation. Call emergency services (if you can) and prepare for delivery. If the mother's contractions are 2 minutes apart or less, delivery is imminent. If labor goes on longer, help the mother fight stress (A) and alleviate back pain (B) as needed.

STEP 2 Thoroughly wash your hands and arms, and be sure the birthing area is clean and covered in sheets or towels. If you have a delivery kit in your disaster medical supplies, get it out.

STEP 3 Get the mother comfortable, and let her find a position for delivery (see suggestions below). Reclining is traditional but not the most effective position; instead, have her squat (C) whileholding onto the back of a chair or sit on a chair (D) with most of her rear hanging off. Place soft pillows on the floor under her, should the baby emerge quickly or slip from your grasp.

STEP 4 When the baby's head is showing, gently cup and support it as it emerges. If the umbilical cord is around the neck or head, gently slip it off. Don't pull the baby out; just catch them—they'll be very slippery!

STEP 5 Gently wrap the baby in a towel and clean them off (this also stimulates the baby to breathe if they haven't already (spanking only works in movies). You can also use a suction bulb to clear the baby's mouth and nostrils. Have mom lay down (if she was using the chair), give the baby to the mother to hold (skin contact is good), and keep them both warm.

STEP 6 Wait for the placenta to be delivered 15 to 30 minutes later. You can gently encourage it by massaging the mother's lower abdomen in slow circles. Don't pull the cord or placenta; once delivered, check to see see if it is fully intact (if not, the mother may experience more bleeding and need additional medical care). Your delivery kit may also include a bag to carry the placenta to a doctor. Get medical care for mom and baby, if it's available.

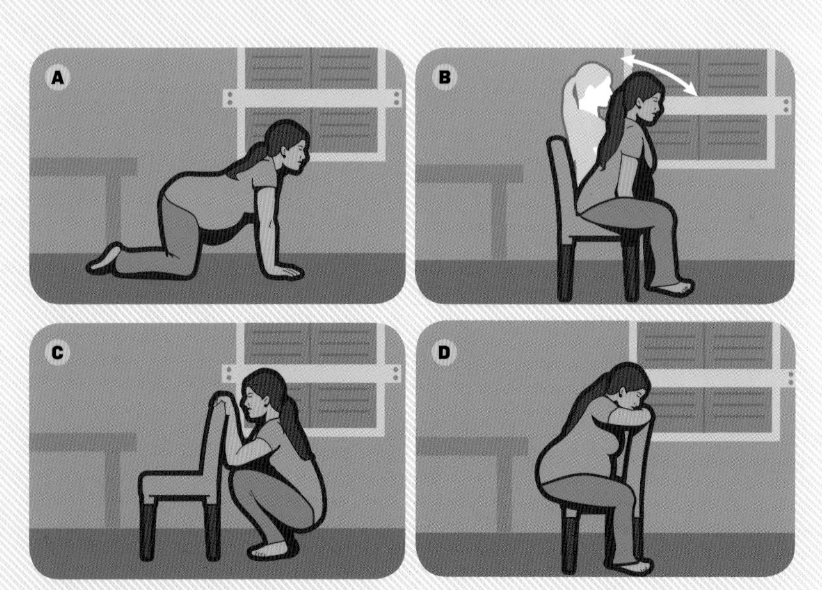

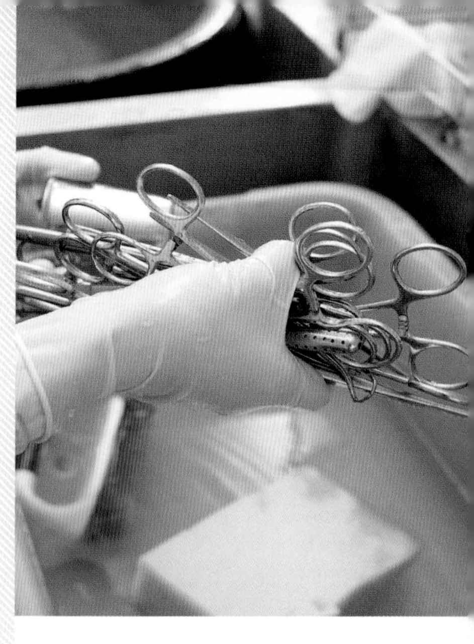

24 USE BOOZE

Since the earliest brewers learned to distill, alcohol has caused many problems for humanity. People have been poisoned by strong alcoholic concoctions, damaging their bodies beyond healing. People have made awful decisions, resulting in maiming or death. And mean drunks have treated others in the most inhumane ways imaginable under the influence of potent booze. But that same fire water has helped people too. Distilled spirits have cleaned wounds, dulled pain, prevented infection, and disinfected water, tools, and surfaces. Used respectfully and in moderation, liquor is a useful asset. And since we're in a section on emergency medicine, it's only fitting that we talk about the use of liquor to disinfect medical tools. Scalpels, forceps, and a host of other metallic medical tools can be effectively disinfected by laying them in a pan of high-proof alcohol for several minutes—no autoclave or cauldron of boiling water is needed. And while you wouldn't want to drink that liquor after it had a fistful of bloody tools soaking in it, you could still use it for something like lighting a fire.

25 STOP BLEEDING BAREHANDED

A hemorrhage can be a deadly medical emergency, killing in mere minutes. With a quick application of the proper bleeding control techniques, however, it's possible to stop further blood loss and potentially save a life. Sure, a proper trauma dressing would be a great piece of medical material to apply to the wound, but here are two other ways to go.

TRY DIRECT PRESSURE This instinctive response is often the right one. When medical supplies are absent, use your bare hand or a piece of cloth to apply heavy pressure to the wound. It's best if there is a dressing over the wound, one that can be constricted such as an Israeli bandage, but don't delay treatment by rummaging around for something. It's also helpful to elevate the wound, if it's on a limb.

USE PRESSURE POINTS This technique is always used as a supplement to direct pressure and it does require some education in human anatomy. For limb wounds, learn where the femoral arteries and brachial arteries run (through the groin and the inside center of the upper arms, respectively). You'll also want to learn how much pressure to apply—squeeze hard, like crimping off a garden hose!

26 CREATE A POWER BALL

When flat direct pressure over the wound is not enough, you may have to use wound packing techniques to staunch the flow of blood. Basic wound packing involves the forceful insertion of gauze into the open wound. It's going to be messy, and yes, if the patient is conscious they will probably scream, but it's this or ratcheting down a tourniquet (and that's not an option for torso injuries). For larger wounds, such as the exit wound from a large caliber gunshot, use an EMT trick called the "power ball" to stop bleeding. Wrap up the end of a gauze roll to create a ball of cotton, then jam it down into the wound. Follow the power ball by inserting all of the gauze that the cavity will hold. Again, this an aggressive and invasive act, but it can compress tissues near the wound and squeeze off severed veins and arteries. Finish by applying another flat dressing over the surface of the wound and find more advanced medical care for your patient.

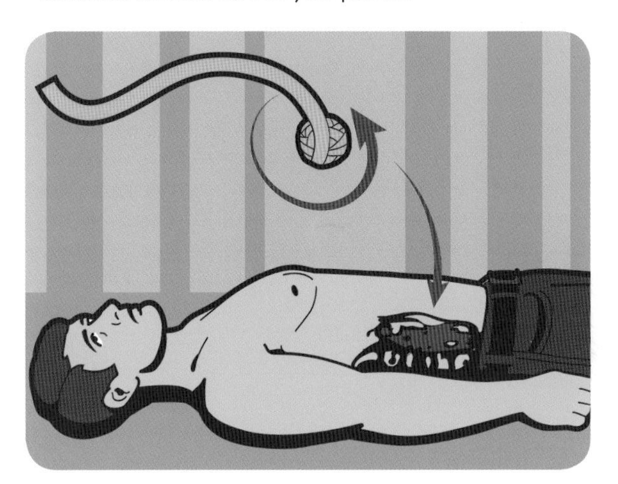

27 REHYDRATE WITH POPSICLES

Kids often run around dehydrated, as most of us do. In hot weather or due to illness, children may become dangerously dehydrated, complaining of a headache and other symptoms. You've probably heard the saying that you can lead a horse to water, but you can't make him drink. The same can be said of children: they may not want to drink, or their small stomachs may stage a revolt, causing the child to vomit up the beverage they were given.

If you have a working freezer in your emergency location (or sub-freezing conditions outdoors), you can bring out the popsicles as our colorful hydration heroes. These cold treats work around two common problems: a refusal to take fluids, and a tendency to gulp them down. What kid can resist a sickly sweet, unnaturally colored frozen treat? And since you can't guzzle them down like a sports drink, popsicles slowly deliver water and sugar to those in need (kid or adult). Make your own popsicles with Kool Aid, water, and freezing air temps during winter emergencies. Keep your generator and freezer running for frosty treats during troubles in warmer weather.

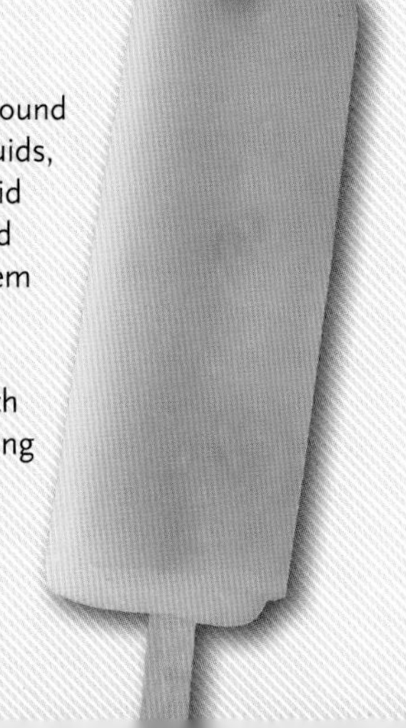

HACK HAZARDS

DENTAL DISASTERS

Ever tried extracting your own tooth (or someone else's) with a pair of pliers or a multitool? Well, don't! Pulling a tooth without the proper training and tools is the stuff of legend and movies. Unless you have advanced gum disease and your teeth are falling out of their own accord, leave them there. Extraction requires training, experience, the right tools, and a clean setting—I doubt you'll have any of those in the wake of a disaster. Pulling baby teeth by tying a string around the tooth and giving a pull is easy. Those teeth are made to come out. You might even be able to pull a healthy tooth with a great set of pliers and a few minutes wiggling it to break the connective tissues. But a rotten, splintered, infected tooth that you're thinking of pulling is likely to be even more rotten, splintered, and infected by trying this method. Find a dentist—you'll be glad you did.

Quick Tip

You can safely add a little sugar or rehydration salts to water for proctoclysis, but alcohol and other substances can be dangerous as they directly hit the bloodstream. The light buzz of a normal drink could be fatal.

28 USE THE BACK DOOR TO HYDRATION

This is an . . . unusual technique, but it might also save a life or two. Let me set the scene: You're on a remote backpacking trip with a couple of friends, several days walk from civilization. One of your pals slips and cracks their skull on a rock. They're unconscious. Your healthy friend goes for help while you stay with your buddy. Days pass and your friend does not wake up. Remember the Rule of Threes? Three days without water can kill. But you can't pour water down an unconscious person's throat—they'll drown. You don't have any idea how to give intravenous fluids, nor do you have an IV kit. How do you save your friend from dying of dehydration if they can't wake up to drink? The answer lies with your trusty hydration bladder, and what you're about to do with it is a procedure called proctoclysis. This procedure does not require any medical training or specialized equipment, and it can be used for several reasons: If someone can't stop vomiting and can't keep any liquid down; if they've sustained trauma to the mouth or throat and cannot take fluids by mouth; or if they are in shock and lost consciousness from dehydration—tube 'em.

STEP 1 Muster your courage and cut off the mouthpiece from a hydration bladder hose.

STEP 2 Beg pardon of your comatose patient and insert the tube into their bottom as they lie there. Use tape or your hand to hold a short length of the tube in place, then press their buttocks together to maintain a better seal.

STEP 3 Hang up the hydration bladder for a slow gravity feed (don't squeeze the bag), and administer at least two quarts (2 L) of water a day. Only about one in four patients react adversely and reject the procedure by voiding their bowel contents during this action, so the odds are in your favor here!

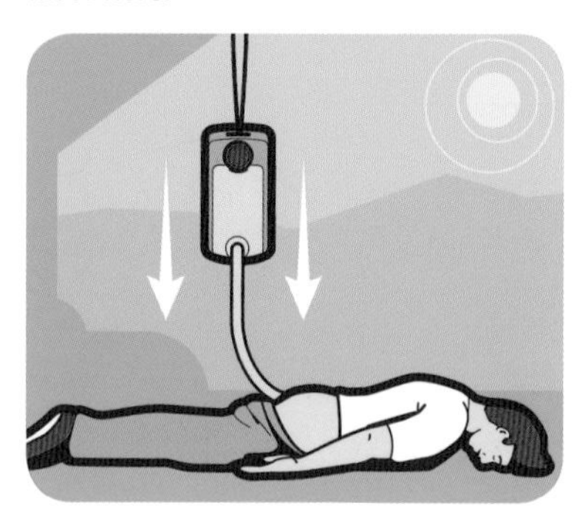

29 BRING TAMPONS TO THE RESCUE (SORT OF)

Plenty of people (men included) carry tampons in their first aid supplies. You could be a true hero to a lady in need someday., and these cottony wonders have many other uses. Plenty of people in the tactical community recommend tampons as an effective plug for puncture wounds and gunshot wounds.

Unfortunately, tampons are designed to soak up a small volume of blood, not control a hemorrhage. And while they do expand to fill smaller wound cavities (like a stab from a knife), they don't usually have enough mass to plug the void caused by the pressure wave of a gunshot wound.Tampons may come apart during removal. Most medics agree that the bleed you're facing now takes priority over an infection that you may or may not face later, but they'll also agree that wound-packing with proper materials will beat an improvised dressing every time.

30 PERFORM OLD-SCHOOL SURGERY

During the American Civil War, field hospitals had limited equipment compared to hospitals of the day, and amputation was often used for traumatic injury on a limb. Although the modern perception is that these doctors were heartless fiends and ignorant butchers, this is a false stereotype. Roughly 70% of the soldiers treated on each side of the conflict were suffering from injury to the limbs. The huge soft-lead ammunition they were firing would commonly flatten out upon impact and cause damage that we don't see in today's gunshot wounds. Nearly severing limbs on their own, these gunshots left little choice for the field surgeons. Today, in austere settings (far away from modern medical care), it's possible that you might face a situation where amputation is warranted. Should the time arise, don't undertake this grisly work unless you're sure you can follow through to the end.

STEP 1 After determining that the limb must go (due to massive trauma or gangrene), assemble a group of people to hold the patient down or find a way to strap them to a table (and you will still need at least one more person to help). Apply a tourniquet high and tight on the limb to be taken. Mark the path you will cut around the limb with a marker, and disinfect the skin with iodine.

STEP 2 With the sharpest and most disinfected blade you have, cut to the bone around the limb. If bleeding appears to squirt in pulses, tighten the tourniquet further. Now pull the cut tissue toward the torso, causing the bone to be exposed (you'll need help with this).

STEP 3 Using the cleanest and sharpest saw you have, cut through the bone. Saw close to the tissue that will remain, so that a bone will be covered by tissue when you release the leg or arm muscles. Do your best to tie off visible blood vessels with suture material (if you have it), though many blood vessels will retract upon cutting and be hidden. Bind the wound with sterile dressings.

STEP 4 Starting one hour after the amputation, release the tourniquet a little at a time until you can remove it without major bleeding. Change the dressing as needed (once or twice daily). Understand that this procedure might kill your failing patient, but keep in mind also the success rate of Civil War doctors. Even though no one knew anything about the importance of sterile conditions, more than 70% of lower leg and arm amputees survived the procedure!

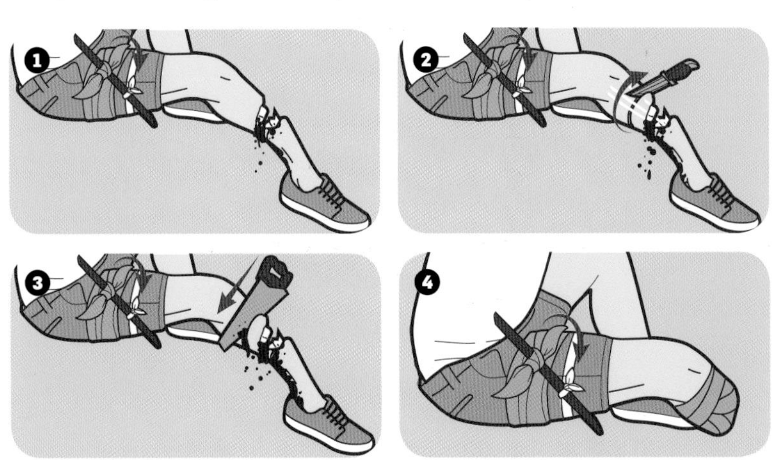

BUDGET SURVIVAL

FREE MEDICAL TRAINING

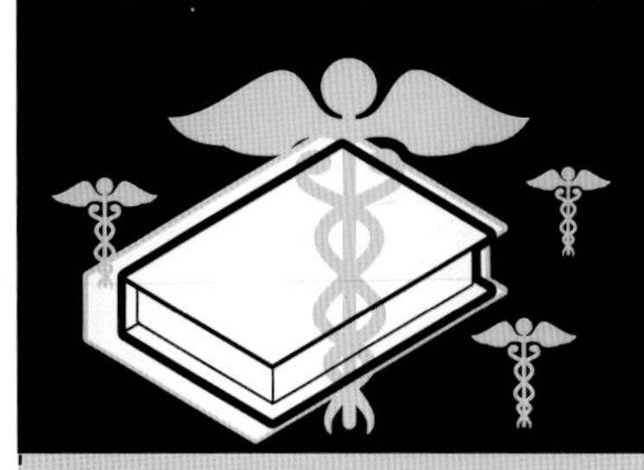

If you're willing to work hard and be a beneficial member of your community, you'll get more than just a pat on the back from your buddies. Your local rescue squad or CERT (Community Emergency Response Team) is probably looking for a few good team members, and most of these organizations provide excellent medical training for free. Of course, it's your civic duty to honor the intent of the training and serve the community for some period of time (not just take free training and run away). And once you're out there helping your neighbors in need, you're getting real world training that can never be simulated in a classroom. Serve the people and get some great training.

Worth Every Penny

BETADINE

This potent iodine solution is a little pricey, but it's also an excellent disinfectant for many different types of wounds and injuries. Carry some in your kit, as one more useful medical tool.

31 PACK YOUR GEAR

Planning which items to put in a med kit is a lot like planning a bug-out bag. Ask a hundred different people and you'll get a hundred lists, with plenty of similarities and a few major differences. What follows is a general list of supplies that the average person could use, with very little training. But do keep in mind that a mountain of medical supplies won't help you if you don't know what to do. Even though it may seem like a daunting task to learn emergency medical skills, it's not. Anyone can learn to perform lifesaving skills. So, get these supplies and the training to go with them! First aid is the most likely "survival" skill you'll ever use.

PROTECTION

- ☐ Non-latex gloves
- ☐ Glasses and N95 or better masks
- ☐ Disinfectants such as Lysol spray and hand sanitizer
- ☐ Antiseptic wipes

MEDICAL SUPPLIES

- ☐ 4x4 inch nonstick gauze pads and 8x10 inch trauma pads
- ☐ QuikClot ACS (clotting sponges), Israeli dressings, and CAT tourniquets
- ☐ Triangle bandages, several sizes of gauze rolls, and medical tape
- ☐ Assorted flexible fabric bandages (band-aids) for small cuts, scrapes, and scratches
- ☐ Dry ACE bandages and metal clips
- ☐ Tweezers and EMT shears
- ☐ Eye pads and eyewash bottles
- ☐ Space blankets

MEDICINES

- ☐ Burn gels, tubes of antibiotic ointment, and anti-itch cream
- ☐ Dextromethorphan and Guiafenesin as cough medicines (the latter also works as an expectorant)
- ☐ Pain-relieving medications such as aspirin (also good for thinning the blood), acetaminophen (which can be used to lower fevers too), and ibuprofen (which also brings down inflammation)
- ☐ Anti-allergy medications such as Benadryl or Sudafed; epinephrine pens for life-threatening allergic reactions
- ☐ Antibiotics, including Doxycycline (for unknown origin fevers and skin infections), Azithromycin (aka Zithromax or Z-pak, for major infections including pneumonia), Cipro, Keflex, and Augmentin
- ☐ Antacids, laxatives, and anti-diarrheal medications (the last is especially important since diarrhea can be a common companion after a disaster)
- ☐ Prescription pain killers as options for when OTC analgesics aren't able to reduce pain enough
- ☐ Any other OTC medicines that your family regularly uses

32 ADD THESE EXTRAS

The usual gauze, ointment, and bandages certainly belong in your disaster medical kit, but there are plenty of other items that may save the day—items you may not expect. Here are some key things to consider.

LIGHTING Everyone forgets about a light source, until someone gets hurt after dark. I like to keep an LED headlamp in the top of each of my med kits. This way, whichever kit I grab, I can strap the light around my head and have hands-free lighting while providing first aid. And don't forget to pack spare batteries in an easy-to-find spot, in case your light runs out of power.

VITAL MONITORING You can learn a lot about your patient by taking their temperature and pulse, as well as listening to their chest. Add a blood-pressure cuff, stethoscope, and two old-school thermometers (non-electronic) to your kit. If your budget isn't tight, you could also add a pulse oximeter. This small device clamps onto a finger and can give you great insight into someone's lung function.

DENTAL SUPPLIES Teeth are the gateway into the body, and when you have a problem with your chompers, you can't get away from it. Add a dental module to your disaster kit, containing a dental pain reliever, temporary filling material, floss, and basic dental tools (like a mirror and an explorer). Your pain reliever could be oil of cloves, benzocaine gel, or Eugenol extract.

BOOKS A good disaster medicine book can provide direction when professional medical care isn't available. You'll need a guidebook on prescription meds. Several publishers put out pocket guides for nurses and doctors, updated each year, to remind medical professionals of the right prescription and dosage for various illnesses and injuries, along with alternate medicines. You'll also need a book on emergency medical techniques, such as *The Survival Medicine Handbook* by Dr. Joseph and Amy Alton.

33 KEEP IT HANDY

While you can't control what happens during a disaster or which hardships and injuries you'll have to endure, you can control the gear you buy and where that gear is located. Keep your gear handy, even if that means building a modular system. Sure, it'll cost you twice as much to have a complete kit both at home and in your vehicle. But here's another price tag to consider. What is your life worth, in dollars, or that of your family? When you consider how much you value your family and even your friends, it's a no-brainer. Spend the money. Keep a bad-ass medical kit at home in an easy to reach spot, like the top shelf of the hall closet or some other cool, dry, dark spot. And keep an equally epic kit in your vehicle. The kit at your house won't help you one little bit, if mayhem catches you miles from home.

Worth Every Penny

EMS RESCUE KNIFE

More than just a folding blade, a rescue knife includes a strap cutter and glass-breaking tool—and some have even more features useful for rescuing and aiding folks in a disaster.

DUCT TAPE

1 ARCTIC SUNGLASSES ▲
This stylish eyewear is based on eye protection worn in the Arctic. The narrow slits restrict the amount of damaging UV light that your eyes receive from sunlight bouncing off the snow, and it's enough protection to prevent snow blindness. Simply measure around your head (where a blindfold would go), peel off a strip of tape twice as long, and fold it in half. Adhere the sticky sides together, leaving a small bit of sticky tape exposed at the end to stick the goggles together. Lay the tape against a hard surface, cut two narrow slits for your eye holes, and you're done. In the absence of other protection, you can also use tape on your nose and cheeks to prevent sunburn and offer protection from windburn or frostbite.

2 TINDER Need something to help you start a fire in wet weather, or you're just running low on tinder? A crumpled ball of duct tape will burn for a minute or two when lit with an open flame. Duct tape responds best to the flame of a lighter or match. The secret to its flammability lies with several of the materials that go into this wondrous product. It's typically made from a cotton mesh, coated with a polyethylene resin on one side, and sticky rubber-based adhesive on the other. Now, guess which ones will burn? The answer: All three!

3 CHEST SEAL A gunshot wound or stab to the torso can create a tension pneumothorax, also known as a sucking chest wound, as air fills up the chest, but outside the lung. As soon as this traumatic injury is diagnosed, it's critical to seal the entrance wound (and exit wound, if there is one), otherwise the air entering the chest cavity will collapse the lung. Since duct tape sticks to bloody skin and it makes an airtight seal, it can be a quick fix for this life-threating complication to a major injury.

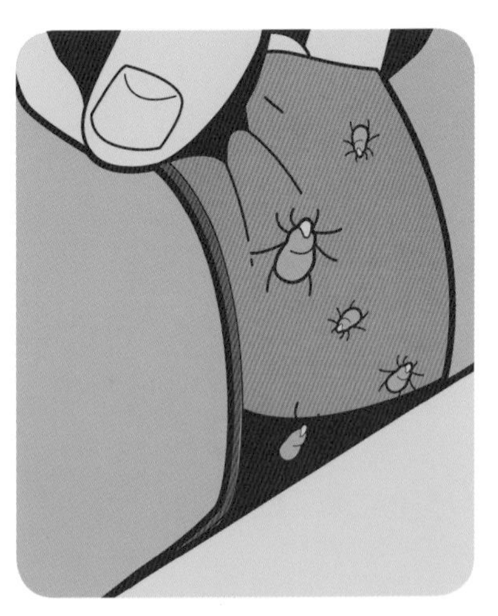

4 TICK REMOVER ▲ Depending on the species, an expectant momma tick may lay an egg mass with as many as 4,000 eggs in one spot. When these hatch in warmer weather, this "pocket" of tick larvae can be like a land mine for outdoor adventurers. As soon as you step in the wrong spot, you may have dozens or even hundreds of baby ticks climbing up your foot and leg. The easiest way to remove these unwelcomed hitchhikers from skin and clothing is duct tape. Just peel off a strip, and press is repeatedly on the affected area to remove the tiny ticks. Be very thorough in your tick removal; With certain tick species, even these hatchlings can carry diseases.

5 ROPE Even cheap duct tape has a lot of strength, but by twisting the tape, you add even more muscle to it. For best results, twist it as you peel it off the roll and use a continuous strip of tape for your entire rope. Splices will be weak spots! Military-grade tape has a 40-pound (18-kg) breaking strength while the strength of less expensive tapes is in the 20-pound (9-kg) range.

6 WOUND CLOSURE You can make your own butterfly bandage strips by cutting small rectangular pieces of tape, and adding a smaller bit in the center (sticky side to sticky side). Use several of these strips to close long lacerations and a few to close smaller cuts. Make sure you stick these strips to clean skin and leave them in place for several days. You may tear open a healing wound by peeling these strips off prematurely.

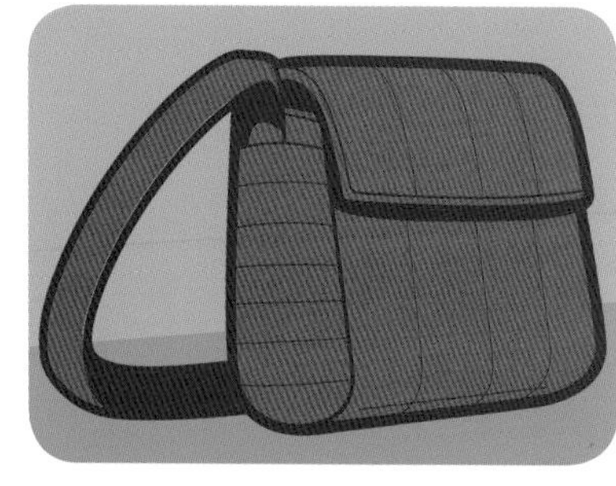

7 POUCHES AND BAGS ▲ Since duct tape is so flexible and it sticks to itself so well, it's easy to form it into a multitude of shapes. From shoulder bags and pouches, to water bags and other containers, duct tape is really only limited by your imagination. Make a foraging bag to carry your meal back to camp, or a water bucket. When stuck together completely, duct tape holds water out or in, as needed.

8 TRAIL MARKERS ▲ Reflective or brightly colored duct tape is a great material to blaze a trail through the wild or mark a clandestine route through urban and suburban areas. Tear off little pieces and stick them to trees, rocks, signs, or structures so you can easily find your way back or lead others to follow your footsteps. Make your sticky signs easier to spot by keeping them all at the same height (like eye level) or in predictable spots (bottom right corner of signs in urban settings). Add a permanent marker to the mix, and you can draw arrows or other symbols, or write words.

34 PLAN FOR A QUAKE

In at least one respect, earthquakes are just like every other natural disaster: There's nothing you can do to stop them. Where and when they happen is completely out of your control, as is the severity of the event. What you can do, however, is prepare for them. Californians have been bracing for "the big one" for decades, but people in many other parts of the world are dangerously underprepared for the threat. Earthquakes can happen anywhere and anytime, without any warning at all. By being prepared for this particular disaster, you're taking an active role in your family's survival and you'll know what to do as soon as you feel the quake. Expect them, prepare for them, and persevere. You may also find out that being prepared for earthquakes will leave you more prepared for almost every other type of disaster.

35 GET THE RIGHT TOOL

If water runs out of your cracked walls, or you smell gas after a quake, your pipes are broken, you need to stop these utilities with a shutoff wrench. It should be made from non-sparking metal, for safety when turning off LP and natural gas (the shut off should be at your outdoor gas meter). These tools also have a wrench for the valve that is your municipal water shutoff (usually located under a round metal cover by the street). You'll only need to turn this off if the water main valve inside your home fails to turn off and you have a burst pipe; or if the burst pipe is between the street and your home's main shutoff valve inside.

36 SEEK THE TRIANGLE

Where do you go if you're indoors during an earthquake? Many disaster search-and-rescue professionals advise us to seek the "triangle of life." This controversial concept involves the triangular voids that solid objects create in earthquake debris. Imagine what would happen when a ceiling collapses on some earthquake victims. Those who hunker down next to sturdy objects such as heavy desks and couches are often saved, because the objects take the brunt of the weight from collapsing building materials. Being under the desktop may seem like a more logical hiding place, but it's actually more dangerous under there, and even possibly deadly: Flimsy furniture can become a lethal deadfall trap when the weight of debris is added on top of it. It's safer to be beside the desk, because even if the furniture is completely crushed, the ceiling will still be partially supported by the desk. And if you're lucky, you'll be crouched in a triangular void near the desk—with enough room to breathe. Cover your mouth and nose with cloth, and hang in there until rescue arrives. Call out or knock so they know where you are.

37 USE A VEHICLE FOR SAFETY

If you're driving during a minor earthquake, you may not even feel it due to the vibrations of the vehicle and the road. But if it's a big quake, you'll know it. The first thing to do is to stop driving if you are in a relatively safe spot (not on a bridge or under an overpass). If possible, pull over in an area where nothing can fall on your car (such as light poles, bridges, or overpasses). The more open the area, the safer it is. If you're stuck under an overpass, get out of your car and lie flat beside it. Should the structure collapse, it will crush your car, but usually not all the way to the ground. The car's frame and body may leave a safe zone immediately surrounding the vehicle. Once the earthquake has stopped, be aware that there may be aftershocks, so stay on guard. Listen to the vehicle radio for updates that may affect your route to safety.

38 WATCH FOR FALLING OBJECTS

Unless the ground opens up and swallows you whole, it's usually not the earthquake itself that harms you—it's falling objects and collapsing buildings that injure and kill people.

AVOID GLASS Windows and other glass used in homes and businesses can break unexpectedly during a quake, and these broken pieces can be deadly if they fall on you or you fall onto them. Understand that the triangle of life doesn't work if you're outside, hunkering against an exterior wall on a home or business. Because the debris from windows, walls and roofs will fall straight down, the area of highest risk is directly outside these buildings.

LEAVE THE TREES Shaken by their very roots, trees commonly lose heavy branches or fall during strong earthquakes. If you can't flee the forest when this disaster hits, run for shorter trees; there will be fewer and smaller branches overhead. If you can't get out of the woods, lie next to a fallen log bigger that you. Branches and tree trunks may hit the log instead of you. Try to lie on the uphill side of the log, as the quake may make it roll downhill.

DODGE POWER LINES Utility poles are engineered to handle a lot of stress, but they can only stand so much. Fallen power lines can electrify the ground for some distance. And whether they are sparking or are lying still, avoid them like the plague. Power lines can electrify damp ground for a great distance.

HACK HAZARDS

AVOID UNDER THE BED

Every kid knows how to hide under a bed when they get scared, and plenty of people fall back on this—even in adulthood. Unfortunately, the small space underneath a bed will be made even smaller if the ceiling collapses on it. Never get under it, and teach your children never to crawl under the bed in an earthquake. Instead, if an earthquake should happen to wake you from your sleep, simply roll off the bed, and then stay near its edge. If the quake is strong enough to cause damage, the bed will be able to hold up some of the debris, thus creating a safe void around its perimeter. To make sure that children and other family members won't hide under the bed in earthquake zones, you can use that space for storage and fill it up. Whether you pack your disaster supplies under the bed, or just bins of clothing and bedding, the space is best left occupied.

Quick Tip

Lots of furnishings in your home (and their contents) can become dangerous falling objects in a quake. Take some time to secure bookshelves, televisions, and other large items with safety straps.

39 BE THE BURGLAR

If your home is really your castle, you should be able to defend it like one. And this "castle" mentality can start by identifying the weakest points. This is a great exercise in home security, for good times and bad. You don't need a crisis to spur this task into action. Imagine that you're the burglar, trying to find the easiest entry points into the home. Walk around your home during daylight hours, and also at night. How would you get inside the house quietly? How could you enter if noise didn't matter? That flimsy back door with the burned-out light above it might as well be a welcome mat for burglars, home invaders, marauders, and all other ne'er-do-wells. Use a critical eye to find the weak points in your armor, and your home will be one step closer to the castle it should be.

40 PUT ON A SHOW

A great way to avoid being looted is to look like you've already been looted. Board up a first floor window completely, and source some broken window pane glass from somewhere else. Carefully distribute the glass under the boarded up window (wearing thick gloves), and now it looks like your home has been breached! Continue the charade by leaving other signs of a break in. Scratch up the paint around the lock on your front door. Rip down a window blind on a first floor window, and mess up the room that the window looks into. Flip over the furniture in that room and make a mess, to give it that ransacked look. For a finishing touch, haphazardly fling some clothes and belongings around the yard and the scene will be set! Whether you're leaving the home for a safer location (the best choice) or hunkering down, robbers will naturally assume that all the "good stuff" in that house is gone and pass on by.

41 FORTIFY WITH WOOD BLOCKS

You should certainly keep all windows and doors locked (including garage doors), if you are concerned with looting and robbery. Sturdy doors and top notch deadbolt locks are a wise investment for your home. But if find yourself trying to secure a home after a calamity hits, you're likely to have plenty of raw materials in the wreckage. Scavenged blocks of wood and longer pieces of lumber can help to secure doors and windows with surprising efficacy.

For doors that swing inward, nailing or screwing a block of wood to the floor will make it much harder to break down the door, especially if you keep it locked. Screwing a block diagonally at the upper corner of the door will help too. You can also wedge a long board in the track of sliding doors to keep them closed tight. Windows can be secured with blocks that are screwed into place to prevent the lower section from being raised. Again, these measures you can take after the fact, and you should always opt for proper locking mechanisms such as deadbolts, but these tricks are better than nothing.

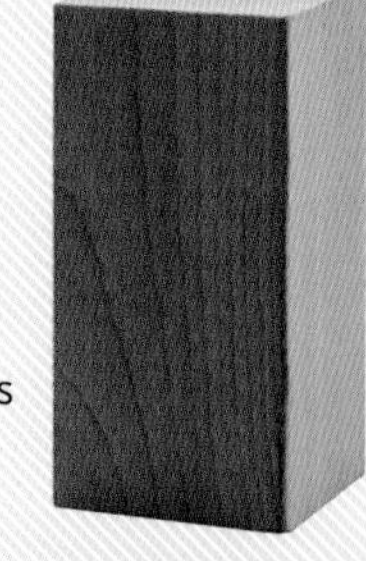

42 FAKE A WALL SOCKET

While it's usually the best policy to keep your wad of cash and fistful of gold in a secure location (like a bank account or a bank lockbox, respectively), you may need these commodities during a crisis, and the bank may be locked up tight. One crafty place to hide a small cash stash is a dummy wall receptacle. Buy an "old work" electrical box, an electrical receptacle, and a cover plate at your local home improvement store. At the height of other receptacles and on a wall with no wires inside, trace the outside of the box with a pencil and cut out the rectangular hole in your drywall. Insert the box and use a screwdriver to tighten the tabs that hold it in place. Stick your loot in the box, cover it with the receptacle and screw that down. Finish with the cover plate and you're done! For best results, buy the same color and style of receptacle and cover plate used throughout the home, and don't brag to people about your cool new "wall safe." As a matter of fact, never discuss your valuables with anyone outside your closest trusted circle of family and friends.

43 DISCOURAGE CREEPERS

Generous lighting around your home will make the dwelling a less appealing target to thieves that prefer to skulk around in darkness. And while the light show won't discourage every bad guy, it's worth the trouble if it chases away even one bad guy. Lighting can be simple or complex, as your budget allows. You could have motion-activated lights installed around the exterior of your house, or simply leave on a few lights inside the home when you're out of the house. There are, however, a few catches that come with lighting, and those are the complications that occur when a disaster has knocked out the power. If your lighting was dependent on the electric grid, it's gone. And if your lighting is self-reliant (whether powered by batteries or generator), then people will be drawn to your lights like moths to the flame. You may not want that kind of attention, so you'll have to consider the pros and cons quite seriously.

44 PLAN IT OUT

After a crisis, you won't be in a position to build a compound, block walls or guard towers; but you can make the area you're in more secure and more defensible.

DECIDE WHAT TO DEFEND
Basically, you are marking the boundaries of your protected area. Consider the role existing walls, waterways, buildings, and fences can play in your defense.

ESTABLISH ENTRY AND EXIT
This may mean blocking off a driveway or street with derelict vehicles (if things are really that bad). If vehicles are operational, several could be parked to create a "gate" to keep out other vehicles.

UPGRADE EXISTING STRUCTURES This can be anything from locking gates in fences to boarding up windows and doors around the perimeter. Look at your perimeter from the outside, try to figure out ways in, and do your best to seal them off.

45 BUILD A DIY SAFE ROOM

If your budget is unlimited, you could opt for a professionally built safe room in your home. This vault could have an undetectable entrance, a secret exit, its own air supply, and a host of other bells and whistles. It would be a glorious place to hide during a home invasion or some other scary situation. But unfortunately, most of us can't afford something this lavish. This is where DIY safe rooms fill the gap.

Choose a basement or second floor room to fortify. If you're handy with carpentry tools, you can reinforce the wall framing around the door, and install a heavy security door with several sturdy locks and reinforced hinges. You could even have the door swing inward, and use lengths of lumber to bar the door (like you see in movies). Add a layer of thick plywood to the interior walls where they adjoin other rooms or hallways, since anybody can kick or punch through drywall (aka sheetrock). The room also needs an emergency exit of some kind, if that's possible. Stock the room with food, water, a bucket to use as a toilet and a big medical kit with trauma supplies. Keep a spare mobile phone in there or have a landline phone installed so you can call for help. Understand that this room is your last line of defense, not your first. Your property should have deterrents that keep people away from the house. The house itself should have many features that keep people from getting in. This room is the innermost layer of your defenses, and a room that you hope you never need.

46 GET SOME TRAINING

You can watch self-defense videos, read karate books, and flip through gun magazines until your eyes bleed, but none of that will prepare your body to go through the motions it must take in a defensive situation.

PRACTICE, PRACTICE The only way to get real skills and experience is through training, training, and more training. After you drill a certain technique or movement into your mind, by doing it over and over, you'll have "muscle memory" of that action. When the time is right, you'll just respond, like an instinct or a reflex. Again, this only happens through training, which should occur in a variety of settings.

TRAIN UNDER STRAIN "If it ain't raining, you ain't training." Whether you're striking, grappling, shooting, kicking, or performing any other martial skill, you need to train when and where it's uncomfortable, dark, dirty, wet, and even when you're sick or very tired. By training under adverse conditions, you won't be distracted by those conditions if you face them in a real crisis. You'll be ready to defend yourself and your loved ones.

47 STAY AT RANGE

Your enchanted knife may have a +9 against ogres, but let's get real. Who wants to be that close to an ogre? If those two sentences don't make sense to you, allow me to put it a different way: Unarmed fighting and hand-to-hand combat skills have a very real place in self-defense, but they shouldn't be the first thing you pull out of your toolkit. A weapon that can be used at a distance (where you're out of the reach of your foe) makes a lot more sense than going toe-to-toe with an assailant.

First, find out which weapons are legal in your area, and how and when you are permitted to legally use force to defend yourself (this is a disaster chapter, and it assumes that the rule of law is still in place; see Chapter 3 for the Mad Max stuff).

Second, figure out which of those legal weapons make sense for you, your family, and the types of situations you expect to face.

Third, get that training! Whether it's firearms or something else, train until you can hit your target every time and then keep training. You don't want to get rusty. Just make sure that you have access to the weapon, while keeping it secured from children. The weapon doesn't help much if you can't reach it when you need it.

48 IMPROVISE A WEAPON

The average home is loaded with objects that could be used as weapons. In fact, anything can become a weapon if you understand the vulnerabilities of the human body and you're able to improvise. You could choke a bad guy to death by stuffing a teddy bear down his throat. You just have to be creative and serious about your survival.

Stocked with knives that can slash and stab, cleavers that could take off a hand, rolling pins that can bludgeon someone, and plenty of other heavy or sharp kitchen tools, a kitchen is a potential arsenal. Don't forget the pots and pans either, particularly ones containing scalding hot food or water—and as a distraction, you could unload a fire extinguisher in their face. In a living room, you could give the bad guy the Jason Bourne treatment with a tightly rolled-up magazine, bash them with a chair (WWF style), push a bookcase on top them, or go in for the attack with a fireplace poker. Bedrooms have weapons too, hard cover books can block and strike, pens and pencils can stab, and we already know what a teddy bear can do. Even a bathroom, full of cleansers and plumbing, can be a deathtrap.

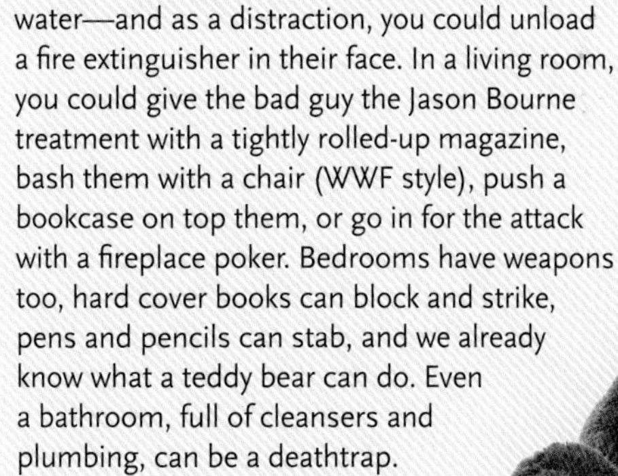

In summation, anything is a weapon in the hands of a creative and motivated defender—you just have to be open to the possibilities.

49 MASTER DIRTY FIGHTING

Preventing violence is the best self-defense, but you can't always avoid a fight. If you're attacked and have no weapons, prepare to fight dirty.

TAKE THE KNEE Need to disable a huge aggressor? Kick them as hard as you can in the knee. This is a weak point on anyone, but someone big and tall will carry even more weight on their knees. A powerful knee shot will hurt them immediately, and potentially disable them for some time, unable to chase you or continue the fight effectively.

KICK A GROIN A soccer kick to the fork can definitely jolt your attacker. Even if your foe is a lady (though she's not acting very ladylike), the groin is a tender, nerve-rich area on anyone. Just keep in mind that adrenaline, drugs, or alcohol will dull the pain of your strike, and your assailant won't go down the same way that a kick will drop an unsuspecting fellow.

JAB THE THROAT Predatory animals go for the throat when fighting or hunting prey, and you can too. A swift punch to the throat can leave your opponent breathless and distracted. If that's not an option (for example, your hands are bound), use the Dracula approach and bite their throat with an unexpected savagery.

52 GET TANKED

One of the most unorthodox sources of fresh water in every home is the toilet tank. This one is the least savory, so you may want to save it for a last resort. And to clarify, we are talking about the tank, not the toilet bowl. The tank of every toilet has one gallon (3.8 L) or more of the same water that was coming into your house before the water stopped flowing. And even though there may be some muddy-looking sediment at the bottom of the tank or moldy fungal growth around the tank rim, this water is safe to drink if it recently came into the tank. Just dip the water out with a cup and drink heartily. If you find that you are bothered by the water's proximity to the toilet bowl, or if the water has been sitting in there in the tank for weeks, you can filter and disinfect the tank water before drinking it.

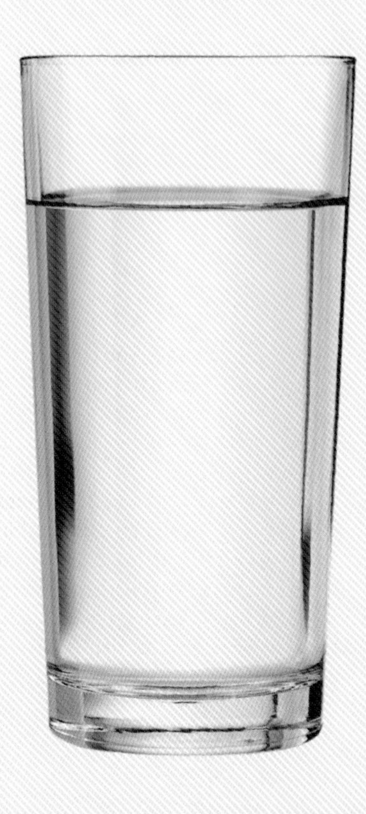

50 FIND WATER

When a disaster knocks out the supply of drinking water coming into your house from municipal supply lines, water can still be found in many places throughout the average home. One of the easiest place you'll collect it is from the pipes themselves. Whether you have a two-story house, a single-level home, or an apartment, there will be water in those lines. To get the water out effectively, open the highest faucet in the house (to allow air to enter the pipes), then open the lowest faucet in the system—this may even be a spigot outside the building itself. While the water is still running, fill some clean containers which should be standing at the ready nearby, before you open the valves. With a little luck and some effort, you'll get a few quarts out of the average plumbing system in a typical home, or even a gallon or two from a larger home or one with larger diameter pipes.

51 DRAIN A HEATER

Aside from the plumbing in your residence, there's another place where lots of water can be found in an emergency: The tank of your water heater. You can get between 40 and 80 gallons (150–300 L) of water from your home or office water heater by opening the drain valve at the bottom and catching the water in a shallow pan. You'll want to use this water soon, as warm water sitting there is a great bacterial breeding ground. If the heater is electric, you'll want to turn off the power to it. If the power is on, or comes on later, the dry heater elements will burn up the unit. The drain valve is usually threaded and the right size to attach a garden hose. To make water collection easier, cut a short section of garden hose (from the "female" end), rinse it out with bleach water, and screw it onto the tank spigot. Open the valve and you can move the hose around to easily fill buckets or other vessels.

53 CATCH SOME RAIN

Catching rainwater is an ancient practice that still makes sense for modern people, and you already have a tool in place to catch that rain—namely, your roof and gutters! The average roof on a single-family home is roughly 1,500 square feet (150 sq. m), which may not seem like a lot of rain harvesting space, but when one inch (2.54 cm) of rain falling upon one square foot (0.1 sq. m) of surface area yields more than half a gallon (2 L) of water, it adds up quick. Just a small rain shower can yield several hundred gallons of water, though it's not a perfect solution. Sometimes there's too much rain—and more often, there is no rain. Another issue is contamination: The birds, bugs, and other beasts do their business on your roof, contaminating the water with bacteria, viruses, and other pathogens. This means that effective filtration and/or disinfection are needed before you use the water for drinking or bathing.

54 MELT SOME SNOW

In a wintry emergency, you may have water all around you in the form of snow, but you won't be able to gobble it down directly without getting hypothermia. Snow is mostly frozen air and only about one-tenth frozen water. This means that you'd have to eat ten handfuls of snow to have one palmful of water in your belly. Not only would you have a monumental brain freeze, but you'd dangerously chill your core temperature. For both safety and comfort, melt that snow into liquid water before you drink it. Scoop snow into a pot and melt it over a fire, or place it on a black plastic trash bag in the sun to use solar energy for melting—and afterward, consider disinfection as well, since the falling snow may have picked up pathogens after lying around. You can't afford to risk hypothermia, illness, or dehydration in a cold climate calamity.

BUDGET SURVIVAL

WATER COOLER JUGS

Aside from breathable air, potable water is the next major thing your body needs to keep going—on average, you'll only live about three days before succumbing to dehydration, so in a disaster scenario, you'll need all the supply you can get your hands on. Grab a few water-cooler jugs ahead of time for yourself and your family, and store them safely in case things get bad.

- These are among the few "cheap" disaster preparations.
- It's safe for your whole family.
- Water is easy to ration into smaller portable bottles.
- The containers are refillable (and empties are available too).
- Each of these is 5 gallons (19 L) and the container can last indefinitely, properly secured.

Worth Every Penny

WATER FILTERS

Few items protect your health and safety as well as a reputable and effective water filter. These products can screen out the many organisms that could impair or kill you in a crisis.

55 DISINFECT YOUR WATER

When it comes to disinfecting your drinking water in an emergency, you can't afford to make any mistakes. You have to get it right. Thankfully, there are many different ways to kill or remove the bacteria, viruses and other pathogens that are lurking in your local waterways. Here are some of the main methods you can use to turn that ditch water into a clean drink.

BOIL FOR DISINFECTION Glass bottles, tin cups, soup cans, pots, ceramic containers, and many other fire-proof vessels can allow you to boil the water over or next to a fire.

GO PRIMITIVE Running your water through a home-made sand filter or boiling it with hot stones are ancient skills you can fall back on, when nothing else is available. But they aren't as reliable as other methods.

USE CHEMICALS Iodine tablets, chlorine tablets, household bleach, potassium permanganate, and other products can disinfect the water chemically, providing you with safe water.

GO COMMERCIAL Any of the water filters on the market will improve your situation and screen pathogens from your water. Make sure you purchase a filter that works on the smallest bugs (viruses), and you are covered for all the bigger ones.

HARNESS THE SUN Using sunlight's UV rays for something good, solar disinfection kills or disables many pathogens, making the water safer than it was. Not 100% safe, mind you, but safer than before.

USE ULTRAVIOLET Small light "pens" and other devices can be used to zap clear water and destroy most (if not all) of the pathogens therein. This is a nice back-up method when other methods (like filtration) may be failing.

56 USE YOUR SHIRT

Want to improve your water-filtering abilities in a crisis? Save those old flannel shirts! People around the globe use fabric to filter their water, and scientists are finally catching onto this ancient tradition. In one NIH study of the people using cloth to filter pond and river water in Bangladesh, four layers of cloth successfully reduced the incidences of cholera in their family by nearly half. Further lab tests showed that a filter made of four layers of worn cotton material held back as much as 99 percent of all cholera bacteria. (Oddly enough, four layers of the older fabric outperformed newer cloth or the use of more than four layers.) Of course, this doesn't mean that we should trust our family's health and safety to cloth filters alone. Bacteria and other pathogens can still get through, so use cloth to pre-filter the water and then use a store-bought water filter (or chemicals) to finish the job, or just boil it.

57 PUT WATER IN THE SUN

The UV rays in sunlight are capable of disinfecting water, but there are a few sticking points. The water needs to be clear; this technique won't work on muddy water. You'll also need a clear plastic (not glass) container. Finally, you'll need a full day of sunshine, or two full days of clouds with no rain. Once these conditions are met, an ordinary item like a clear plastic bag can be filled with clear water and placed in the sun to kill most (or possibly all) of the creepy crawlies that were swimming within. The method has been called SOLDIS (short for SOLar DISinfection) and it doesn't require fancy equipment, toxic chemicals, or fuel to perform. Do keep in mind however, that SOLDIS becomes less effective as you travel away from the equator and you'll have to use a perfectly clear plastic bottle or bag. Two-liter clear plastic bottles are the biggest vessel you should use.

58 EMPLOY IODINE

Two common forms of iodine can disinfect your water: Tincture of iodine 2% or povidone iodine 10%. It also helps to have a clean eye dropper for measuring.

STEP 1 Use 5 to 10 drops of tincture of iodine 2%, in one quart of water. Use 5 drops for clear warm water, and up to 10 for cold or cloudy water. 10% Povidone iodine solution is weaker, so you'll need 8 to 16 drops per quart of water. Use fewer drops for nice looking water and 16 drops for swamp water.

STEP 2 Using an eye dropper, add the right number of drops of iodine to your water, based on the type of iodine and the water's condition. Follow the cross-contamination fighting instructions too.

STEP 3 Allow the water bottle to sit in the shade for one hour, and then drink. Iodine disinfection is not recommended if you are pregnant or nursing, or have thyroid problems or a shellfish allergy.

59 FIGHT CROSS-CONTAMINATION

Your bottle may be full of disinfected water, but what about the threads of the bottle that you are going to put your lips upon? People still get sick after using chemical disinfection techniques, and the culprit is usually the dirty water bottle itself. Rinsing water bottle threads is a smart way to fight cross-contamination and prevent water borne illness. Once you've added your chemical disinfection drops or tablets to the bottle of raw water, screw the bottle lid back in place and shake up the water. Once the chemicals have mixed with the water, turn the bottle upside down and unscrew the cap far enough so that a little bit of the chemically treated water escapes. This will flush out the threads of the bottle and cap. Wipe down the exterior bottle with this released water and you're as good as you can easily get in a crisis situation.

60 COOK LIKE A HOBO

Bottles and cans are abundant in the wild and after a disaster, and they can be collected and cleaned out to boil your water in a pinch. Glass bottles, beverage cans, and metal food cans will boil your water when you place them in the ashes next to a fire. Metal containers can also be placed on a grill over the fire. Don't try to suspend glass containers over the fire, as this intense heat can break the glass. You can even use snare wire or a piece of a coat hanger for a bail (handle) on a tin can cookpot. Use the tip of a knife or another sharp tool to pierce two holes near the opening of the can, on opposite sides. Cut a piece of wire and thread it through the holes. Bend each end so that the wire stays in place, and you're ready to hang your hobo cookpot over the fire! Be aware that some food cans will have a clear or white plastic lining, which is not something you want inside your "cook pot." Place these cans in the fire for 10 to 20 minutes to burn it off, then sand or scrub the interior clean.

61 BUY A WATERBOB

The waterBOB is a remarkable prepper product that is well worth the trouble of tracking down. It's a large plastic bladder, sized to fit into a standard bathtub (dirty or clean) and it holds up to 100 gallons of sparkling clean water (no nasty bathtub taste). To use it, just unroll the plastic catchment bag inside your tub and attach the fill sock to the faucet. Fill the bladder to capacity and close it. In 15 or 20 minutes, you'll have a massive water reserve that is clean and protected from contamination by activities in the bathroom or your unsavory bathtub residue. To get the water out, the kit also includes a siphon pump which you can use to dispense the water easily into bottles, jugs or other containers. You can also use it in odd shaped bathtubs, since the heavy-duty 10-mil food grade LLDPE plastic can handle the pressure.

62 DIG A SEEP WELL

If you have source of surface water that is muddy, stagnant, or otherwise afflicted, this filtration technique does not filter out contaminants, but it can filter larger particles from the water which makes most disinfection techniques work better. Dig a hole about one foot away from the edge of the questionable water source, and dig down about a foot (30 cm)—or deeper in dry terrain. This well can be dug in dry areas also, such as dry creek beds, to allow subsurface water to collect in the hole for emergency drinking water. Now, you play the waiting game. The hole will fill with water asit seeps through the soil. Let the water sit for a few hours, or overnight, to clear out some of the sediment. Collect the water and disinfect it with the best method you have available.

63 DON'T BE MISLED

There are plenty of myths about water in survival situations. These tall tales circulate in movies, books, even cartoons. Before you put too much faith in these pop culture practices, discover what is real and what is not.

Cactus Water

MYTH Based on my intense study of historic cartoons (particularly Bugs Bunny), you can just chop the top off a cactus and it will be full of cool clear drinking water.

REALITY While cacti do contain water (as do all plants), they are hardly a bucket of drinkable H_2O. In fact, that cactus is more commonly filled with a bitter gelatinous pulp that would make you sick if you tried to consume it. Instead, you should learn to identify trees and vines that will actually deliver drinking water in the springtime and other seasons.

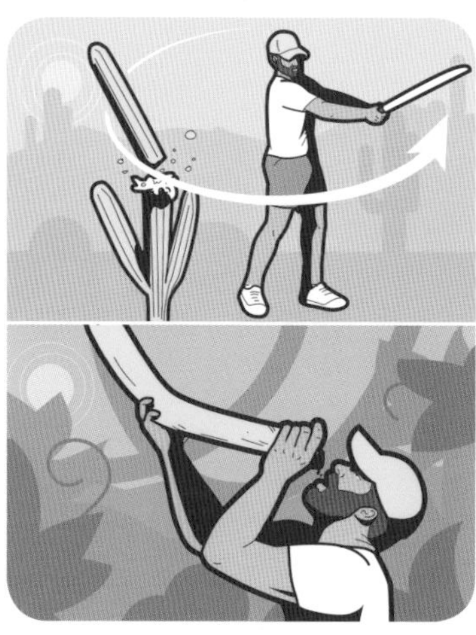

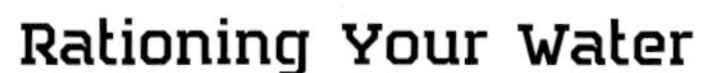

Rationing Your Water

MYTH Rationing your water is critical, especially in the desert. If you drink all of your water, your body will just waste it!

REALITY Dead people have been found in the desert, with water still in their canteens. Despite literary and TV examples of rationing water in emergencies, the best place to store your water is in your stomach. In a harsh situation, your body knows what to do. It will automatically concentrate your urine, dry up your feces, and thicken your blood to survive.

Drinking Your Pee

MYTH Many survivalists believe that it's okay to drink urine when you run out of water. They've even seen it on TV survival shows, so it must be true!

REALITY Hold on a minute, pee drinkers! Before you chug that golden glass of urine, understand that it has a dangerously high salt level, comparable to sea water. Drinking either of those will alter your electrolyte balance and cause very adverse physical reactions. Don't do it.

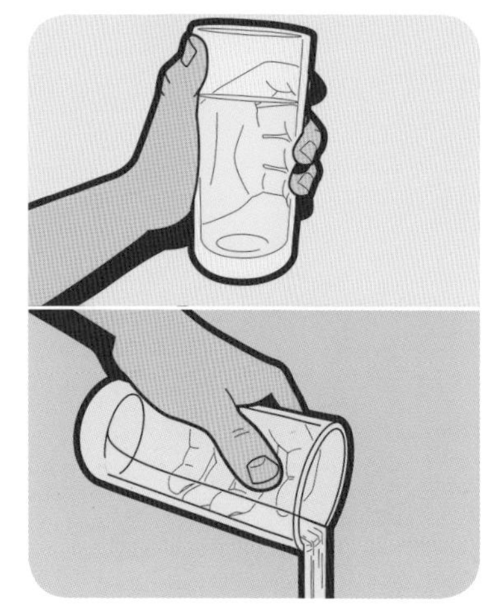

HACK HAZARDS

DIRTY WATER

A sip of raw water may not seem dangerous, but what if it carried the wrong organisms into your body and you were without modern medical care? There are four main groups of pathogens and parasites that we don't want to ingest in water. The virus is the smallest of all pathogens, with more than 100 known species that are transmissible through drinking water. Common waterborne viral diseases include rotavirus, enterovirus, norovirus, and hepatitis A. In addition, bacteria commonly enter the waterways through dead animals in the water—and also through animal and human feces. Those pathogens that can be transmitted by water include Cholera, Salmonella, Campylobacter, Shigella., and Staphylococcus aureus. Cryptosporidium and Giardia are also two of the most common protozoan pathogens found in raw water.

Quick Tip

After all the trouble you will go through to find and disinfect water in a survival situation, don't squander it! Water is a life-giving resource that we should always try to conserve, in a disaster setting or not.

64 COOK ON A RACK

When the storm of the century knocks out power and gas lines (or you've had to shut them off for safety), it may not seem like your faithful kitchen oven can help you cook anymore. But it can, and here are a couple of ways.

BUILD A BACKYARD GRILL After setting up a fire pit from rocks, bricks, cinderblocks, and other non-flammable materials, pull your racks out of your oven, and rest them over the top of your fire pit to turn the contraption into a functional grill. Light a fire underneath and commence cooking. The heavier gauge the wire, the more weight and heat your rack can handle. If it does start to sag, try flipping it over (to bend it the other way), decreasing the weight that it supports, or doubling up by adding a second rack on top.

SMOKE OUT YOUR OVEN If a grill isn't quite what you're looking for, you can even drag your poor old oven out into the yard entirely—with its racks still in place. Shovel some hot coals into the bottom of it, set your food on the racks above, and you'll be able to bake foods and even use it as an improvised meat smoker.

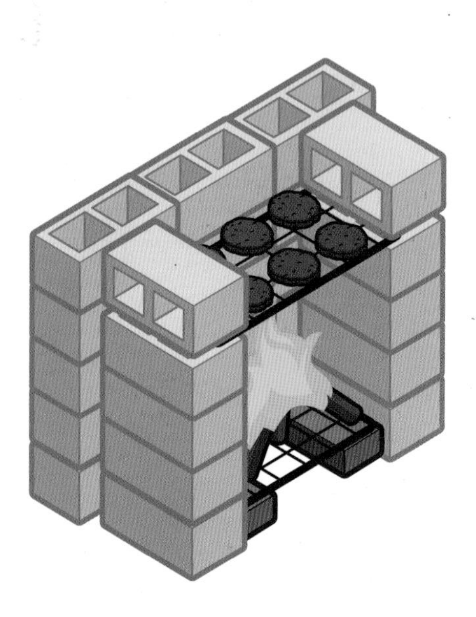

65 SPLIT WOOD FOR A SWEDISH TORCH

You don't need a chainsaw to make all of the dangerous cuts in a single log for the classic "Swedish torch." You can make this vertical campfire from split pieces of firewood. Just take a single log of fire-sized wood, and split it into five or six pieces. Place these back together, as if you were trying to reassemble the log, but packing tinder, oil and kindling sticks inside. Fuss with this "stuffed log" on solid ground until it stands steadily on its own. Light the tinder, which will light the oil and kindling, and in a few minutes, the split wood pieces will start to burn. You can enjoy this as an alternative to a normal campfire, a way to burn a fire on top of snow, or set your frying pan on top to cook a meal. The Swedish torch is both a fire and a stove!

66 TRY A WAX STOVE

A shallow metal can (like one for tuna, or lozenges, or mints), some wax, and a few strips of cardboard can turn into a quick cook stove with a long burn time. Just follow these easy steps.

STEP 1 Fill the can with coiled strips of cardboard, packing it as tightly as possible.

STEP 2 Pour in melted wax (any kind will work, but beeswax is best). Be careful when handling the hot wax, and don't completely drown the cardboard under wax. A little bit of cardboard should be sticking up as a wick for easy lighting.

STEP 3 You can stove now with a match and watch your stove flame up, or let it cool to use later.

STEP 4 Set up bricks or rocks around the stove to set your cookware above the flames. Use a flat item, like tin foil, to extinguish the stove if your cooking is done before you run out of fuel.

67 BUILD A BLOCK ROCKET

If you've got wood to burn, and you can source some cinderblocks in the rubble, you can build a cinderblock rocket stove in just a few minutes!

STEP 1 Find three standard cinderblocks, each with two holes. A fourth "block" can be pieced together from cinderblock caps and bricks, or you can use a hammer to knock the end out of a fourth standard block. If you're lucky, you might even find an "H" shaped block that is ready to go.

STEP 2 Fit the blocks together as shown. One will go on the bottom, with the "H" shaped section above it. A side block allows fuel and air to enter, and a top block provides a chimney effect.

STEP 3 Add a crushed tin can for a fuel rest and air intake; and some kind of grate over the top hole to set pots upon (without sealing off the chimney). Light your block rocket with some dry sticks and crumpled paper!

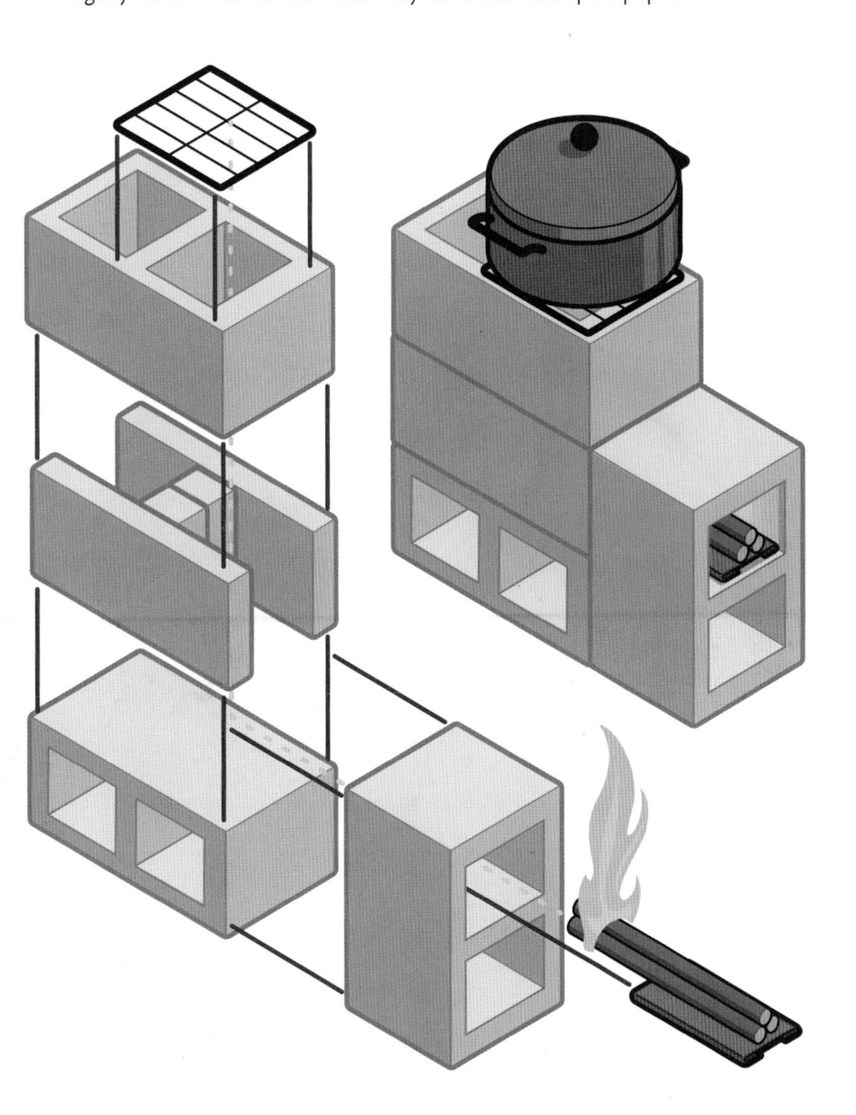

68 USE ROCKS

Ancient doesn't necessarily mean outdated or obsolete. The use of hot stones for cooking is probably as old as cooking itself, and we shouldn't rule out any useful survival skills, just because they aren't modern. These are some of my favorite ways to cook without utilities, and I often use them even when the gas and electricity are still available. Just make sure you gather your rocks from a high and dry location, since waterlogged rocks tend to explode when heated.

BOIL WITH ROCKS By heating up small egg-sized stones, you can use tongs or a ladle to drop them into containers to boil water and cook food. This technique makes the most sense when you don't have metal containers that you can place over a fire to boil—such as pumpkin soup boiled in a pumpkin.

BBQ BELOW GROUND Dig a pit, fill it with burning coals or hot stones, and suspend racks of meat, veggies and other foods above the heat. Seal the pit to keep the heat inside and patiently wait for the cooking to complete. This is a bit different from the steam pit, as it's a dry cooking method that infuses the food with a rich smoke.

STUFF WITH STONES Cooking a larger carcass? Add extra heat by stuffing it with hot stones. A steam pit or similar setup can also be enhanced by adding hot stones to improve its cooking abilities.

69 COOK ON A CAMP STOVE

For those who already have a camping stove and are familiar with its use, firing up the cooker during a utility outage with be familiar and easy. Camping stoves come in a wide range of sizes and styles, with various features and fuel requirements. Some burn small propane bottles, while others use liquid fuels. Do your research. Find the best choice for your needs, and consider which fuels will be readily availablc in a crisis. Maybe you only need a small one-burner stove to boil water and heat up a few cans of soup. Or if you're cooking for a crowd, a multi-burner stove may be just the thing you need. Plan ahead by getting any accessories that make sense, such as adapters that allow you to use different sizes of fuel tanks or accompaniments that make the stove easier to use.

70 HEAT UP WITH CHEMISTRY

Sometimes it's not practical or safe to heat food with a flame-based cooking method. If there's any chance of a gas leak or if you're stuck indoors in tight quarters, fire just isn't reasonable. Thankfully, there's an alternative. The flameless heater pouch (commonly seen in military MREs) is able to harness a safe natural phenomenon: Chemically created heat. When iron rusts, iron atoms combine with oxygen to create iron oxide. This oxidation process actually gives off heat, though it's very slow under normal circumstances. When magnesium dust, salt, and a little iron dust are combined, adding water creates a very fast oxidation process (and a lot of heat). In just a few seconds, the flameless heater reaches the boiling point. To use the heater, add the directed amount of water and insert a pouch or can of food into the bag. Quickly close the bag and allow it to steam for ten minutes. Once heated, your meal is ready!

HACKS THROUGH HISTORY // CHIMENEA

Named after the Spanish word for chimney, the chimenea is a bulbous free-standing fireplace. Today, we commonly see them throughout the world as a backyard decoration in outdoor entertaining areas. When they are being used, this fixture is little more than a convenient way to enjoy a campfire while amusing guests on your patio. But these are hardly a new invention, and they are much more than just a lawn ornament. These clay stoves actually date back to the 1600s, where they were used for both cooking and home heating. Traditionally, these were placed inside the home near a window or under a smoke hole in the roof, to heat the home in cooler weather and as a cook stove. We can honor the heritage of this handy portable fireplace and use it as a very efficient cooker, if we find ourselves in need of a way to prepare a meal. Just light a fire inside with available scrap wood or tree branches, place a grill over the top opening, and set your food on the grill to cook. Roast meat on a spit, sear some kabobs, or cook a pot of rice with your chimenea.

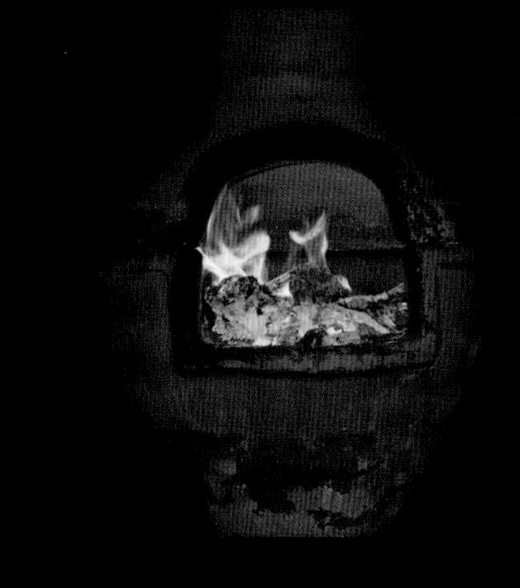

71 MAKE A CARDBOARD OVEN

Can't afford a factory-built solar oven? You can make your own, though maximum temperature will only be half as hot as a commercial model, but the price is right. To make your own solar oven, you'll need foil, a cardboard box, a black cooking pot, a clear lid for the pot, tape, scissors to cut the box, a clear turkey cooking bag, and a clothes pin. The heart of the operation is the pot, which absorbs the heat from sunlight reflected by the aluminum foil, while the pot sits inside the heat-resistant bag for a "greenhouse" effect. Cut the top from the box so it can be propped up, then tape aluminum foil on the interior of the entire cardboard box. Place a section of the turkey bag over the opening and tape it down. Place your black pot of food inside the box and keep it aimed toward the sun (move it every 30 minutes during the day).

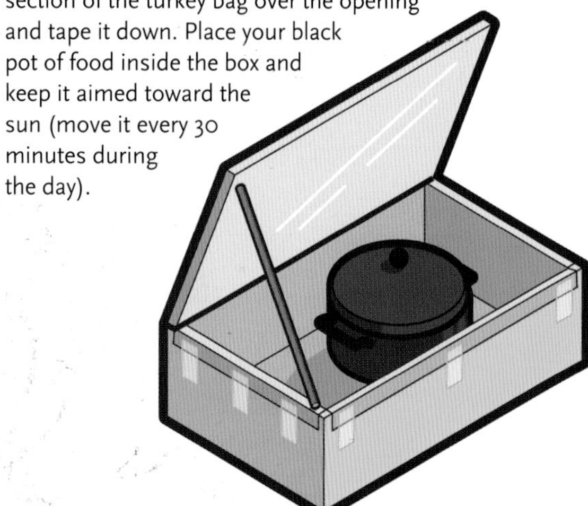

72 COOK IN YOUR CAR

A sunny day can turn a parked car into an oven, so why not use that heat? You don't have to do anything to turn your vehicle into a solar oven, and while it's usually not hot enough to cook meats or bread, it will heat up canned goods, MREs, and leftovers. Park your vehicle so that the windshield is facing south (in the Northern Hemisphere). Place your food on the dashboard and wait a few hours. If you place your lunch items out at breakfast, and set out your dinner foods at lunch, they'll have plenty of time to heat up. It doesn't have to be summer for this effect to work. With a 70 °F (21 °C) outdoor temperature, the interior can reach 104 °F (40 °C) in 30 minutes and 113 °F (45 °C) in one hour. And on a hot sunny day, the interior can exceed 150 °F (66 °C).

73 HACK A DISH

For those who are great fabricators, you can use your metal working skills to turn an old satellite dish into your new parabolic cooker.

STEP 1 Decide how your dish will be set up and moved to follow the sun (kist like the box cooker, you'll need to move every 30 minutes or so, to continue tracking the sun). You could build a tripod to support it or mount the dish on a pole with a bracket.

STEP 2 Decide what you'll be cooking. If it's just meat, bolt a metal spike onto the arm so you can impale a big hunk. For more versatility, mount a flat piece of plate metal that you can set pots and kettles upon it. Strip the electronics and wiring from the arm of the satellite dish.

STEP 3 Finish the project by covering the inside of the parabolic curve with mirrored tiles or strips of reflective metal, or glue on some aluminum foil. For the best effect, choose a dark-colored cooking pot with all metal construction. Plastic or rubberized handles can melt in the intense heat. Cover the dish when adding, stirring, or removing food, so you don't get burned. A parabolic mirror can melt plastic and leave metal extremely hot on a bright day! Depending on the satellite dish size, your cooker may bake like an oven or slow-cook like a crock pot.

74 BUILD A PENNY STOVE

Strong alcohol is a common and environmentally-friendly fuel that you can use with complex or simple cook stoves, but it doesn't get much simpler than a penny stove. Here's how to make one.

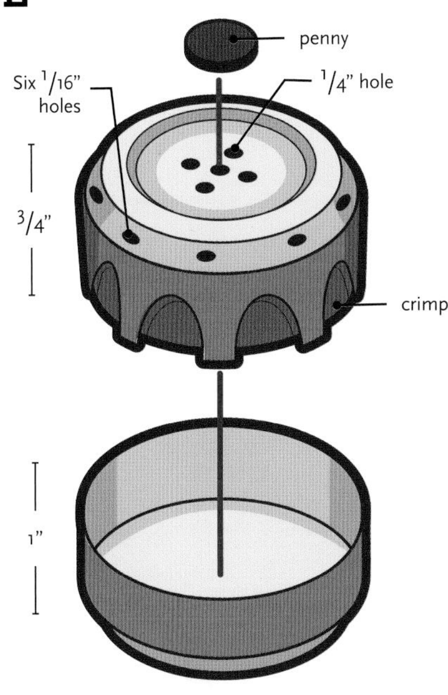

STEP 1 Gather two aluminum cans, tin snips, a hammer, a nail, a small coin like a penny, and high-proof alcohol.

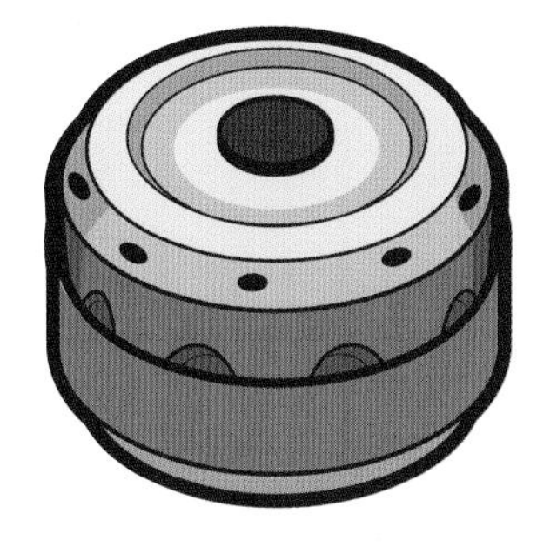

STEP 2 Cut around the bottom of each can with tin snips, 1-1/2 inches (4 cm) from the end. Crimp the cut edge of one piece, and force the crimped one inside the other.

STEP 3 Use the hammer and nail to punch a dozen holes around the top perimeter, and several holes in the center of the top.

STEP 4 Pour your alcohol in the center holes, but not so full that it spills. Denatured alcohol is great, 90% isopropyl alcohol is marginal, and anything less won't work well. Set it on a steady fire-proof spot and light it. Cover the center hole with the coin and suspend your cook pot over the burning stove.

HACK HAZARDS

SOLAR BURNS

Solar cooking is a gentle way to simmer your food with free sunlight energy, but it's not risk free. The same light that steams your veggies can also blister your skin and permanently damage your eyes when concentrated by a mirrored collector. Use something to cover the mirror component of larger solar cookers and wear gloves when you add or remove food. Don't look into the mirror when it is uncovered. This is no joke. Amplified sunlight can burn the surface of your skin just like a fire. And when you rush to douse cold water on your burn (as the pain will drive you to do), your outer layer of skin may slough off—just as if you've been burned by some kind of fuel. But this horrible injury is easy to prevent. Approach the dish from behind and slip a piece of cloth down over the mirrored surface. This provides all the protection you need.

75 COIL A SOLAR WATER HEATER

Anyone who has ever killed their prized plants by watering them with a scorching hot garden hose will know exactly how hot it can get. After several hours of sun exposure, the water inside a dark colored garden hose can reach temperatures that will nearly scald human skin and definitely cook any plants you water. But if you need hot water in a crisis, that black or dark green garden hose can make a great solar hot water heater, pressurized or not. So let's say that the water isn't running, but you have a large rain barrel that has an attached garden hose. Just lay out your water-filled garden hose in direct sunlight and wait. After an hour or two, test to see if it's hot enough. When it's ready, start spraying. This can give you a few gallons of hot water for dishes, laundry, or bathing during a utility outage.

Worth Every Penny

STOVE CHARGER

The BioLite stove can actually use heat to produce electricity. While burning any available wood scraps, the thermoelectric element can run small lights or even charge your phone.

550 CORD

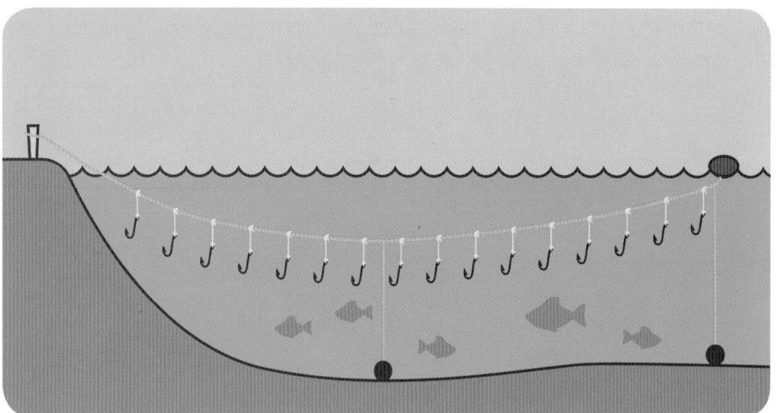

1 GET THE BOOT Often called paracord, 550 cord is a tough yet slender line that was originally used in WW II for parachutes! Once on the ground, creative war fighters found hundreds of uses for the sturdy cordage, including bootlaces. Cotton and leather boot laces were no match for cord with a 550-pound breaking strength, then or now. You can also take this cord out of your boots and cut off a few short sections, using the short ones to strategically re-tie your boots. This gives you several feet of available cord, and your boots stay on!

2 START A FIRE For those who burn the ends of 550 cord (a great way to keep it from unraveling), you already know that 550 cord is sort of flammable. Whether your cord is made from nylon or polyester, either of these plastics will burn once they get hot enough. But for one enterprising company, "sort of flammable" wasn't good enough. There's a product on the market called 550 FireCord, which has an additional red colored strand inside. This can be stripped from a cut piece of cordage to yield flammable tinder or left in place to help a strand of 550 burn even better. For best results, light your cord with an open flame like a lighter or a match.

3 SET UP A TROTLINE ▲ Need to some catch fish? Use a trotline for survival fishing! Tie a piece of 550 cord so that it is securely anchored across a waterway, above or below the water. Use existing shrubs or drive stakes into the mud for land anchors. Use rocks and floats out in the water for aquatic anchors. From the 550 line, you can drop multiple hooks on regular fishing line to multiply your chances of making a catch. And for those who need to use this technique under the radar, set every part of the trotline so that it stays below the water.

4 CREATE SURVIVAL SNARES Setting snares to catch game animals definitely takes a lot of practice, but it's also a great way to maximize your chances of catching something to eat in an emergency. You can use complete 550 cord (or strands from it) to make a wide range of trap components and snare lines, with just a little research and practice. And it you're dealing with an animal that can chew through the cord (virtually all mammals, for example), then use the 550 to make a lethal trap—it's more humane, and your quarry won't have time to chew the line.

5 GO FISH ▼ Short bits of 550 cord may seem like trash, but they can become surprisingly nice fishing lures with just a little bit of work (and a sharp hook). By sliding part of the outer jacket down and cutting it off, you'll expose more of the white inner strands on this remarkable rope. Slide the shank of a fish hook up through those strands until the eye emerges, then melt the end of the cord with a lighter. Shred the exposed white strands and your lure is ready for the water. And if you're short on fishing line, remove a long inner strand of 550 for your fishing line.

6 BAFFLE THE BEARS ▼ One great use for 550 cord is bear bagging. In backcountry areas with bruins and other animals that want your food, hanging it in a tree downwind of camp will keep it out of reach and reduce nighttime animal prowlers around your tent. To hang your bag of food, tie a rock to the end of 100 feet (30 m) of 550 cord and lob the rock over a tree branch. Untie the rock and tie on your food sack. Hoist the bag up and tie it to a different tree so that it hangs at least 12 feet (3.5 m) off the ground, 5 feet (1.5 m) down from the branch and 5 feet (1.5 m) from the trunk.

7 MAKE STRAPS, BELTS, AND MORE ▶ 550 cord bracelets have become a common item in the outdoor skills community, but you can make more than ornaments if you have some cord and some weaving skills. Simple braiding and plaiting techniques can turn a roll of this cord into belts, straps, collars, and other useful items. And if you can knit or crochet, go nuts with this durable and flexible cordage material! People have woven sandals from this cord, even bikini tops. Your creativity and imagination are the only real limits.

8 CUT ZIP TIES ▲ You've been kidnapped and bound with zip ties! It's a good thing that your 550 cord boot laces can also be put to good use as a saw. Zip ties can be cut by aggressively working 550 cord across them. To make your escape, remove your 550 laces, and tie them together with a large loop on each end. Thread the cord through one zip tie. Place each foot in one of the cord loops, and move your feet like you're peddling a bike. This will saw the cord back and forth on the zip tie, heating the plastic to its melting point, and eventually breaking through the restraint.

76 DO THE RESEARCH

Most people only think about flooding after a scary weather prediction has been made, though this isn't the best time to get ready for high water. Get yourself and your family ready right now, long before the storm clouds gather. The first thing you'll need to do is research the local flood history and learn the flood risks for your neighborhood and immediate area. Has your home or neighborhood flooded before? Have local levees ever failed? Is there a dam at or above your elevation? After answering these questions, determine your property's height above the nearest body of water. If forecasters project flooding of a certain height, you'll need to know if that water could reach your home's elevation. Finally, determine the main roads and alternate routes you'd take to drive to higher ground in the event of a flood. You don't want to take the low road when you're running for higher ground.

77 FIGHT BACK AGAINST FLOODING

Snow melt can cause predictable local flooding every year at the same time, while large hurricanes can dump flood waters upon an entire region. Flooding can even happen in the blink of an eye as a violent flash flood caused by a storm in another area, or the failure of a dam. Get your family and your home ready before the floodwaters come.

MAKE A MOVE As discussed with hurricane preparedness, move your important items and documents to the highest point in your home for the best chance of their survival.

GET UNPLUGGED If you're fleeing before the flood hits, turn off your main electrical breaker, or at least unplug your electrical appliances. Power and water don't mix well.

THINK OF THE PETS In the event that you cannot take your pets as you evacuate, do not leave them locked up in your home. Find a neighbor who is staying put and willing to watch your pets. Never leave your pets home alone.

WALK WITH CARE Murky flood waters can often conceal sharp and dangerous debris. If you do have to walk through flood waters, it's best if you wear sturdy boots and long pants for protection. Walk slowly and use a stick to feel your way along.

PREP FOR A LONG TRIP Flooding can wash away bridges and cover roads with standing water, thick mud, and dangerous debris. Without a safe alternate route, this can block you from returning to your home. Be prepared to stay away for some time, if you are forced to evacuate your home.

BEAT THE MOLD Often laden with sewage and other filth, flood waters are quick to breed mold in flooded homes. When drying things out, use fans and dehumidifiers to dry out the home as quickly as possible. Aim your fans to blow the air out of windows and doors, rather than inward, for faster drying and less mold. Purchase mold-killing sprays and related products before flood season, as they are likely to be sold out after flooding occurs.

HACK HAZARDS

DRIVING THROUGH WATER

It's not the lightning that you have to worry about. Flooding is the chief cause of death associated with thunderstorms, accounting for more than 90 fatalities each year in the U.S. More than half of these losses occur when vehicles are driven into dangerous flood waters, especially at night when visibility is hampered. As little as 2 feet (0.6 m) of fast moving water can sweep away most vehicles, even SUVs and trucks. And forget about trying to wade through swift flood waters: It only takes 6 inches (15 cm) of fast rushing water to knock a person down and sweep them away. The two best ways to deal with flooding are to evacuate before an expected event, or shelter in place. Never try to drive through flood waters. Turn around and find some other way to get home; or at least find some high ground and stay put. It's not worth losing your life.

Worth Every Penny

SAND BAGS

These can protect one of your biggest investments: your home. Get the materials and prepare to make traditional sand bags (or purchase sand bag alternatives), well before flood season.

78 CHILL IN A CELLAR

Air conditioning is a treat of the modern age, and while people from impoverished nations would call A/C a luxury, some of us truly can't live without it. Heat-related illnesses are one of the leading causes of weather-related death in the United States. The 1995 summer heat wave in Chicago claimed more than 700 lives, and a similar two-week weather pattern killed 655 people in California in 2006. So what's your Plan B for keeping cool when a summer storm knocks out the power? For ages, our ancestors have survived in some of the hottest places on earth (without the cold breeze blowing from an air conditioner), and they did it by going underground. For those with a basement in their home, cool air naturally created by the walls and floor can turn that area into a hot-weather haven.

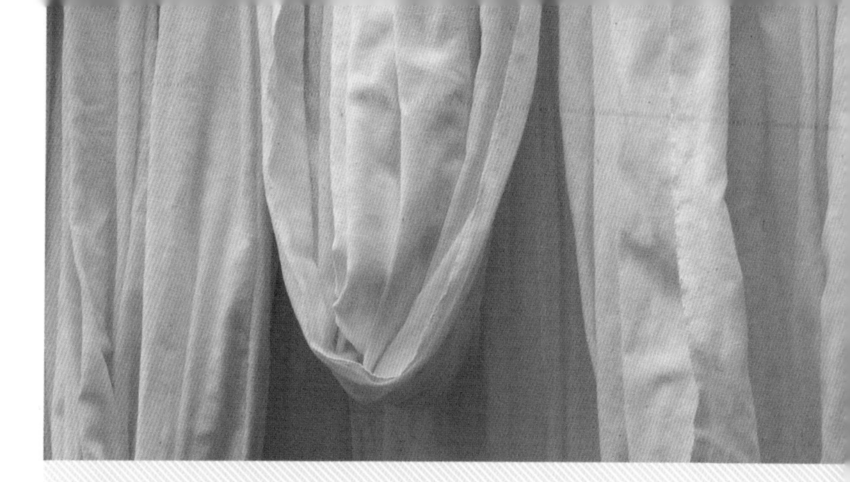

79 BLOCK SUNNY WINDOWS

Don't give up, if you don't have a cool (yet funny-smelling) basement as a summer disaster retreat. It's creepy down there anyway. For those who can't go underground, you can block some of the heat coming into your home by dimming the sunlight.

REFLECT THE LIGHT The same principal that allows a reflective panel in your car windshield to keep the vehicle interior cooler means we can hang up light colored or reflective material in sunny windows to reflect away the light and minimize heat gain. Grab that reflective thing from your car and cut it into the size and shape of a small window. Hang up shiny space blankets in larger windows.

IMPROVISE If you're lacking silvery materials, hang up white sheets or similar light colored cloth. Then, once the outdoor temperature drops, open up your windows during the night to ventilate your home and allow the cooler evening air inside.

80 COOL THE SWAMP

In the ancient days of woe, people had plenty of reasons to drop dead—but it usually wasn't caused by a lack of central air conditioning. Why not? They had plenty of low-tech solutions to find relief from the baking heat.

MEET ANCIENT AIR CONDITIONING Early Egyptians were known to hang damp lengths of cloth in their doors and windows, a primitive version of today's "swamp coolers." As the moisture evaporated from the cloth, the breeze passing through would be naturally cooled. These damp sheets also added some needed humidity to the arid desert breeze.

TRY IT AT HOME On unbearably hot nights, you can even tie damp sheets over your bed (almost like a pup tent) so that cool air will descend on you, or try sleeping in damp sheets. You can plan ahead for disasters by purchasing some white cotton bedsheets when you see them on sale, as they serve so many purposes.

81 DEAL WITH DISCOMFORT

It's hot as Hades, your power is out, and your family is getting more irritable by the second. How can you focus on your tasks when you're absolutely miserable? Pull a page from the Navy SEALs playbook: Train yourself to rise above discomfort. The saying "get comfortable with being uncomfortable" has been attributed to these top tier operators, and their brutal training is the epitome of being uncomfortable. Long days of rigorous training in nasty conditions and grueling psychological drills prepare them for the unexpected and the miserable. You don't need to mimic the extremes they endure, but it can't hurt to step outside your comfort zone either. Subject yourself to situations that are not so pleasant, and stay focused on your tasks. Try to ignore how uncomfortable you feel and push on toward success. Don't go to extremes, but learn to enjoy the little things that are going right, and ignore what doesn't feel so pleasant. If you can stay focused even when things are uncomfortable, you're better prepared to handle any tough survival situation—even the summer heat!

HACKS THROUGH HISTORY // **CLAY POT COOLER**

When power goes out, the ability to keep your food cool can mean the difference between eating well and having to throw out spoiled meals. Storing your food in basements and root cellars can make a big impact, but so can a smaller contraption: The clay pot cooler. Often known as a zeer pot, this is a modern take on technology that is actually more than 4,000 years old. Start by placing a medium terracotta pot inside a larger one, and filling the void between them with dry sand. Pour water in the sand to dampen it and place your food inside the inner pot. Cover it with a lid or a damp cloth, and set the nested pots in a shady place, ideally with some air flow. Through evaporative cooling, your food will then stay significantly cooler than simply keeping it in the shade.

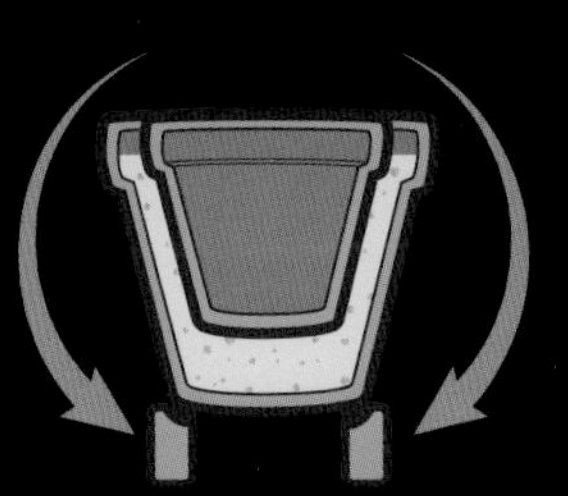

82 WIRE UP A HEAVY LIGHT

The average vehicle battery carries 12 volts of electricity and a whole lot of amperage when fully charged, and it can make an unwieldy (yet long lasting) flashlight in a pinch. You'll need a bit of electrical tape, along with some insulated wire and a 12-volt bulb taken from the car.

STEP 1 Cut two pieces of wire, and strip each of the four ends.

STEP 2 Tape one wire end to the side of the bulb and tape the end of the second wire to the small lead button at end of the bulb.

STEP 3 Now connect the wire from the end of the bulb to the positive battery terminal and the other wire end to the negative terminal on the car battery. The light should burn for quite some time (a 2-amp bulb and a 100-amp-hour battery will burn up to 50 hours). Be careful, as this can be both a fire and shock hazard!

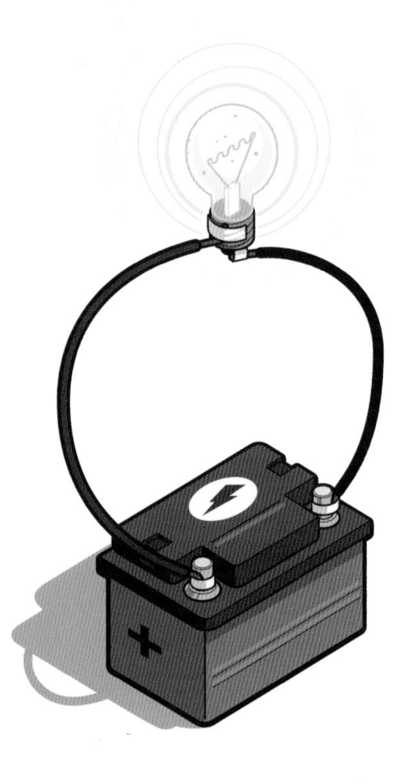

83 GET LIGHT FROM OIL

Burning plant oils for light dates back thousands of years, and one simple way to replicate this is to make an oil candle in a canning jar.

CREATE A LAMP Pour a small amount of cooking oil into the bottom of a food jar, about 1 inch (2.5 cm) and drop in a cotton ball. Move the cotton ball to the center of the jar and light it with a long fireplace match or stick. Don't use drinking glasses for this, as they can break from the heat.

TRY A TORCH For a brighter outdoor light, wrap some toilet paper around one end of a green wood stick so that it looks like a giant Q-tip. Soak the head in cooking oil (or any other oil) and light it up as a torch. The average sized torch head will burn about 15 to 20 minutes, and look just like the ones in the movies. Be careful; this is obviously a fire hazard.

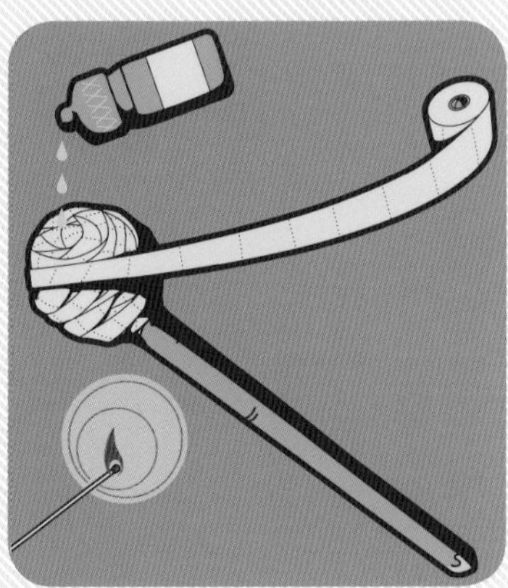

84 CREATE SOME CANDLES

I never knew how many different ways you could make candles until I started making them myself. You can create molds for various shapes of wax candles, and all of them will provide light and comfort.

CREATE STICK CANDLES Rolling up flat sheets of wax around a wick will give you a serviceable candle. Dipping candles can be fun too, dunking a wick repeatedly in melted wax to build up layered taper candles.

FILL UP A JAR The easiest way to make a candle, by far, is simply pouring melted wax into a fire proof container and inserting a wick before the wax hardens. Use a food jar as you would for an oil candle, to take advantage of the clear glass. If you don't fill it to the top, your wick will burn inside the jar giving you a candle that resists the wind. Or pour some hot wax in an empty tuna can and add a wick. Either way, it's so easy to do!

85 MAKE LOTS OF LIGHT

When an emergency arises after dark, you'd better have ample sources of light. Here are five modes of lighting that just might save you.

CHEMICAL LIGHTS These single-use lights can come in 30-minute high-intensity versions, long lasting dim versions, and many colors. Their best attribute is that they pose no risk of fire whatsoever. As a final point, you can get a brighter light by heating light sticks in hot water (though it shortens their "burn" time).

GREASE LAMPS Any type of lard or shortening can be combined with a plant fiber wick in a fire-proof vessel to create a grease lamp. Also called slush lights, fat lamps, gras lights (think Mardi Gras), and many other colorful names, these portable lamps are rooted in ancient history. Just don't spill it once the lard melts, or let the wind blow it out.

OIL LANTERNS These lights use fire and oil, the way that a grease lamp does. But being enclosed in glass, they're less a fire hazard and more weatherproof. Oil lanterns can burn on kerosene, liquid paraffin, or lamp oil. They can also work on vegetable oils, but not as effectively. Just make sure you never put gasoline, white gas, Coleman fuel, lighter fluid, alcohol, paint thinner, or similar low-flash point liquid fuels in the tank—the lamp will blow up!

BATTERY LANTERN Looking like an old-school oil lantern, modern battery powered lanterns eliminate the fire hazard and some provide extra features, like SOS strobes and energy saving modes.

SOLAR LIGHTS You can bring in your cordless solar lawn lights indoors for evening illumination, or invest in a dedicated solar powered lighting source. Either way, these lights store up the sun's power during the day, and return it to you again at night for home lighting.

86 BRING BACKUPS

I'm a big believer in multiple flashlights, and having the right light for each job. These are the three types of lighting that everyone should carry.

REGULAR FLASHLIGHT Bright beams, extended battery life, and rugged construction can be found through a variety of different models and across many brands. This handheld light is good for any number of situations.

HEAD LAMP My favorite for most tasks, the headlamp gives us hands-free lighting, often with a long battery life. Head lamps are ready to stream illumination exactly where I'm looking, while keeping both of my hands free to work. You can even strap a headlamp onto a water jug or bottle for a DIY lantern.

TACTICAL LIGHT Nothing helps you out in those "bump in the night" situations like a high lumen, ultra-bright tactical light. These lights can reach out in the darkness and give you the visibility you want and need. Look for lights that also have multiple features like battery-thrifty low intensity settings.

87 GET MORE LIGHT

Having already mentioned three different light sources you should carry, it only seems natural to mention three ignition sources to bring. Why three? By carrying three, you now have one to lose, one to break and one to use.

BUTANE LIGHTERS These modern marvels can light more fires that a huge box of matches. Just store them in some way that doesn't press the button, which would cause all the butane to escape.

MATCHES Each match acts like a little piece of kindling, helping the baby fire to burn. They also provide an open flame like the lighter, though most matches aren't that reliable when moisture is an issue.

SPARK RODS Ferrocerium rods can throw a lot of sparks, but that's their problem. Not every tinder is able to light from sparks; some require an open flame. Still, a spark rod can be a useful backup to matches or lighters.

88 PASS THE CHIPS

Snack chips are delicious and packed with calories, and it's the reason they are calorie dense that allows them to become amazing fire starters. Unless they are some kind of healthy chip, they are made with a generous amount of oil (most chips being fried in fat). This means that we can use these greasy chips for a phenomenal fire starter. Just apply an open flame to the edge of a chip and hold it for a few seconds. As the grease begins to vaporize, the chip begins to burn like a torch. Add this chip and a few more to your fire lay for a campfire or use them to light your charcoal for a grid-down barbeque. And the best part is that they don't even have to be fresh! This is a great use for the old rancid chips you found while scavenging for food in the back of your pantry.

89 USE A BATTERY

That same battery which can be a source of light can also be used with jumper cables and tinder to start a fire.

MAKE SPARKS FLY Carefully clamp your jumper cables to the positive and negative terminals on the vehicle battery. Then touch the metal jaws of the free ends of the cables together. For best results, make this contact over a nest of fluffy tinder material that is sitting on the ground.

STAY SAFE Don't clamp or hold the jaws together, as this can create a closed circuit and heat up the battery to a dangerous level—acidic explosion, anyone? Just sweep the jaws past each other, touching them as they pass. The shower of molten metal sparks that will result from this contact will be intense and startling, so wear gloves and goggles if you have them.

TRY AN ALTERNATIVE If this is too scary, sharpen both ends of a pencil and clamp the jumper cables to each end; in mere moments, the pencil will burst into flame.

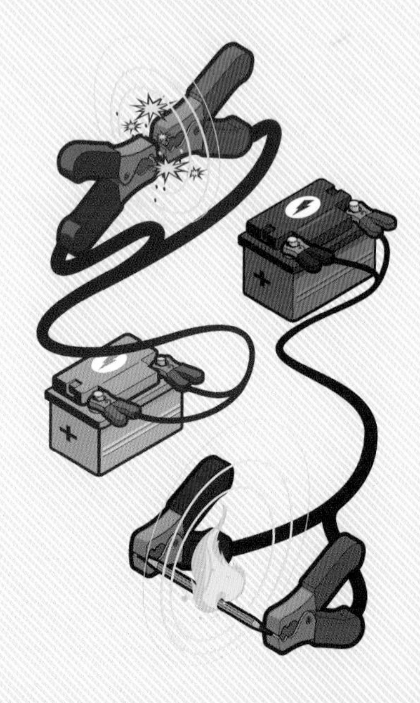

90 BRING A FRESNEL LENS

There's only one way I know to level the playing field in an emergency: redundancy. And while we've mentioned bringing three fire starters to the party, why not carry one more? The Fresnel lens is a small thin plastic magnifying "glass" that can tuck right into your wallet. Use it just as you would use a standard magnifying glass to make fire. Focus a blinding pinpoint of sunlight on the flat spot in some dark tinder, angling the lens to make the dot of light as small and round as possible. Manipulate the lens at different angles and at different distances from the tinder until you have the perfect dot, and the smoke should start to flow from this hot spot immediately. Blow gently across the tinder while you are magnifying light on it. Your extra oxygen and air movement will cause burning fibers to spread their ignited red glow.

91 MAKE CHAR CLOTH

For easier fire starting, a great resource you can make is char cloth. This is the same "char" that you'd use for traditional flint-and-steel fire starting, and it's easy to make. Get a small metal box, like a candy tin, and poke one small hole in it. Fill the can with scraps of dry cotton or linen cloth, fluffy plant-based tinder, cotton balls or even crumbly rotten wood. Chuck the can into a campfire and let it cook for about 5 minutes or until smoke stops jetting out of the vent. Use a stick to roll the can out of the fire, cover the pin hole, and allow it to cool before opening. The contents should have become brittle and black, and shrunken in size. If properly burned (long enough but not too long), it will be excellent at catching sparks from ferrocerium rods, flint and steel, and optical methods.

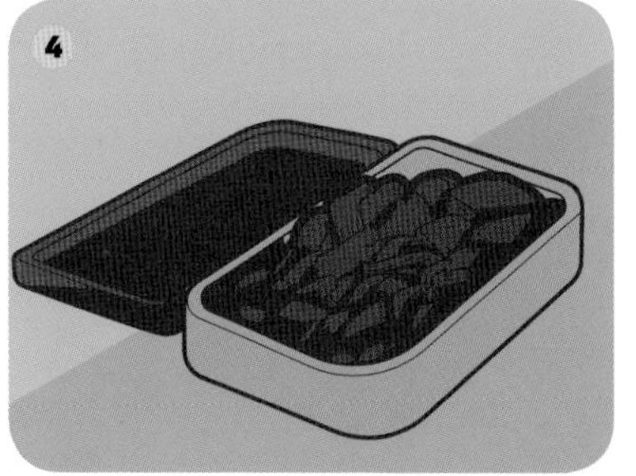

BUDGET SURVIVAL

WAX FIRE STARTERS

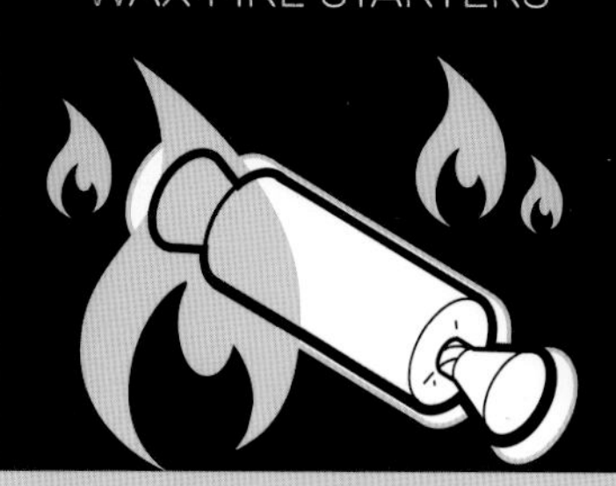

For a diehard DIYer, buying fire starters at the camping store is out of the question. You'll want to make your own from the creative use of household materials. Make your own amazing fire helpers by tightly rolling up some ordinary paper towels and cutting them into short sections. Tie each one with a bit of cotton string and dip them in a container of melted wax. Once cooled, these can be stored with your fire kit, and the cotton strings can be used wicks for easy lighting. Here are just a few of their benefits.

- It's cheap to make them.
- They're easy to make.
- You can make them in small or large sizes.
- When properly soaked in wax, they're waterproof!

Worth Every Penny

TORCH LIGHTERS

Those little butane lighters that act like blowtorches will start a fire in any almost any weather, and are capable of lighting a wide range of materials on fire. Enjoy responsibly!

92 LEARN ABOUT PET CARE

When your pet is injured or ill, and emergency conditions are preventing you from visiting the local veterinary clinic, your best friend will need your help. You'd better be prepared to give it. Get some training in pet first aid!

SEEK CLASSES Many organizations offer low-cost training in pet first aid and related topics. You don't need to be an EMT or medical specialist to join in. These are classes for the general public, designed to show you exactly what to do for your pet in their time of need. Through these workshops and programs, you can learn to diagnose common ailments and problems in pets.

OFFER AID You'll also learn to render first aid to your furry, feathered, or scaly friends. Just a little bit of education can go a long way in a crisis. Don't let your busy schedule stand in the way; find your local educators and sign up today.

93 KEEP THEM WARM

In a cold catastrophe or during the nighttime lows, a utility failure can mean cold temperatures for us and our pets. One trick to help regulate their body temp is to play dress-up. Find appropriate sized clothing for children, teens, or adults, and see if you can get your pet to wear it. Patient dogs are the easiest to dress up, while persnickety cats are the worst. But do your best to dress them in human clothing to keep your pets warm. And whether they let you dress them or not, make a bed with a warm water bottle for them to curl up against and give them extra food. Their bodies can burn the extra calories for metabolic heat, while they soak in warmth from external sources like the bottle. When all else fails, or maybe earlier than that, you can curl up with your pet for warmth.

94 MAKE DIY DOG FOOD

You ran out of dry kibble during a calamity? Long before the commercial availability of mass produced dog food, people fed their dogs many of the same foods that they were eating. And just as we crave good taste and variety, so do our pets. That's why they beg for table scraps!

KEEP IT SIMPLE Which human foods can you safely give your dog? Cooked meats and cooked eggs are great sources of fat and protein for poochie. Many fresh or frozen vegetables can be finely chopped and added to their food for fiber, vitamins, and minerals.

LEAVE OUT SWEETS Avoid onions, garlic, and avocado. They don't need sweets either, so skip the grapes, raisins, and of course chocolate. These and a few other people foods are toxic to dogs. You'll also want to skip the canned veggies and fruits. High in sugar and sodium, their mushy texture can also cause stomach upset.

95 SPLINT YOUR PET

While it's universally recommended to take an injured animal to a vet, there are circumstances that prevent it and require you to support your pet's movement temporarily.

STABILIZE WITH STICKS If you can determine that it's a minor injury, treat it as you would a sprain on a human limb. Wrap the injury, above and below, with an Ace bandage for stability and support. When the injury is more severe, bind the area with a bandage and a stiffener. A piece of a wooden ruler (or even a few well-padded sticks) can be incorporated into the wrappings to become a splint.

UPGRADE YOUR CARE For large animals, wrap a thick magazine around the area and bind it in place for a tubular splint. Then, as your situation improves, get your pet to the vet. Leaving a pet in a makeshift splint may prevent their injury from healing properly, causing more pain and suffering in the future.

96 MAKE A PLAN

The time to build and test your family's emergency communication plan is not after the disaster has hit. It is the time well before a crisis strikes. Since most of us have never gone without listening to the news or communicating with our friends and loved ones for a long period of time, we don't understand that communication can be just as critical a topic as food, water, or medicine. And since your family may not be together during a disaster, you'll need to plan how you will contact one another. This plan should include the use of various communication methods, to account for a variety of different scenarios. Make sure everyone in your circle has a card with family phone numbers and email addresses in their wallet, purse or backpack. Include the contact info of a friend or relative who lives out-of-state for household members to notify they are safe.

97 GET ON THE RADIO

Walkie-talkies provide instant communication in an emergency situation when mobile phones and landline communications are down. They aren't perfect and may only work over a short distance, but some communication is better than none!

KNOW THE PROS These little gizmos work whether the grid is up or down, unless they were bathed in the unholy pulse of an EMP. But even that can be circumvented by storing the units in a Faraday cage until needed. They allow direct and immediate communication with people who may be several miles away. Their batteries may be swapped out with the batteries from a flashlight or some other sources. And modern walkie-talkies can offer weather alerts, hands free operation, and SOS signals.

CONSIDER THE CONS The advertised range of the units is under perfect conditions: dry air, direct line of sight, and no vegetation blocking the signal. If there is abundant vegetation, high humidity, or atmospheric interference, your best results may only be 1/10th of the advertised range. Even if you're within your working range, terrain can and probably will block the transmission. Your batteries will go dead eventually and you need both units to be operational; lose or break one, and it's over.

CHECK THE WEATHER While you can't communicate back and forth with this item, weather radios with the NOAA bands can provide vital information in a crisis, and the occasional music is a welcome distraction in a tense situation.

98 CONNECT AFTER A CRISIS

The ability to communicate with your friends, family and loved ones—anytime, anywhere—is one of the most undervalued aspects of the modern lifestyle. When an emergency cuts off this ability, we can feel caught off guard and very vulnerable. But if we are unable to reach out to those we wish to contact, there are a few things that can help us in this disorienting situation.

KNOW THE NUMBERS By having a phone programmed with names instead of dialing the actual phone numbers every time you call, many of us may find ourselves forgetting those important numbers. Take time to memorize them, or keep a "cheat sheet" someplace handy.

USE SOCIAL MEDIA If the crisis is localized, you may be able to reach to friends and family outside the affected area. After the 2011 Tohoku earthquake and subsequent tsunami struck eastern Japan, phones were out and thousands of people were displaced. Many people connected with family by social media and email to signal that they were still alive.

CONSIDER A COMMS HOBBY HAM radios and CB radios can provide you and your group with news from around the world and short-range communication. Of course, the HAM radio setup will take a good amount of equipment and practice, but CBs are simpler and cheaper.

PLAN A DISTRESS SIGNAL This would be something that only you and your people know about, to signal a problem to any group member, such as leaving the "welcome" sign hanging sideways outside their home and plenty of other distress signals. Some even use a code word to say if you are getting alarmed or perceive a threat.

HACKS THROUGH HISTORY // DEAD DROP

Imagine an event where communications are knocked out. Your neighborhood has become unsafe and you decide to flee, but you need to leave information for those who were planning to rally at your home. In the past, people who weren't in the same place at the same time would jot down secret hand-written messages to be left in a prearranged spot for their recipient to collect. Even now, this concept has continued to have value for spies and others in the intelligence community. Today, it's called a "dead drop" when people use a secret location to transfer information or an item when they can't meet together in person. We can also use the trick of dead drops to selectively communicate in the aftermath of a crisis. Pick an out-of-the-way spot and a weatherproof container to leave messages for family, friends, neighbors, or anyone else, when it's not possible or practical to talk face-to-face.

PLASTIC BOTTLE

1 CAGE A CRAWFISH ▲ Minnows, crawfish and other small aquatic animals just can't seem to find their way out of this simple trap. Cut the end off of a plastic bottle, with just a little bit of the side wall attached. Place a small rock in the bottle as a weight and some meat scraps as bait. Turn the bottle top around, and insert it inside the bottle. Poke several holes through both of the pieces (keeping the holes aligned) and use wire or string to "stitch" them together. Place it in slow moving water, and watch the trap fill up with crustaceans and tiny fish.

2 GRAB YOUR GOGGLES ▶ Larger plastic bottles (such as 2-liter soda bottle) provide us with a lot of real estate for repurposing, and when those same bottles are see-through, they're pretty easy to turn into goggles. First, cut a piece of paper with scissors or a knife, to act as a template for your eyewear. Start big and keep trimming them down until you have a good facsimile of wrap-around sunglasses. Next, use a marker to trace your template onto the side of a plastic bottle. Using the knife or scissors again, cut out your goggles and pierce a hole on each side. Use string to tie them in place, and now you're ready for blowing sand and wind.

3 BOIL IN A BOTTLE When all else fails, you can still disinfect your water in a plastic bottle, but it's hardly a desirable technique. Start by filling your bottle with some raw water from your local waterway. Use some wire to dangle your plastic bottle high over a fire (using a tripod made of sticks will help) and wait for it to boil (without a cap on top). The plastic will deform, darken, and put loads of nasty flavor and contaminants in your water—but at least the bugs will be dead. Again, this is a last-ditch method for killing pathogens in your water.

4 USE A CAP WHISTLE ▲ Something as basic as a whistle can be a very useful signaling device, so it's a good thing you can turn almost any plastic bottle cap into a shrill little whistle. While there is some finesse involved, once you get the hang of it, it isn't hard at all. Hold the bottle cap with both hands, placing your thumbs over the open side of the cap. Squeeze your thumbs together tightly and bend your thumbs so that there is a "v" shaped gap between your thumb nails. Place your lips on your bent thumb knuckles and blow as if whistling hard. When you aim the jet of air at the top edge of the cap, it will whistle loudly.

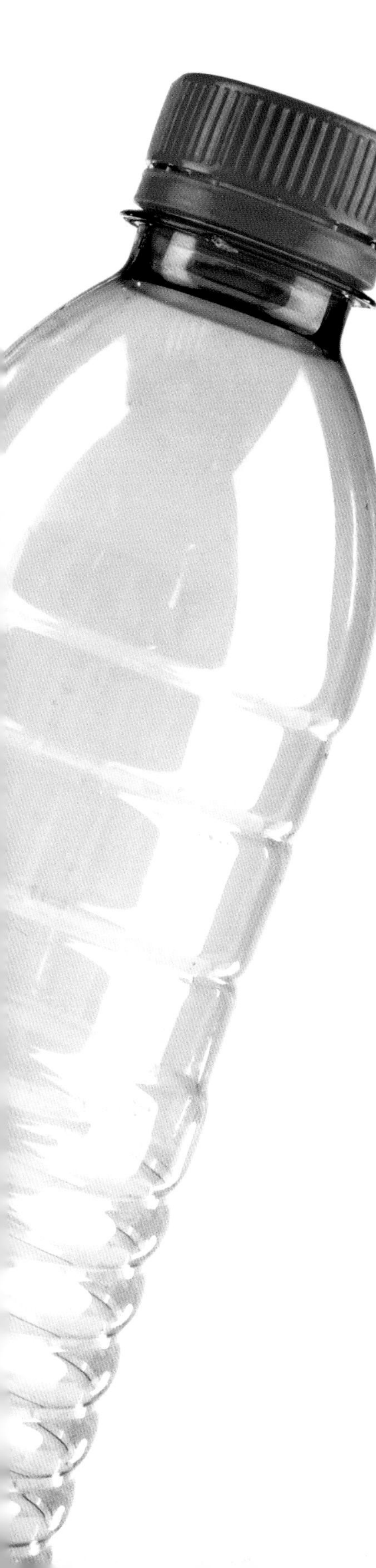

5 GET CORD FROM A BOTTLE Plastic bottles are commonly recycled to make all kinds of fibers, so it shouldn't come as a shock that you can turn a plastic bottle into cordage on your own. With the careful use of scissors or a sharp knife, you can cut both ends off of a plastic bottle and begin spiral cutting the sidewall of a bottle into a long flat ribbon of plastic cordage. Try your best to cut the plastic strips into a uniform width for consistent strength. A plastic strip will be tricky to tie knots into (try the sheet bend knot or water knot for best results), but it gives you a source of cordage where fiber may be scarce.

7 TRY A FISH FLOAT An empty plastic bottle can assist in trotline fishing, netting, and even hook-and-line fishing. Use large plastic bottles as net floats or floats along a trotline. They are more buoyant than chunks of wood are far easier to see. Medium-sized bottles are a better fit for smaller fishing nets, particularly the kind you would cast by hand. The smaller bottles will work just fine as oversized bobbers for hook and line fishing. If you have a color choice in your bottle selection, colorful bottles are naturally the most eye-catching as floats, but any of them can be fish-catching when you're working a productive waterway.

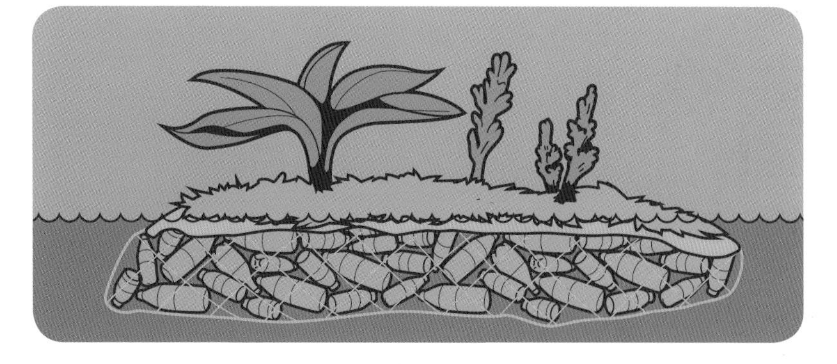

6 BECOME AN ISLAND ▲ Creative (and very brave) off-grid enthusiasts are using air filled plastic bottles bundled inside discarded fishing nets to build their own floating islands covered with sand and even vegetation. And while this is quite the ambitious project, we can use drastically scaled-down version of this concept in a watery emergency so you can tread water a little longer. Air filled plastic bottles have very little weight, yet great buoyancy, so stuff them inside your clothing for a makeshift personal flotation device. If you have a bit of string you can salvage, tie the bottles together at the neck to keep from losing any of them, and then stuff the bundle into your shirt. Even a small amount of buoyancy helps!

8 DISINFECT IN A BOTTLE The SOLDIS method of using sunlight for water disinfection can work in many vessels, but the most practical one is a clear plastic bottle. Choose one that is newer, or with very few scratches and scuffs. The more beat-up the exterior of the bottle, the less light passes into it. You also don't want to go too big. Clear plastic 1-liter and 2-liter bottles are the upper range for reliable solar disinfection. You can ramp up the amount of light by placing a mirror or some reflective surface behind the filled bottle. Only use crystal clear water and leave the bottle in the sun all day, if possible. This method isn't 100-percent effective, but better than drinking raw water.

99 PREP RIGHT

The weather forecasters say a blizzard is on the way, so what will you do? Make a mad dash to the grocery store for milk, bread, and toilet paper—or get out of town?

LISTEN TO THE PREDICTION Find out if there is a cause for alarm before you barricade yourself or flee. Listen to multiple meteorologists to get an average prediction of the upcoming storm. When will the snow start falling and how long it will last? How much snow is expected and how cold will it get? Have all the information before you go "Chicken Little" on your family.

SEE IF YOU'RE REALLY READY Find out just how prepared you really are. Take stock of your food, water, backup lighting and heating methods, alternative power, and all other necessities before you make a decision to stay put. Riding out the storm while underprepared can be really uncomfortable, or downright dangerous.

100 STOCK UP

Well before the storm, clean out your pantry and make a shopping list. Buy the things that you know you'll need first; leftover funds can go toward the wants.

CANNED GOODS High-calorie foods are often canned, able to be eaten as-is, and last for years if properly stored. Look for hearty stews, soups, and pasta.

DRY GOODS Dry pasta is a high-calorie dry staple, and you only need boiling water to prepare it. Rice, oats, beans, powdered milk, cornmeal, flour, and hard candy are also great.

FATS Olive oil, lard, ghee, coconut oil, and shortening last a long time in cold conditions, and provide the calories you'll need in a chill.

DRINKS Cocoa, tea, coffee, and other hot beverages are an important source of warmth, calories, hydration, and morale. Stock an ample supply of family favorites.

101 RAKE A ROOF

Every year, people try spraying water on their roof to remove excess snow. Deep snow on your roof can be heavy and lead to dangerous structural stresses, but the last thing you want to do is spray water up there in an attempt to remove the stuff. Whether the water is hot or cold, it will chill as you spray it onto the snow and add a startling amount of extra weight. As the snow drinks in the water and becomes a slushy mess, you're far more likely to suffer ice damming or structural collapse.

Instead of breaking out the garden hose and making the situation much worse, why not invest in a "roof rake" in blizzard country? This long-handled tool is used to literally rake the snow off your roof, removing weight rather than adding it. You can even make arrangements with a snow removal company to do the work for you—either way, it's a lot cheaper than buying a new house after yours is crushed. And if you happen to be replacing your roof before winter, consider a metal roof. It's more expensive than asphalt shingles, but the snow can slide right off and a roof like this can last for decades.

102 PUT SNOW TO WORK

While all due caution should be exercised when you're dealing with a blizzard, it's important to understand that the snow isn't actually out to get you. When used in the right way, snow can actually become a very valuable resource for your family's survival. Here's how.

KEEP FOOD COLD When the power goes out, use snow to keep your food cold. Move your refrigerated food to coolers and fill in the empty space with snow or ice. Keep these coolers in a cold garage or nearby shed, both for easy access and for protection from hungry animals. Dispose of any perishable meats, poultry, seafood, raw eggs or leftover foods that have been above 40 °F (4 °C) for several hours or have an off scent or texture.

MELT A DRINK While you shouldn't eat snow (yellow or otherwise), fresh snow can be melted to yield safe drinking water. Just remember that snow is one part frozen water and nine parts frozen air, so it will take a lot of snow to keep a group fully hydrated. (Good thing you're in a blizzard, right?)

HEAL WITH COLD Sprains and strains are common injuries, and relief may be close at hand. Fill a plastic zip-top bag with snow and wrap it in cloth. Use this bundle as a cold pack to reduce swelling and pain from sprains, strains, and other orthopedic injuries—and to dull the ache of a migraine.

SIGNAL WITH SNOW Various colorful liquids and powders can be used to dye the snow to create massive ground-to-air emergency signals. Mix food coloring with water and fill up a spray bottle to dispense the liquid. Make a huge "X" or write SOS; just ration your coloring to make sure you'll have enough to finish.

103 HANDLE OUTAGES

You're snowbound and the power is out. It's time to put your plans into action. I always plan for the worst while hoping for the best. This way, if things aren't completely horrible, I'm pleasantly surprised. Here are the first things to do when the power goes down in a blizzard.

LIGHT UP Turn on some safe alternative lighting. Be wary of candles if you have clumsy or rambunctious kids or pets (or adults). Use battery-powered lighting for safer illumination.

MIND YOUR MOBILES Start conserving cell and tablet power. You'll likely be using your devices to access the world outside of snowmageddon. Use that power wisely. Rather than wasting battery power with constant browsing or gaming, just send periodic updates to let people know that you're snowed in without power, but safe for now.

CONSERVE HEAT Begin using heat conservation and alternative heating methods. It's easier to keep the house warm, than to try heating it up again from freezing.

104 MAKE POWER

Providing your own power makes a lot of sense for all kinds of reasons, but think about human nature and the kind of issues you might face in a disaster that goes on for some time.

STAY LOW-KEY A noisy generator, or solar panels on your roof, will provide you with power during an outage, but these items (and the fact that your house is lit up a night) will advertise that you have your own power source. If desperate people become more frantic, they'll wonder what else you have, if you were prudent enough to have the equipment to make your own power.

MAKE YOUR CHOICE Determine whether it makes sense to even have power when your neighbors don't have it, and whether that power should come from a high profile source (like that loud generator) or something else. In my mind, low-profile is better than yelling "Hey, look what I've got!"

105 ADD AN OUTLET

Vehicle engines aren't meant to be electrical generators, but they can be. A trained professional can install an inverter (to turn your alternator's DC power into AC current), and place eletrical outlets in your vehicle. These can be stationed in your car trunk or in the bed of a pickup, and they're capable of operating small appliances while the engine is running. This setup isn't recommend for long term use and you'll need some gasoline to keep the vehicle running, but for short term power needs, it's one of the easiest generating systems to use. Turn on the engine of the vehicle and plug in your ordinary electrically powered gizmo. It's just like a receptacle in the wall, only this wall can drive around the town. Keep in mind that you are consuming a lot of fuel to charge your phone or run a blender, but having the option for emergency power can add a little more peace-of-mind to your prepper planning and be handy on campouts, and you can take the power with you!

106 CHARGE A PHONE

One great product to buy (before the mayhem starts), is a battery-operated mobile phone charger. This can turn a few ordinary batteries into several full charges on your phone. But in the event that you didn't manage to pick one up, there's still a chance for you. Here's a quick hack.

STEP 1 Grab an ordinary plug-in phone charger designed to work in vehicles, some electrical tape, a 9-volt battery, and a bit of wire.

STEP 2 Strip both ends on a short piece of wire, and tape one bare end to the larger (female) terminal on the 9-volt.

STEP 3 Tape the other end to the side terminal of the car charger. Now touch the end terminal on the car charger to the smaller battery terminal (the male one), and plug in your phone. The car charger will step down the power from 9 volts to the amount needed for your phone and the charging will begin.

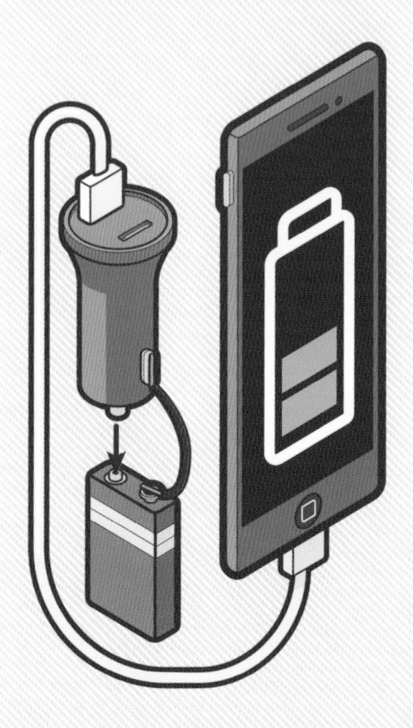

107 HACK A CAR ALTERNATOR

If you liked wiring up your phone to a 9-volt battery for charging, you'll love this. By pulling one (or more) car alternators from available vehicles, you can use them as small generators. While they're not as efficient as purpose built generators, they do produce electrical power (that's their job in your vehicle). Rig up a pulley between an alternator and a stationary bike wheel. Pedal the bike and power is made! Or divert some water from a higher area into a pipe with a nozzle shooting water at a Pelton wheel attached to the alternator. The harder the spray, the faster it spins —and the faster you can make the alternator spin, the more power you get. There are many different ways to cobble together equipment that will make an alternator turn, and if you have a battery to store that power, you can use it any time you like.

108 GO MICRO

For our remote ancestors, muscle and fire were the only sources of energy that they could routinely harness. Then came metal and electricity, and ultimately, the high-tech world we live in today. And despite its technological sophistication, the modern lifeway has many vulnerabilities. Any number of disasters could leave us scrambling to find alternative energy sources to power our useful devices. We are left with two choices in this sobering survival arena, make the power ourselves, or make do without it. Since the average American home is filled with electrically powered tools, appliances and other devices, a back-up source of electricity might be a great investment. If you live near a fast flowing water source (like a mountain stream), it may make sense to start doing research on micro hydro generators. These wheels turn from the force of the water, thereby turning a small generator and producing electrical power.

BUDGET SURVIVAL

SOLAR PANELS

Small solar panels have come a long way in the past few years. Little folding units are now lightweight and easy to carry, yet capable of producing enough power to charge up your various smaller devices (such as mobile phones). These gadgets turn the sun's abundant energy into electrical power, and some kits even include small batteries to allow you to save your power for nighttime use. Some kits even come with an LED built into the panel. Here are a few perks of mini solar panels.

- They're very lightweight.
- They are small to begin with or can be folded down small.
- You can use them in full sunlight or on cloudy days.
- They are affordable.

Quick Tip

This may not be the tip you'll want to hear, but living without electrical power is a possibility. Just ask the one billion people on Earth who currently go without electricity every single day of their lives.

109 DIG A CAT HOLE

For those with an urgent need to relieve themselves while on the move, a cat hole is one of the best ways to be responsible about survival sanitation. Use a stick, shovel, or trowel to dig a hole that is roughly 6 to 8 inches (15–20 cm) deep in the local topsoil. Squat over your hole and make yourself a bit lighter. Wipe up and bury all of the evidence. Use your awesome counter-tracking and camouflage skills to blend the disturbance in the landscape, and no one should be the wiser. In a camp setting where you might be there for a day or more, throw some sticks or a small log on top of your cat hole to prevent people from stepping in your "landmine." And if you forgot the toilet paper, don't worry. You can wipe with a stack of dead dry leaves or virtually anything else that mirrors TP.

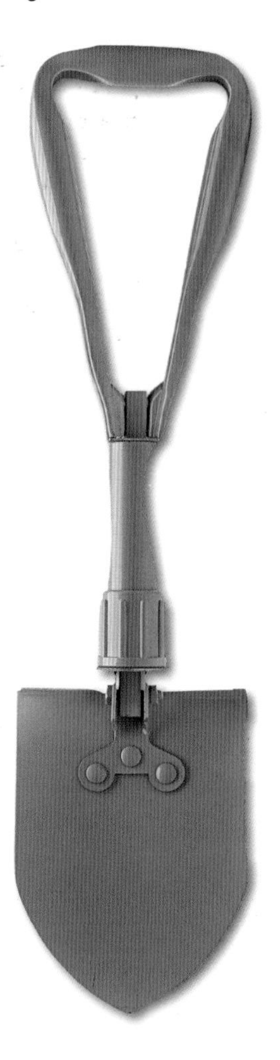

110 USE A BUCKET

The bucket toilet is a relatively safe short-term solution for emergency human waste management, and it's easy to put together. Grab some plastic trash bags, a 5-gallon (20-L) bucket with lid, twist ties, duct tape, and some toilet paper.

STEP 1 Place one trash bag inside the bucket and tape the edge of the bag opening to the side of the bucket.

STEP 2 Add a second layer by inserting and taping down a second bag.

STEP 3 For comfort, place some foam pipe insulation around the rim of the bucket or buy a special bucket toilet seat from a disaster supply store.

STEP 4 Replace the bucket lid after each use. When the bucket is about half full, tie up the inner bag and outer bag. Seal the knot with duct tape and write "Human Waste" on the duct tape with a marker. Place bags out of the way and out of sunlight until you can properly dispose of them.

111 BORROW KITTY LITTER

Borrowing the cat litter isn't exactly what we are talking about here (since I doubt your cat will want it back after you've borrowed it), but we're borrowing the concept of waste absorption. After just one strong "accumulation" in a bucket toilet, the need for odor management, liquid control, and modesty will be obvious. Even the cat has he decency to bury its waste, and we should be no different from—or even better than—a household pet.

By sprinkling a bit of cat litter into a bucket toilet after depositing solid waste, we hide our shame and some of the stink. The litter also soaks up some of the moisture that can be present in these toilets. And in the absence of cat litter, shredded newspaper, and saw dust will work. Dirt and sand can also be used, though they will make the bucket much heavier to carry outside for burial or other disposal.

112 BUILD AN OUTHOUSE

To serve the bathroom needs of a large family or group, particularly for a long span of time, your best bet is to dig a pit and build an outhouse over it. Dig a deep yet narrow hole, downwind from your cabin, camp or home. Make sure you are at least 50 yards (50 m) away from shallow wells and waterways. Use an area above the highest flood level. In areas with a high water table (like wetlands), keep the hole shallow. The bottom of the hole needs to be at least 6 feet (2 m) above the water table. Once your hole is done, build a seat or an entire outhouse building. The most basic build is a wooden box over the hole with an open top and open bottom, with a toilet seat attached. Place tarps around it for privacy, or build a little building to cover the hole, if you have the skills and materials. Whichever way you go, sprinkle a bit of dirt, wood ash, or powdered limestone down the hole when it gets too stinky. And move the setup when the hole is looking full. Bury old outhouse holes under a mound of dirt, and it all goes back to soil.

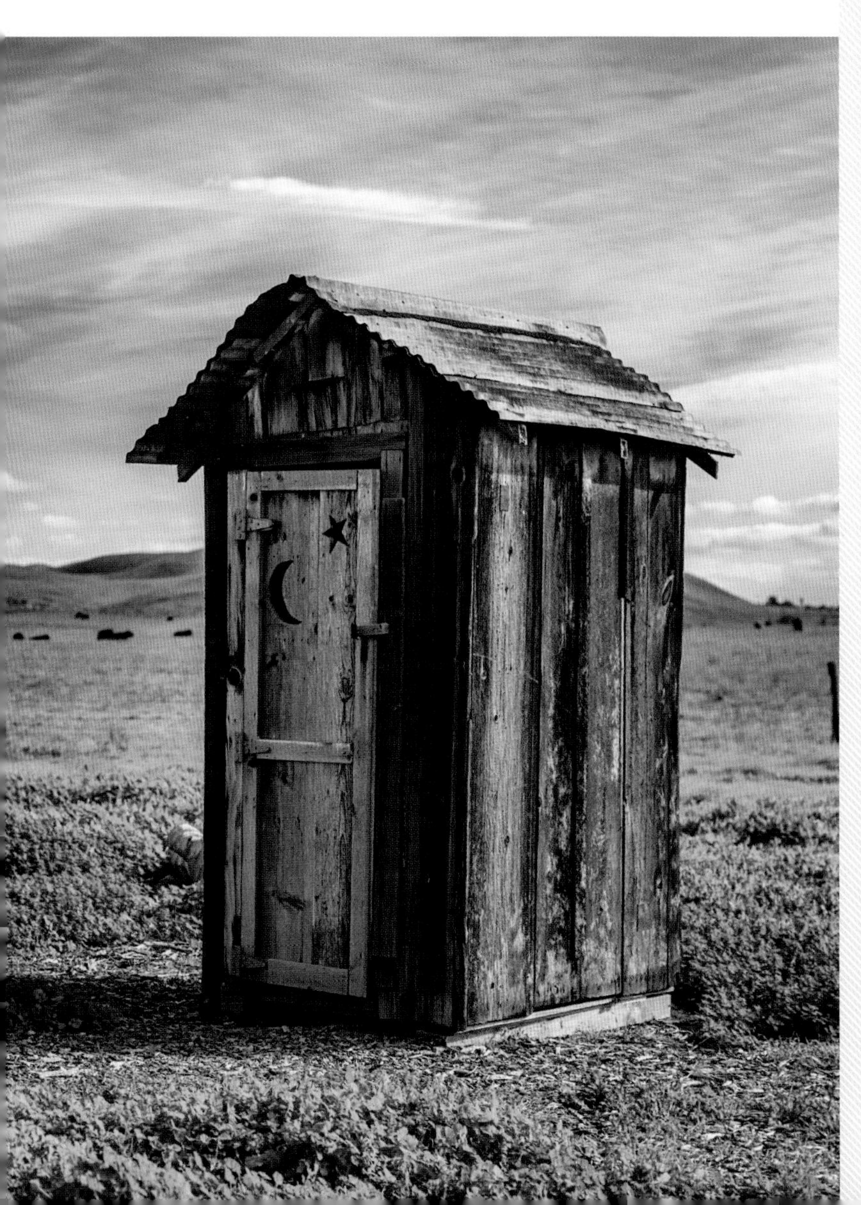

113 IMPROVISE SOME TP

When there isn't a square of toilet paper to spare, you've got to get creative when it comes to improvising toilet paper. In the days of yore, old timers would hang various mail-order catalogs in the outhouse (after they had done their shopping). Sheets of paper would be torn free and softened with a simple technique that will work on newspaper and many other modern paper products. First, crumple a page into a tight little ball, then open the ball up and flatten it back out again. Repeat this "crumple and flatten" technique a few times, until your paper becomes soft and absorbent. Various grades of pulpy paper can be given this treatment and repurposed. Just don't try to flush them down a functional toilet. They don't dissolve like regular toilet paper and they may clog the line. Instead, bury your used TP in the nearest compost pile. Those with a strong nose could also burn the dried used toilet paper, if they have an area where they can safely burn paper trash.

Worth Every Penny

EXTRA TP

If you shop at one of those bulk discount stores that sells mayo by the pallet, grab a big case of TP. It never goes bad, it's a great trade item, and you'll have plenty when you're in need.

114 SEEK A SOAP ALTERNATIVE

Many different kinds of soap can be interchangeable for dish, laundry, and hand soap. I've bathed with dish soap and washed my clothing with bar soap. If you happen to have some kind of liquid soap, this can be added directly to your wash water. If the soap is solid, like bar soap, you can rub it on wet clothing directly, or you can shave off small pieces of the bar and allow them to melt in the water before laundering clothes or washing dishes. When you're done, dump your soapy water and rinse water into the top soil, at least 50 yards from any water source. Even biodegradable soap is harmful to aquatic life. And if you don't have any soap, use hot water and a cloth to scrub the dishes or your body. This will remove a lot of dirt and oil, which is far better than removing none.

115 MAKE A BUCKET SHOWER

As we've seen, the humble 5-gallon (20-L) bucket can serve as a toilet, but it can also provide a bath for improvising survivors. For simple bathing, take a sponge bath with a bucket of warm water, though that's not very close to the showers we are accustomed to using. For an actual shower from a bucket, you'll need a pair of 5-gallon (20-L) plastic buckets that can fit together, some rope to hoist the bucket into the air, and something to pierce small holes in the bottom of one bucket. You'll also need a structure to hold the bucket above head height, and of course, some warm water to wash with.

PREPARE YOUR BUCKETS Using a tiny drill bit or small nail, poke about ten little holes into the center of one bucket bottom (A). This will be your shower head. Tie the rope to this bucket handle and find a place to hoist the bucket up in the air. This could be a sturdy tree branch, or in a treeless location, set up a tall tripod of sticks, lumber, or pipes (B).

SET UP YOUR SHOWER If you make a tripod, the shower can be set up anywhere and you have a structure to which you can attach tarps or sheets for a modesty preserving shower curtain. It's also helpful to choose a spot with a hard surface to stand on. Setting the shower up without a hard surface underneath will result in the bather standing in a messy mud puddle.

GET CLEAN When it's shower time, place the perforated bucket inside the solid bucket. Get them into position under the support and fill the inner bucket with warm water. The intact bucket keeps the water in the perforated bucket until you're ready. Hoist the rope, sliding the shower bucket out of the intact bucket, and secure the end of the line (C). Take your well-earned shower, and enjoy it.

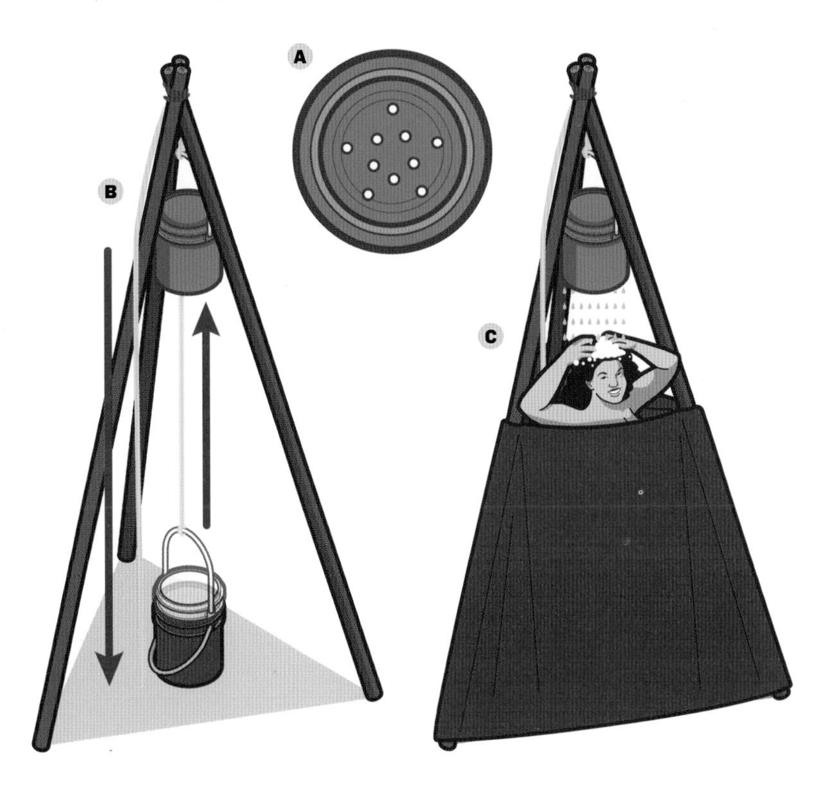

HACK HAZARDS

SCALDS

The modern water heaters and scald protector shower heads in our homes do a great job of providing steady hot water and a safer way for us to bathe. But when these are out of the picture, the hot water we can create will not be so consistent. Whether you are trying to heat up some wash water over a fire, or you've created an elaborate solar water heating system, be aware that scalds are a common occurrence when working around hot water. Make sure there are no trip hazards in your path if you are carrying pots of hot water. If you're creative enough to build a water-heating system, add a thermometer so you can see what temperatures you are dealing with before the water hits anyone's skin. And be ready for burns: A bucket of cool water can lessen the pain of a scald immediately and prevent additional burn damage.

Quick Tip

If you can't take a full shower or bath, find a way to "spot clean" yourself. Use baby wipes or a soapy rag to scrub your most offensive parts while you dream of a day when you can bathe once again.

116 COLLECT WATER

If you can spare the water to wash a few items of clothing, your skin and your clothes will thank you for it. In addition to wearing out your clothing prematurely, dirty clothes can harbor fungus and bacteria. This can lead to fungal skin rashes, infections and other skin maladies. Rain water is great for clothes washing, and a simple set up can collect the rain for you and give you a wash basin.

DIG YOUR OWN BASIN Just dig or find two holes in the ground, side by side is ideal. Line the holes with a plastic tarp. Once they're full of rain water, use one to wash clothes and one to rinse them.

FIND A STREAM Another option is to use the water from a stream, river, or lake in containers. The water doesn't need to be potable, just free of mud. Use buckets, bins, pots, tubs, or another other watertight containers for your wash basins.

117 DO THE DISHES

One of the best ways to wash dishes in the absence of utilities is a "three-bucket" system.

STEP 1 Line up three buckets in a row and fill the first two with warm water and the last one with cold water. Add a scrubbing brush to the first and second buckets. Add some soap to the second bucket, and a splash of bleach to the third bucket.

STEP 2 Scrub away the majority of food residue in the first bucket with your scrubber. Then scrub it even more in the soapy second bucket.

STEP 3 Shake off the soapy water and dunk the dish in the third bucket which contains bleach water. It's fine if the dish lingers in the bleach water for a minute or two.

STEP 4 As a final step, pull the racks out of a household dishwasher and place them in direct sunlight. Use them as convenient dish drying racks with the bonus of UV disinfection from sunlight.

118 WASH THE CLOTHES

Washing clothes may seem pretty darn low on the list of survival issues if you're living in an off-the-grid situation, and truly it is. Shelter, security, safe water and many other topics take precedent over laundry. There is, however, a valid reason to make time for this tedious task. The oils and dirt that build up in clothing, especially when wearing the same clothes repeatedly, tend to destroy most clothing fibers quickly (not to mention stink them to high heaven). If you only have a few items of clothing, it makes sense to take steps to ensure that they last longer. Rub the clothing articles against each other or against themselves, since you probably don't have an old fashioned washboard handy. You could also use a hot rock heated by a fire to warm up your wash water, making it more effective and more comfortable to work in.

119 BE YOUR OWN TRASH COLLECTOR

It's not uncommon for rural households to burn their trash or dig a huge hole in the back 40 acres for a private dump. These may be on option for some folks in some situations, it's hardly a remedy for all. So how do we dispose of trash during and after a disaster? The best route begins with trash separation. Divide your trash into dry and wet.

START WITH DRY Cardboard from food packaging, empty bottles and cans, and anything else that can be reused or repurposed should be culled from the dry trash. Store the cardboard and rinsed out containers where you can keep them clean, dry, and out of the way. Other dry trash can be compacted into a bin or box, and dealt with later. Unless there is a lot of food residue in it, this trash shouldn't stink and it shouldn't be very attractive to mice, rats, roaches, and other pests.

DEAL WITH WET Trash with food residue, and trash that is actually wet (like spoiled food, and leftover food scraps) will draw pests and become a health hazard as it decomposes. This "wet" trash will need to be dealt with in a safe and timely manner. Options include a small, backyard burial, burning in a small burn barrel or pit (if conditions allow and the trash is flammable), or disinfecting and deodorizing the trash, and storing it until you have an opportunity to dispose of it properly. This latter option involves putting the trash in a sealed bucket with a splash of bleach, or a layer of wood ashes, or any other odor-controlling substance that is inhospitable to bacteria and fungus. But before you designate anything as trash during an emergency, ask yourself if there is some other use for the item. Maybe that spoiled food could be handy as trap bait. One man's trash . . .

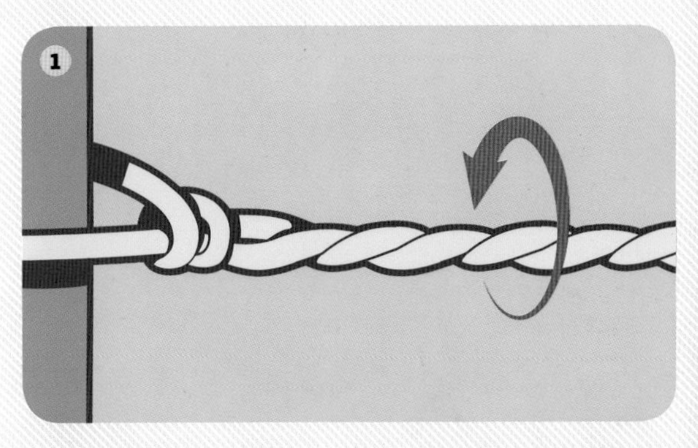

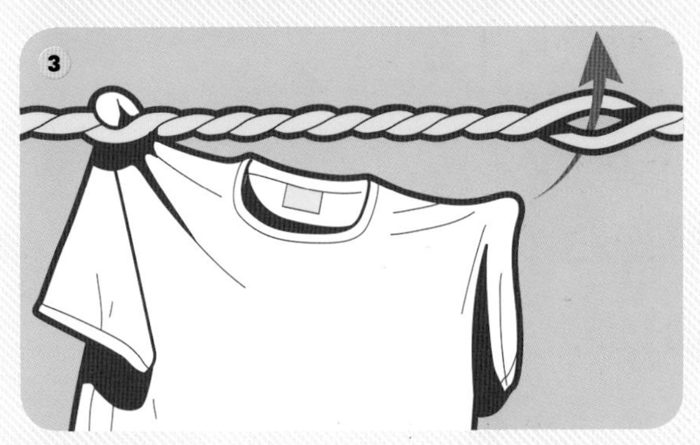

120 TRY A PIN-FREE CLOTHESLINE

This old camping trick has been around for decades, if not centuries. Take a long cord (550 will work nicely), and fold it in half, effectively doubling it. Find two points to tie the cord so that it is stretched tight at eye level when standing. Trees and shrubs work great. Tie one end of the doubled cord to the support. Start twisting the cord from the free end. This may take a minute or two, but once the two cords are twisted around each other tightly, tie off the free end and your clothes line is ready. To secure clothes, spread the twisted lines apart and insert a corner of the clothing item. Do this several times on heavy garments, or just once on small things like handkerchiefs and socks. Let them air dry, and the laundry is done. This twisted line keeps your clothing in place, even if conditions turn windy.

121 UPGRADE A MUD ROOM

If your home has a "mud room" or some similar feature, you can use this as a great decontamination area. After you've been outside walking among the sickos, enter the room and kick off your footwear at the door. Walk further in and strip off your clothing. Use liberal amounts of hand sanitizer on your hands before changing into your inside clothes.

This can prevent the spread of disease into the home on contaminated clothing and shoes. If it's a bigger room, you could even turn the mud room into a quarantine room. Place food, water, bedding and a bucket toilet in the room, before your potentially sick friend or family member comes over. Lock your inner door and make them stay in the quarantine room for a few days to see if they become symptomatic. No, they won't like it, but that's the price of admission to your sanctuary.

122 MAKE A CHEAP SUIT

Concerned about the flu or some even more sinister pathogens? You'll need the right supplies for protection. You can use some or all of these simple items to create a DIY protective suit, should the horseman of pestilence ride through your town.

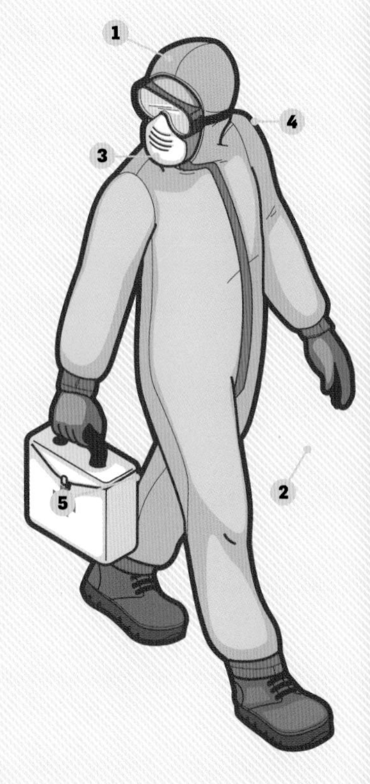

STEP 1 Start by hitting your local hardware store for a set of Tyvek coveralls. These are tough, tear-proof, and almost waterproof. They're commonly available and can also be purchased with head and shoe covers.

STEP 2 Grab a little duct tape to tape the joints of your suit.

STEP 3 Add a standard medical mask, such as an N95 mask or even an N99. Grab a big box of them at one of those warehouse stores, and you'll have plenty extra for other people to wear.

STEP 4 Add work goggles to the outfit, especially ones with an anti-fog coating and vents.

STEP 5 Finally, nitrile gloves will protect your hands, without causing latex allergies.

123 USE A SHIRT GASKET

Basic surgical masks are one of the cheapest defenses against airborne diseases. The common N95 mask protects against 95% of the particulates larger than 0.3 microns in size. The next masks are N99 masks (99% effective) and N100 masks (99.7% effective). But none of these help much if they don't make a tight seal around your nose and mouth because of facial hair. Whether it's just shaving stubble or a full beard, air will seek the path of least resistance—gaps created between your mask and your skin. But here's a helpful option: Put a spare t-shirt over your head, just so that your face shows through. Put on your mask over the shirt so the fabric acts as a gasket. It's not a perfect solution, but it will help.

124 KNOW YOUR FOE

Many organisms can be harmful to human life, but the two most common troublemakers are bacteria and viruses. Both can kill us if we are exposed to the wrong species, yet these are each very different forms of life. Bacteria are the oldest creatures on Earth, found in a wide range of shapes and sizes, some helpful to human life and some lethal. Viruses are small infectious agents that enter living cells of animals, plants, or even bacteria, and then replicate inside them until they destroy the cell, spread through the body, and repeat the cycle. The majority of viruses and bacteria that enter the human body are rendered harmless by the protective effects of the immune system.

But sadly, there are plenty of organisms that can completely ravage our immune system. Age-old illnesses like smallpox, ebola, anthrax, and even the plague have been resurfacing as a lethal blight on modern humanity. We also face the risk of being attacked by intentionally spread pathogens as an act of terror. Any of these, or just a particularly catchy strain of the flu, can become responsible for an outbreak, an epidemic, or even a pandemic. These are similar events, and the difference has to do with the scale of the event. Both an outbreak and an epidemic are a widespread occurrence of an infectious disease within a community. According to the Centers for Disease Control (CDC), the main difference between them is the percentage of deaths from the disease, though many factors are considered. Typically, an epidemic has higher mortality rates than were expected for the disease. If an epidemic occurs across several countries and affects a large population in each, it is considered a pandemic. The last influenza pandemic was the Hong Kong flu between 1968 and 1969, which killed 33,000 Americans.

125 GET OILED

According to the legend, thieves' oil is a mixture created by a group of 15th century thieves to protect themselves from contracting the plague while robbing the homes and bodies of plague victims. When apprehended, the thieves admitted to using the formula and disclosed the recipe in order to avoid a torture-filled death delivered by witch-hunting Inquisitioners. Whether the tale is true or not, the essential oils in this blend are truly antiseptic and antiviral, with a high kill rate against airborne bacteria. I use it every year during cold and flu season, and it even smells nice.

MAKE YOUR OWN

40 drops clove bud essential oil
35 drops lemon essential oil
20 drops cinnamon bark essential oil
15 drops eucalyptus essential oil
10 drops of rosemary essential oil

Mix this blend with olive oil to dilute it, and wipe it on your skin. You can also put some in a diffuser to get the oil airborne.

5 TRY BLEACH FOR BAD ODORS

That nearly full bucket toilet or big sack of kitchen garbage can be stinky, especially in warmer weather. Bleach can help to dial down the gag reflex: First, it kills bacteria, who are the real culprits behind any foul stench. Secondarily, bleach has its own strong smell, which can cover other odors. Just sprinkle a little bleach into your bucket toilet after each use, or put a diluted bleach solution in a clearly marked bottle and spray down your garbage before shoving it into a bag.

1 MAKE A DISINFECTING SPRAY ▲ Sanitizing cleansers are common enough in the average home, but you may need something stronger in the event of an infectious outbreak. Ordinary household bleach can be diluted with water to create a very effective disinfectant following the CDC (Centers for Disease Control) recommended 1:10 solution. For a small batch, blend 1/4 cup of bleach with 2 1/4 cups of water. Pour the bleach in first, then add the water to avoid being splashed by the bleach. Use cool or cold water, as hot water can degrade the mixture. Do not add other ingredients into the mixture.

2 ZAP YOUR DISHES Dirty dishes aren't just gross—they can make us sick. In a crisis with limited water, you may consider many shortcuts when it comes to cleaning your soiled cups, plates, bowls, and utensils. Just make sure that bleach is involved in your plans. If water is very scarce, wipe as much of the food from your dishes as is possible, then give them a wipe down with the disinfecting spray we just mentioned. Air-dry them and the bleach residue will (mostly) evaporate away. If you have a little more water to spare, pour just a few ounces of bleach into a bucket of clear water for a dish disinfecting station.

3 DISINFECT DRINKING WATER

Bleach can make water safe to drink, but you have to read the label. Older bleach formulas are 5.25 to 6% sodium hypochlorite, while newer ones are 8%. This will affect the amount you use, and so will the water temperature and quality. Cold, clear water will need less bleach than warm or muddy water. Add two drops of bleach per quart (liter) if the water is warm and clear; use four drops instead, if the water is cold or murky. If your bleach concentration is 8% sodium hypochlorite instead of 6%, your usage range should only be 2 to 3 drops instead. Shake the water bottle, and let it sit one hour.

4 SANITIZE CLOTHING AND BEDDING If you still have power (and a clothes washing machine), it's no problem to toss your germy and disgusting garments and bedding into the wash and add bleach to disinfect the load. If you're dealing with infectious waste or a catchy virus, follow the bleach label for the amount to add to the wash to sanitize fabrics. And if the clothes washer is out of commission, you'll have become the clothes washer. In a bucket or tub, mix laundry soap, water and a little bleach to make a cleansing wash for sick-room bedding and any contaminated clothing you may have.

6 WEAPONIZE YOUR LAUNDRY ROOM ▼ You can turn almost anything into an improvised weapon, if you're quick thinking and adaptable in emergency settings. Bleach stings the eyes intensely and can cause very serious damage to the mucus membranes. I'm definitely not telling you to make plans to throw bleach in someone's eyes, but I can tell you to be alert to any possible weapon that lies within reach, even when you're washing the clothes. And if you mistakenly fling bleach in the face of a friendly rather than a marauder, rinse their eyes with a steady stream of water for 30 minutes. Use clear water and have them move their eyes around so they are rinsed thoroughly.

7 CAMO YOUR CLOTHES ▲ Bleach can strip the color right out of fabric, leaving whitish blotches; use this to your advantage to create a winter camouflage suit from old clothing. Use an eye dropper or some careful dribbling to cover the garments with a multitude of large and small splotches. Strive for irregular sizes and patterns of bleach drops and allow them to sit for a few minutes. Wash the clothes as you normally would, and admire your handiwork. If the bleach took out the color completely, the clothing will have wintery white spots.

8 ENJOY THE JUG Once the bleach is all gone, you still have one great thing you can use: the jug! After a good rinsing, it can make an excellent water jug due to the dense plastic construction. That empty bleach jug can also be cut up in different ways to create everything from a megaphone for yelling louder to a scooper for shoveling dry goods or sand. You could cut the bottom out of the jug and use it as a cloche to protect tender seedlings in your survival garden. The list goes on and on.

128 TOUGHEN UP

How tough is your brain? Mental toughness doesn't have anything to do with muscle mass, or how many protein shakes you can chug. We mean the strength of your will and the toughness of your mind. This is not a tough body, but a tough head. To be mentally tough, you must tolerate the intolerable, suffer the insufferable, and overpower your weakness and your desire to give up. Laziness can be a pitfall to your mental toughness. Survival is hard work and it can require some tough choices to be made. A survival scenario is not a vacation from your job, or some unexpected leisure time. Survival experiences, by their very nature, are tough situations. Taking the easy way out and being lazy will eventually get you into serious trouble. Be as tough as you can, and work as hard as you can!

126 MANAGE MINDSET

The mentality of a survivor is very different from the mindset of a victim. The survivor will tend to take advantage of their own positive mental, emotional, and psychological traits. They will work hard to find the silver lining in their gloomy situation. They will attempt to stay motivated and mentally strong. They will learnto embrace adaptability and find new ways to get the things they need. In short, a natural survivor is "wired" for survival. But then we have the victim. These people are pessimistic, lazy, stubborn, and ruled by fear. For these people, being entangled in a disaster is just another unfair event in a long chain of bad luck for which they do not feel responsible. So which way do you lean? We all have elements of both the survivor and the victim within us. Which one will you allow to be in charge of your fate?

127 FIGHT SORROW

Maybe you or someone in your group lost a pet, or a home, or a loved one during a catastrophic event. Mental healthcare providers have long recognized five stages of grief and loss—denial, anger, bargaining, depression, and acceptance. Denial is often the first stage, where we will refuse to believe what has happened. We then drift into anger, which can manifest in numerous ways. Next comes bargaining, where people often plead their case to a higher power, offering whatever they can to have things restored to the way they were. When this invariably fails, depression is the next natural step. Once this has run its course, we can connect to the final phase of acceptance. There's usually no easy way to speed through these steps, so the hack here is patience, whether you or another is grieving.

129 ATTACK ANGER

Anger can be a common response to a situation that is out of our control, especially when things aren't going the right way. And depending on your unique personality and history, you may show your anger in many different ways. Some people boil over and give in to verbal outbursts and hulk-like smashing. Other people bottle up their anger and withdraw emotionally. It's helps to know how you and your group members show their angry side, so you can identify it when anger hits and have the right response to cool things down. The "outburst" crowd is usually quick to recover, so let them vent. The sullen sulking group may need to be coaxed into expressing their feelings. In any case, the primary function of anger is to let us know that something is wrong and spur us toward a resolution. Put that angry energy to work. Don't let it become another problem.

130 RAISE MORALE

Morale is an ongoing condition that you need to monitor in an emergency, but what is morale exactly? Merriam-Webster defines morale as "the mental and emotional condition of an individual or group with regard to the function or tasks at hand." The task at hand in survival is surviving, so it's important to know how to boost morale. Start with a fair assessment of the level of morale in your group or yourself. Some people may not show their pain or problems, so ask. Next, you'll want to show your support through word and deed. Survival situations are stressful and traumatic, so show them that you are on their side. Find ways to reward yourself or your group, and things to look forward to in the short term. Celebrate the smallest successes (or even the absence of failure). Finally, reassess morale often until you're through the ordeal.

Worth Every Penny

MORALE TOKEN

It could be a religious item, a small keepsake, or a laminated photo of loved ones, but by keeping a token for morale, a survivor can focus on something as an inspiration to persevere.

MENTAL HACK // **PREVENT PANIC**

Panic is the state of being terrified to the point of thoughtless behavior, but each person's version of "thoughtless" can be very different. Some people freeze, while others take off running and screaming. Your results may vary.

If you find your logical mind being swallowed by fear, focus on something you can control: Your breathing. Breathe in for five seconds, hold it for five, and exhale for five. Repeat until calmer thoughts prevail.

WILDERNESS

THE WILDERNESS IS A PLACE OF GREAT BEAUTY, AND WHEN WE VISIT IT, WE MIGHT EVEN DREAM OF LIVING THERE AS OUR ANCESTORS ONCE DID.

We might imagine ourselves as modern-day pioneers, never again setting foot on concrete. But when we leave the safety of modern life, we expose ourselves to the hazards and threats that our ancestors faced. There's nothing imaginary about getting lost in the wild, or succumbing to starvation, or death by dysentery. These hazards are very real, and they still happen in modern times. And if our problems are compounded—say, getting lost and then getting hurt; or running out of food and then losing our gear—the odds of survival are not in our favor. Most survivors can deal with one problem, but when they pile up, so does trouble. Cold, heat, dangerous animals, and hazardous terrain can kill the unlucky and unskilled on a regular basis. And while we can't change your luck, by practicing the skills contained in this section, we can give you some tools to better your odds.

131 BUILD THE KIT

Survival kits aren't just for Rambo types who are slogging through third-world jungles or remote patches of no-mans-land. They are for everybody and should be carried on every outdoor excursion. Here's a basic list of gear to get you started, and from there, you can customize the kit.

SHELTER It's hard to beat a space blanket. Originally developed for astronauts (hence the word "space"), this windproof and waterproof blanket reflects most of the wearer's body heat. An emergency poncho or large trash bag can also provide shelter from wind and rain.

WATER A survival straw or disinfection tablets can provide you with a basic water disinfection system, and these items are lightweight and small. Add a container to the mix (such as a water bottle to hold your survival kit), and you now have a way to transport water, too.

FIRE Butane lighters are a great choice, while waterproof survival matches are a nice backup. Ferrocerium rods (aka spark rods) can also be a backup fire starter, but they aren't capable of lighting everything on fire. A magnifying glass or flint-and-steel kit can last forever, if you don't lose them.

MEDICAL Survival situations are often accompanied by medical emergencies. This makes first aid another important part of your survival kit. Carry the gear to cover traumatic injuries and everyday ills.

COMMUNICATION This group consists of the signal mirrors, signal whistles, and even your mobile phone. These tools communicate your distress and attract attention. Go big, go loud, and go home!

TOOLS Your kit should have duct tape, a multi-tool, cordage, a compass, and any other outdoor tools you suspect you'd need. A backup knife is a great too, as is a tool that can saw wood (and bone, if needed); consider a high-tech add-on such as a solar-powered battery charger for your mobile phone.

132 PACK EXTRAS

A survival kit has no room for luxuries or frivolous items, but there are some unexpected items that can be a great addition to your wilderness survival kit.

HARD CANDY Keep hard candy in your survival kit, for energy and as a motivator. Sugary treats are a great short-term fuel for your body, and a few candies can lift almost anyone's morale.

DENTAL FLOSS The mouth is a gateway into the body, and we need to be able to take care of our teeth. Add dental floss to your kit, for cleaning your teeth and a hundred other uses.

ALCOHOL For larger kits, a tiny bottle of liquor is a great addition, even if you don't drink. A little splash can get your campfire going, disinfect wounds, sterilize tools, deodorize skin, and treat infections.

133 STAY LIGHT

Anyone who's gone out on a long hike can tell you that being overburdened is a killer. When you pack a survival kit, make sure it's got everything you need—but still light enough that you can carry it. A backup item (or two, if they're really small) is a good idea, but consider the trade-offs: Extra items will also bring extra weight with them, which may slow you down and take up space in your kit that you could put to better use.

134 ADJUST YOUR SIZE

There are many styles of survival kit, and it can be hard to decide which one to buy or build. A kit may consist of a few critical items stuffed inside a paracord bracelet or dangling from a necklace. Or it may be a small container that easily fits in your pocket. Then again, it could be something larger, like a pouch that attaches to your other gear. For a hike in the park, a pocket kit should be more than enough—as long as it contains a space blanket, signaling gear, and fire starting equipment. But for a trip into the backcountry, a bigger kit is a smarter choice.

Since they only contain a little bit of gear, survival bracelets are probably best regarded as a backup to more substantial (and easier to open) survival kits. Redundancy is a beautiful thing, so bring more than you think you will need. It's better to have some extra gear and not need it after all, than to need it and not have it with you.

135 PACK A KIT IN A BOTTLE

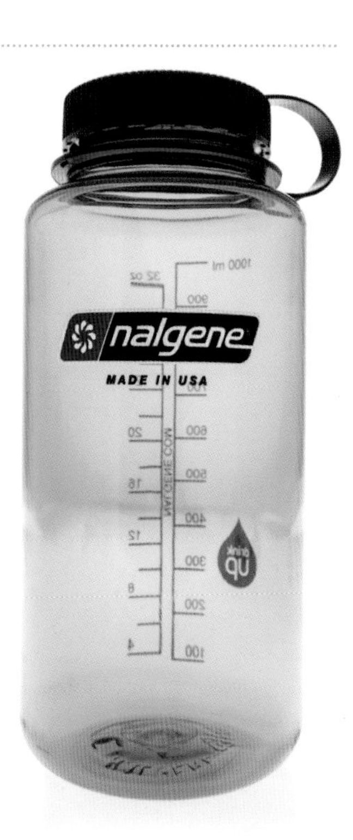

A bottle of water is worth a lot to a thirsty person, but the bottle itself can serve many purposes. One of the best of these uses is a survival kit container. Whether your bottle is plastic or metal, you can fill it with supplies and turn it into watertight survival kit. Consider using a wide mouth stainless steel, single-walled water bottle. This is not only a crack-proof, crush-resistant water carrier and survival kit container, but it has a hidden advantage: It can be used to boil your water to make it safe to drink. Just make sure it's stainless steel or some other fire-friendly metal such as titanium. Never put an insulated or double-walled bottle in the fire—pressure can build in the lining, leading to an explosion!.

BUDGET SURVIVAL

CANDY TIN KIT

Those with a sweet tooth might occasionally have small metal candy tins lying around, and one can make a very handy case for your pocket survival kit. Compact, lightweight, and strong, they are easy to carry and durable enough to survive the rough-and-tumble life in your pocket. The price is right, too: You paid for the candy and ate it, so the tin is basically free. Tins may be round with a friction-fit lid, or they may be some other shape that has a hinged lid. Since they're metal, you can even use these tins to make char cloth in your campfire. There's really just one problem with this budget container: It does not come waterproofed. You can, however, tape the tin shut to resist water.

Quick Tip

Once you build or buy a kit, be sure you take at least one with you on EVERY single trip to the outdoors—you never know when you'll need one, and it's the kit in your pocket, not one at home, that can save a life.

136 LAYER UP

Our clothing is our first line of shelter from the elements, so it should match the wildest weather that the season can throw at you. One easy way to prepare for the variabilities of the lower atmosphere is to dress in layers.

COLD WEATHER For cold weather, don a wool or synthetic shirt and pants, with an extra sweater or hooded sweatshirt. Top it off a parka or similar coat with hood. Choose synthetic fill if the coat may get wet; and round things out with warm gloves, insulated boots, and thick wool socks.

WARM WEATHER In warm weather, choose synthetic, cotton, or linen pants and a long-sleeved shirt (to keep the sun off your arms). Use thin fabrics, loose fit, light color, and keep skin covered for added sun protection. Add a wide-brimmed hat and light work gloves for extra protection.

137 MAKE A MATCH COAT

You too can turn a blanket into a coat, and you don't need sewing skills or even a pair of scissors! In the past, various peoples throughout time and around the world have worn blankets like cloaks, but keeping them in place required extra work—or a free hand. Around the time of the American Revolution, soldiers and other people who needed both hands free began wearing their blankets as "match coats"—garments trussed up to be more like coats than cloaks. Here's how to make your own "period-correct" coat to stay warm in a pinch.

STEP 1 Fold a wool blanket in half and drape it over your shoulders like a shawl or over your head like a poncho.

STEP 2 Wrap the blanket around your torso, pulling one corner far to the left, and the other to the right. Use a large safety pin to fasten it at your throat.

STEP 3 Use a proper belt, or make one out of cord or rope, to help keep it in place around your torso. This effectively gives you a wool coat with two sleeves.

138 BAG YOURSELF

I'm unsure of the exact number of times I've done this trick, but it's safe to say I have made a trash bag poncho quite often. Trash bags are very versatile, and can be made into many useful items with just your hands!

MAKE A SIMPLE PONCHO Tear one corner out of a large trash bag, slide the bag down over your body, and stick your face out through the hole. This creates a surprisingly effective rain poncho that's light weight and still usable for other tasks. By staying dryer, you'll also stay warmer!

FREE YOUR ARMS If you want more mobility, tear a hole in each corner and in the center of the trash bag bottom. Pull this over your head like a t-shirt and it will keep your torso fairly dry, while allowing your full range of movement at the same time.

139 BUY THE BEST

You may look great in your backcountry clothing, but any experienced outdoor enthusiast can tell you: fabric and function are more important than fit and fashion. Purchase the best outdoor clothing you can afford, as your life may depend on it. Select the right clothing for your outdoor activities. It also helps to buy apparel from a store or company with a generous return or exchange policy, in case it doesn't live up to expectations.

WEAR SOME WOOL When you can find it, buy and wear wool clothing for cool and variable weather. This costs more than other fabrics, but it can stay warm even when wet and will resist burning better than synthetic fibers.

SKIP THE COTTON Just because a company sells cotton long underwear and markets the products for an outdoor crowd doesn't mean that it's a good choice. Cotton is actually an unsafe base layer for the outdoors, since it can retain moisture for quite a long time. If it's cold enough to want long johns, they should never be cotton material.

HACKS THROUGH HISTORY // GET WARMER

When your outdoor clothing just isn't thick enough to keep you warm, and you don't have another layer that you can put on, then you can use a very ancient trick to enhance the clothing you already have: By stuffing your clothes with any available vegetation, you'll add more air space to insulate you against the cold. It's like adding another garment to your layers, and it definitely works—we even know that people have been doing this for at least 5,000 years. In September of 1991, German mountain climbers found the naturally mummified body of "Ötzi the Iceman" in the Ötztal Alps. This copper-age fellow lived between 3,400 and 3,100 BCE; and his body and belongings were well preserved by thousands of years of ice. Ötzi's numerous cold weather tricks and techniques were plain to see—including his grass-stuffed footwear. Grass is one of our best choices for natural plant-based insulation, even today. The hollow shafts of grass hold air in their stalks, while the leaves and stalks trap warm air in between them. If you can't find any grasses, you can also use leaves, pine needles, moss, or virtually any other vegetation—as long as it's relatively dry—to stuff into your chilly clothing. Just tuck your pants into your socks, and fill them up. Then tuck in your shirt and stuff it too. You'll look like a scarecrow, but you'll be warm.

1 TRY SOME COMPRESSION
The belt has become little more than a fashion accessory in modern times. But in the backwoods and wild places, a creative survivor can repurpose their gear and make life easier. While most belts won't deliver the pressure needed for a fully effective tourniquet, any belt can be wrapped around a dressing to apply pressure to a wound, to gauze, or other absorbent material for best results. A long belt can even be adapted to serve as an arm sling to support an injured arm or shoulder. It's even adjustable!

2 FLOAT WITH YOUR PANTS ▲
In the event of a water landing, your pants may be used as a flotation device—that is, if you can get them off while treading water. First, get your pants off without losing them, and tie the pant legs together. A basic square knot will work fine. Next, grab the pants by the waistband and lift them out of the water. With a quick motion, slap the waistband down into the water and the pant legs will start to fill with air. Repeat this motion, and then put our head through the pant legs (like a life vest) while holding the waistband closed. If you can grab a cord or shoe lace, you can even tie the waistband shut for better air retention.

3 BREATHE THROUGH A BRA ▲
Dangerous dust in the air? Urban disasters can launch all kinds of nasty particulate matter into the air you breathe, but what do to if you don't have a respirator? Cut a bra in half between the cups. Pierce a hole in the side of the cup where it was cut in half, and thread the straps from the other side through the new opening. Fit the cup over your face tightly, and tie off the strap. Each bra cup can be a surprisingly good filter. It may be a little weird asking for half of a bra, or offering half of yours, but it's worth the awkwardness.

4 USE YOUR SOCKS A pair of dry socks are a blessing to a wet hiker, but they're more than just foot coverings. A sock can become a pouch or a water filter. A pair of thick socks can make fine mittens in a cold weather emergency. Even holed socks can become tick gaiters (a tight covering between your boot tops and pant cuffs) if you cut off the toes. Socks can even help you process acorns: Just fill one with crushed chunks and anchor it in a stream to flush away tannic acid. You'll cook the acorns afterward; ignore the dirty sock!

5 PACK YOUR PANTS ▶ A spare pair of pants may seem like a burden, unless you can get those pants to help you do some of the carrying, too. Grab three pieces of cord, one about a yard (meter)long and two that are half that length. Use each of your short cords to tightly tie each pant leg near the bottom cuff. Next, pull the two legs up and tie the pant cuffs to the belt loops on either side of the zipper. Your final step is to thread the long cord through the belt loops of the pants and use it as a drawstring to close the backpack. By using cargo pants, you can even take advantage of the many pockets to hold smaller items.

6 MAKE BOOT-LACE CORDAGE Our ancestors started using fibrous materials for cordage a really long time ago. Lucky for us, we still have all the heritage materials that our predecessors used, and a wonderful assortment of high tech materials which could be twisted into cord as well. Even if you're caught without survival gear, you probably still have your boots. Bootlaces can be removed and used individually, or they twisted into cord.

7 STROP WITH A BELT Your leather belt can be used as a strop to finish the edge on knives, axes and other edged tools that you have field sharpened. And while a rigger's belt or paracord belt may seem more survival savvy, plain old leather will strop your steel perfectly while the other belts will not. I recommend taking off the belt and laying it on a smooth log. Then just draw the tool edge back and forth across the belt, moving the spine of the tool forward and dragging the sharp edge behind it, keeping the blade pressed to the surface. Soon, all of the burrs will be gone and the edge will be sharp.

8 IMPROVISE BANDAGES ▼ When someone is bleeding and your medical kit has run out of bandages, you'll have to get creative to improvise a dressing for that wound. Your first instinct may be to hold pressure on bleeding wounds with your bare hand, and this is a good instinct. This can help to control the bleed, but the bad part is that you can't hold the wound forever. By grabbing a clean piece of smaller clothing (like a t-shirt), and using it as an improvised bandage, you can help to stop the bleeding and even bind it in place to act as a dressing. Cut strips from a shirt to act as binding, and wad up the rest as padding.

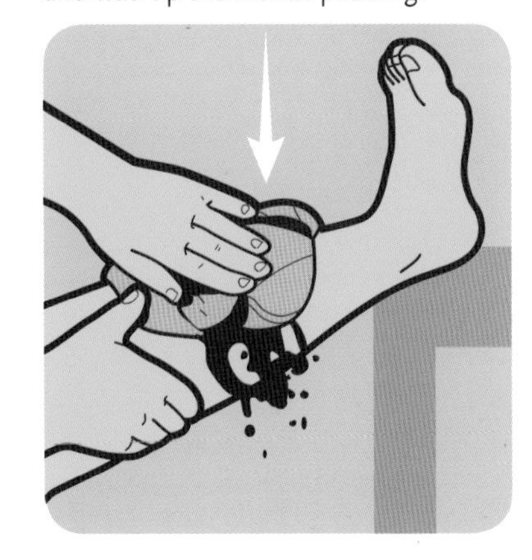

140 MAKE SOME SHADE

Any shade is good shade in a sun-scorched desert, but the best shade is portable. You won't travel very far hanging out all day under the only tree for fifty miles (80 km). But, if you stretch a space blanket or a piece of cloth over a broken branch from that tree, you'll have a makeshift parasol that can go anywhere you care to roam. Now you can bring your "shade tree" with you. Of course, you should still try to work or walk during the cooler parts of the day to avoid excess sweating and heat illnesses that can come quickly from being out in the heat. And if you need more substantial shelter, set up "tents" or sun shelters with tarps and rope. If these aren't available as building materials, then use brush and vegetation to build a brush hut for shade and protection.

141 USE WHAT THE DESERT PROVIDES

At first glance, the desert may seem like a vacuum, empty of life and water. But once you look a little deeper, you'll find an environment full of well-adapted life forms and many natural resources.

MAKE SCORPION KABOBS Like most animals, scorpions have natural predators. This list includes mice, birds, snakes, other scorpions—and survivalists. Using a knife, cut off the scorpion's venomous stinger. Run several of them through with a skewer and roast them over your fire until crispy. The "shrimp of the land" has roughly 4–5 calories per gram, making it far more nutritious than worms or caterpillars. Enjoy!

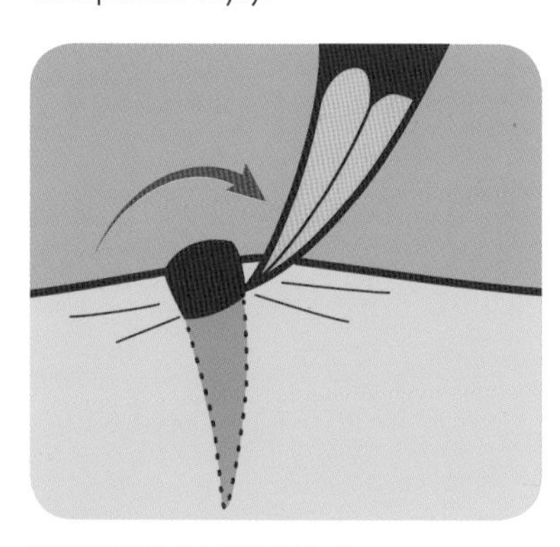

REMOVE A THORN If you've stepped on a thorn in the desert, my condolences. But this painful condition can be remedied, with another thorn. In this "hair of the dog that bit you" treatment, you can use a strong stiff thorn to pick at the skin above an imbedded thorn, to dig it out as you would a splinter. Just take care that you use a sturdy thorn for this procedure; you don't want to break off another thorn in your skin.

ENJOY FRICTION FIRE In the desert, moist wood isn't usually a problem. So grab that sun baked yucca stalk and use it to spin up the fastest bow drill or hand drill friction fire you've ever made. The extreme dry conditions place certain desert plants among the most effective friction fire materials on earth. If you can't rub two sticks together successfully there, then you'd better go back to survival school.

DIG IN THE SANDBOX Need to dig a hole? It doesn't get much easier than in sandy desert terrain. Need to dig a latrine? Done. Need to dig the trench for some primitive cooking or a hot rock mattress? It's so easy. Rather than fighting the sand as if it were your enemy, you can use it to your own advantage.

HACK HAZARDS

DON'T WASTE WATER

You could certainly rig up your canteen for an improvised shower in the desert, or wash the dust out of your clothing with some DIY laundry hacks, but is that really the best thing that you should be doing with your water? I'd say no, and rather strongly. Water needs to be in your food and drink, and as for the rest, you'll just have to do without. Scrub your dirty dishes with sand rather than washing them with water. Use just spit and toothpaste for dental hygiene, instead of using valuable water for repeat rinses. Leave your clothes to bake in the sun for a few hours to kill some off the terrible smell, rather than washing them in water. Unless you're camped out next to a desert lake or river, treat every drop of water like the precious thing it is. The deserts of the world are quick to punish those who don't respect and conserve their water.

Quick Tip

Watch where you put your hands and gear! Scorpions, spiders, snakes, and other desert prowlers need shade too, and they may end up in gloves, boots, or open backpacks that are left lying around.

142 BEND SOME TREES

A flexible sapling can make things, though my favorite has to be shelter. Over the years, I've constructed many traditional indigenous homes out of bent saplings. From complex wigwams and longhouses, to smaller field-built survival shacks, the flexible wood of a bent sapling can make shade and shelter for you and your fellow adventurers. If you don't have time to weave saplings into an elaborate dome and thatch that dwelling with bark slabs or grasses, then try this trick. Bend over a tall yet flexible sapling tree and use a rope to tie the top to the ground via a stake, fallen log or some other anchor. Fling a tarp over the top and secure the edges, or lay sticks against both sides and cover the frame with debris. Either way, this humpbacked hut is easy to build and the rounded shape sheds the rain very well.

143 TIE UP A ROOF

A tarp shelter is one of the fastest survival shelters that a person can construct, but what happens if you don't have a tarp with rings in the corners? Then grab any large piece of fabric or plastic sheeting you can find and use the sheet bend knot to tie it up. Simply bunch up the corner of the tarp and bend it into a "J" shape. Bring the line through from behind the "J", wrap around the entire tarp bend, and tuck the line under itself on top. Pull it tight by hand before putting a load on the line, just to make sure it begins to hold. Tying an overhand knot in the end of the line is a good insurance policy too, in case the sheet bend slips as it tightens for the first time. Once tightened, this knot is surprisingly tough and durable. Now you can tie almost anything to almost anything!

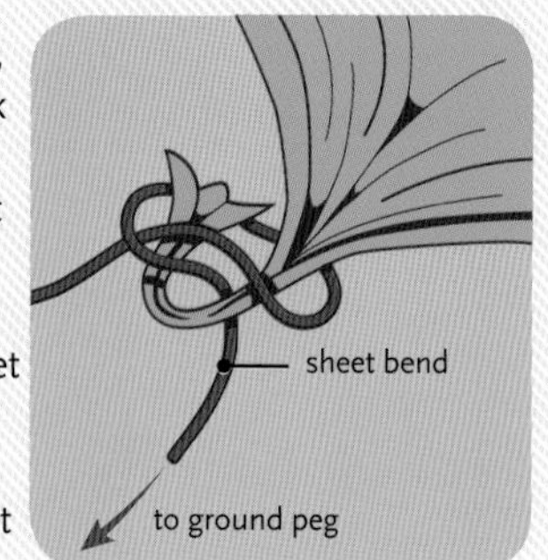

144 BUILD A BIKE HUT

You may feel perfectly at home riding on your mountain bike, zipping up and down those hilly trails. But did you know that your beloved bike can actually help you make a home for the night in the mountains, whether of choice or necessity? By turning your bike upside down to rest on the seat and handlebars, you can use it as a rough-and-ready frame for a two-person tarp shelter. Just spread a tarp over the bike tires, tie ropes to each corner of the tarp, and tie stakes to the free ends of the ropes. Drive the stakes into the ground, adjust the tension, and you're all done! One person can sleep on each side of the bike, and if the tarp is big enough, you might even have room to use a tiny stove under there. Who said camping out has to be hard?

145 MAKE QUICK TIES

If you have functional grommets, you can use little sticks as toggles to create a quick-take-down version of any tarp shelter. For corners, pass just part of a loop through the grommet and insert a wooden toggle into the loop. Pull the line tight and secure it. For edge grommets on a fixed line, leave enough slack on the line to push a loop through the grommet and peg it in place. Though these attachments aren't as sturdy as tying knots, they let you construct a shelter that can be taken down in seconds. If you need to secure a line to a tarp without grommets, a "wart" may be just what you are looking for when you need an easy, yet strong, method of fastening the two together. First, collect a hard nut or small round pebble, and place it under the tarp in the spot you need to attach a line. Be sure to use something that isn't too unevenly shaped or has any sharp or rough edges, so as not to damage the fabric of your tarp. Bunch up the fabric around the object, creating a bump or "wart" in the material, and tie a constricting knot around the wart. Make sure the rope constricts the tarp tightly and pull tension on the wart to test it.

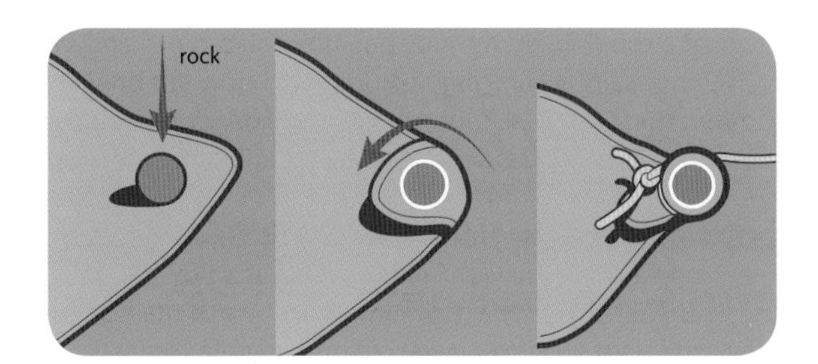

146 TAKE SHELTER, CATCH RAIN

What if your shelter could be more than just a shelter? Wouldn't it be better if it did even more than protect you from the weather? If you have a tarp, a bit of rope, and some small trees or stakes you can tie off your line onto, you can quickly build a shelter that also acts as a water collection rig. This unorthodox tarp configuration is great for rain protection over a large area if you have a large tarp; or it can provide coverage to a smaller area when using smaller tarps. I use a 20-by-40-foot (6-by-12-meter) tarp in this shape over my campfire area when teaching classes. It keeps us dry and produces a stream of water, even in a light rain. To make one, tie opposing corners of a tarp, two up high and two in lower positions. It's not the best shelter for windy conditions, as the tarp can billow like a loose sail in wind, but for calm weather, it works well for both sun and rain. To catch water, just place containers below the lowest point on the tarp. Even one inch (2.5 cm) of rain can produce massive volumes of water (this gives you more than a half-gallon (2 L) of water per square foot (0.09 sq m) of collection space). Shelter and a drink—now there's a multifunction setup!

HACKS THROUGH HISTORY // **SAND PIT**

Constructing a shelter to provide shade in hot desert terrain is great—but you haven't finished the job until you have a cooler place to lie down during the heat of the day. Use any available tool to dig down into the hot soil or sand to create a depression under your shelter. As soon as you lay down in this grave-like hole, you'll notice that the ground is much cooler. And the deeper you dig down, the cooler it gets. Just digging down a few inches can give you a more comfortable place to lay or sit, until the sun backs off and the cooler air of evening descends. And a word of warning, don't try to build huge shelters or dig massive depressions in the heat of the day. Wait until it cools down to do your heavy toil.

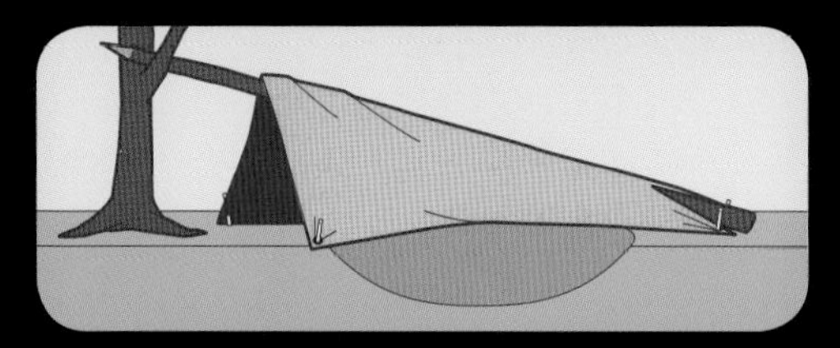

147 MAKE A LEAF BED

Spending a night in the outdoors with no tent or even a sleeping bag? A pile of leaves is all it takes to get you off the cold wet ground and provide a warm place to sleep.

BUILD THE BED Use a tree branch as a rake to pile up leaves, and move them around with a tarp, blanket, or some other conveyance. Pile them up and pack them down by laying on them. Repeat this pile-and-pack procedure until you have a bed that keeps you off the ground, even when your full weight is lying on it. This can even be done between two logs, to minimize shifting and movement of the bedding pile.

UPGRADE YOUR SLEEP In bug country,make your leaf mattress on the ground, then set up a tent over the leaf pile. Leaves can also be used in conjunction with many other kinds of emergency shelters. Stuff them into a hut for bedding and cram them into a stuck vehicle for warmth. Use your imagination and get creative!

Quick Tip

For those who are really concerned about bugs and spiders in the leaves, here's a bit of comfort. The disturbance of raking up and moving the leaves will often scare many of these pests away.

148 RIG A HAMMOCK

Hammocks are one of the most under-utilized shelters, and you can make this "survival bed" with just a bit of rope and sturdy fabric. Start out with one of the long sides of the tarp and roll it up halfway across the entire tarp. Then roll up the other long side to meet the first. Now, grab onto one end of this bundle and bend it to make a "J" shape. Tie a sheet-bend knot with a length of rope. Tie another sheet bend to the tarp's other end, using a second rope. Select leg-thick or bigger trees, about 9 to 12 feet (3–4 m) apart, and securely tie the end of each rope to a tree, as high as you can reach. Open up the rolls you made in the tarp, put a little weight on the tarp to tighten the knots, and settle into your new bed.

149 SLEEP ON A GRASS MAT

Those fancy sleeping pads at the camping store certainly are nice, but you can manage without them. One primitive approach can replicate the comfort and insulating properties of foam sleeping pads, while being portable just like their store bought counterparts. Harvest several armloads of dead dry grass, the taller the better. Grab a bundle of cord too. Find a comfortable place to work and begin trying grass bundles together. Form the grass in to a bundle a little wider than your body, and about 2 inches (5 cm) in diameter. Tie it together with three or four cords, and then form another grass bundle that matches the first. Tie the two together, and keep tying new bundles in a row until you have a mat that is a little longer than you are tall. Roll it up and take it to your camp, you've earned a good night's sleep.

150 BUILD A HOT ROCK BED

It gets cold in the desert at night. And with all the rocks, sand, and dried brush, it's the perfect place to make a hot rock mattress. This type of heated bed is best used in a location with easy to dig soil, abundant rocks, and firewood, and in conditions with a very low risk of wildfire. (Make sure you gather the rocks from a high and dry location, as waterlogged rocks can explode dangerously when they heat up in a fire.)

STEP 1 Dig a shallow trench, a little wider and taller than you are. Bring all of the loose dirt or sand to one side of the trench. This creates a reflecting wall for the upcoming fire, and it keeps the soil handy for the upcoming refill.

STEP 2 Lay some flat stones in the entire trench. This is the rock part of the hot rock mattress. It's okay if the rocks are a bit thicker than the trench is deep, as long as you have enough dirt to cover them all with 3 to 4 inches (7.5–10 cm) of soil after the firing.

STEP 3 Now comes the fire, which should cover all the rocks for 2 to 3 hours. After the rocks have been heated through, rake all the coals off to the side (I like to create a new fire from this). Quickly cover the hot rocks with soil, and let the moisture steam out of the dirt for 10 to 15 minutes. My final trick is to cover the soil with a few inches of leaves or other vegetation, to help insulate the hot rocks and dirt. Top it off with your normal outdoor bedding, and hit the hay.

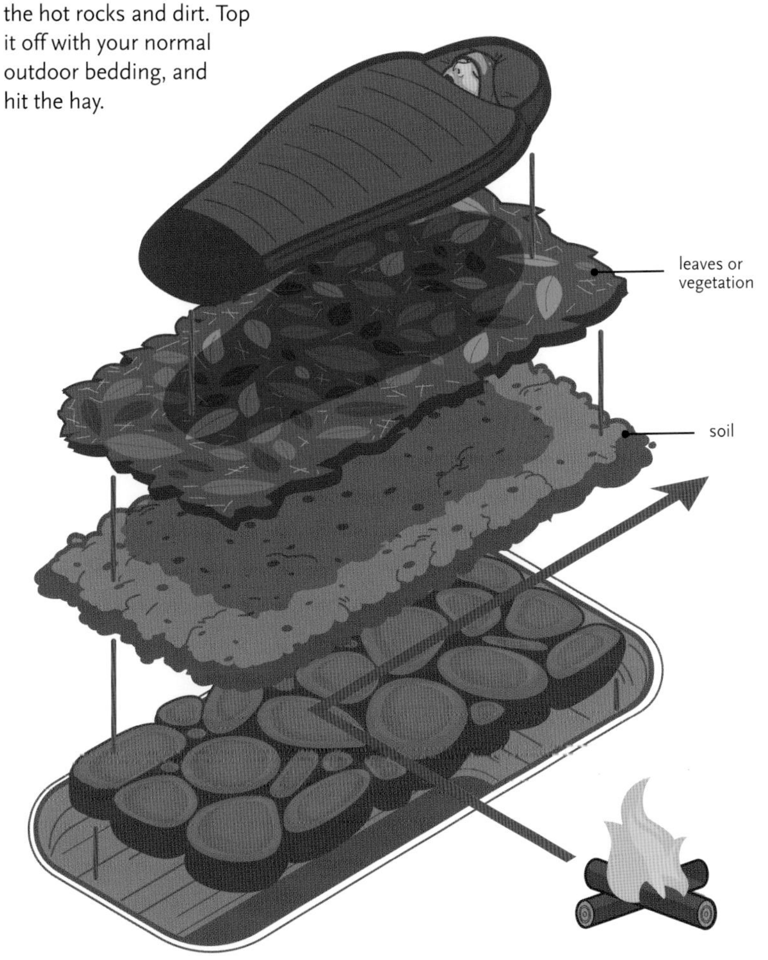

151 SLEEP WARMER

There are plenty of ways to sleep a little warmer in a chilly wilderness setting, and they're well worth the trouble during a frigid evening. By sleeping better and in greater comfort, the body can repair itself more effectively and prepare us for another tough day of survival. Plan ahead for warmth with these various techniques.

BRING A ROCK Sleep with a hot rock wrapped up in cloth or some other insulating material, for hours of warmth.

EAT FOR HEAT Generate extra metabolic heat by eating something with high calories just before bed, and again if you wake up cold.

USE A BOTTLE Snuggle up with a hot water bottle stuffed down inside a thick sock, for long-lasting gentle heat.

CHANGE FOR BED Swap into clean dry clothes before crawling into your bedding, these insulate the body better than dirty or sweaty clothes.

152 EMBRACE THE ROCK

Caves and rock overhangs can make instant shelters for weary travelers in the wild, but how often do you run across them? Not often enough, I would say. So let's utilize a more common rock formation as a shelter—and make a home out of a boulder. Whether huge rocks are jutting out of a larger formation, or they are stand-alone boulders, the first thing you'll want to do is make sure they are stable. You don't want your boulder shelter rolling onto you. Your second task is to add a lean-to on the most practical side of the boulder. This may be the side out of the wind, or the flattest side. Your lean-to can be sticks and vegetation, or just a tarp you have strung up. Either way, it's a quicker build than normal since one "wall" is already there. Add your bedding and your shelter is complete.

153 ADD A WALL

There are many ways you can build a wall in the wilderness, and many reasons to do it. Walls can be defensive structures in predator country. They can also be great fire reflectors, bouncing the heat of a fire toward a shelter or people. The wall can also be part of the shelter itself, especially if it's an insulating wall. To make a simple stacked wall, drive four stakes into the ground in a rectangular pattern. Stack up branches or cut poles inside the stakes, on each of the long sides. As the poles go in, begin to fill the void between the walls with debris. It's easier to place a poles and debris a little at a time, since the debris keeps the poles in place. Once you've reached the top, finish off the wall by lashing the tops of the stakes together.

154 SLEEP IN A BAG

What do you get when you combine insulating material and a giant trash bag? A warm place to sleep that is shielded from wind and rain.

FILL IT UP You can throw together a makeshift sleeping bag in a hurry by filling a giant trash bag with any insulating materials you can find. In the wild, this can include leaves, grass, moss, ferns, and other vegetation. In other settings, you can use crumpled paper, bubble wrap, packing peanuts, or shredded cardboard. Once you've stuffed the bag, burrow down inside and you'll be well insulated from the cold.

ADD A ROOF Ordinary trash bags can work despite their smaller size. Cut the bottom out of one bag, then use duct tape to attach it to another trash bag of the same size. This will give you an elongated tube, which can then be stuffed full of insulating materials just like a larger trash bag. Using the plastic as an exterior will allow this makeshift shelter to resist most of the rain and block much of the wind. Use it as a stand-alone hut, or better yet, use it inside another shelter.

155 FOLLOW THE ELVES

You too can join the ranks of the forest creatures (real and imaginary) that live inside hollow trees and logs. In forest environments and a few other habitats, cavernous trees are ready-to-go shelters that can provide you with the perfect place to get out of the rain and catch some sleep. The tree species that grow into these hollow giants will vary by your location, but if you're lucky enough to stumble across one, use it. In the early part of 2012, a family of three became lost in an old-growth Oregon forest, after hunting for rare mushrooms. Disorientated and unable to find their way back to the vehicle or road, they spent a very rough week sheltering inside a massive hollow log, until they were finally rescued six days later. Dehydrated and hypothermic, they credited their log shelter as a lifesaver in the rainy near-freezing conditions.

156 USE A TREE

When tree hollows are lacking, there's still a way that trees can shelter you (besides chopping them down for a cabin). Seek out the tree with the thickest foliage you can find. If it has plenty of open space under it, that's even better. Build a shelter underneath the spreading branches, close to the trunk. As you use the shelter, you'll find that there is a natural microclimate under the tree, providing extra protection from precipitation. You'll also notice a little more warmth, as the tree shelters you from the wind. If it's safe to do so, add a little fire to your camp under a tree, and the boughs will hold in more heat. Just be aware that evergreens pose two problems. Dead branches with brown needles are a very flammable thing to have over a fire (bad idea), and snow on the boughs overhead will melt and fall down on your fire.

HACKS THROUGH HISTORY // **SHELTER IN A TREE**

Huge trees once grew in old growth forests of eastern America. One hollow sycamore was so large, that settlers Joseph Hampton and his sons lived inside of it for most of the year in 1744. But that wasn't the largest natural tree shelter of the east. In 1749, a French explorer named Bonnecamp described a tree on the banks of the Ohio River, so massive that twenty-nine men could sit side-by side around the interior.

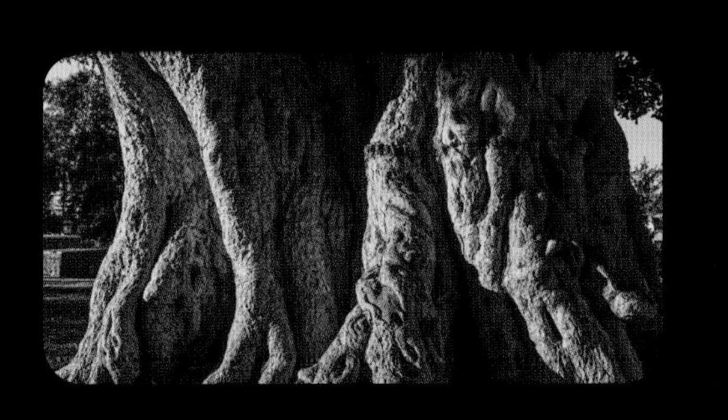

157 GRAB A PIECE OF HISTORY

The town of Mora is located in central Sweden and during the end of the 18th century, many industries sprang up there. Mechanical items such as clocks and sewing machines were once made in the town, though it's an unlikely industry that put this town on the map and persists there today. A man named Frost-Erik Erson began fabricating timber sleds in 1891, and he also started making knives for the workers in his shop to use. These simple knives were constructed from high quality Swedish steel and followed a time-tested Scandinavian woodcarving knife pattern. The knives soon became the most coveted item coming from his shop. Eventually, another local knife maker (KJ Eriksson) merged with Frosts Knivfabrik (Frost's Knife Factory) to be called Mora of Sweden, later renamed Morakniv. And while a number of companies make Mora-style knives, Morakniv itself has become known throughout the world.

158 USE IT WELL

It's been said that "your knife is your life," and I couldn't agree more. When facing an unexpected emergency situation in the wild, your knife may be the tool that makes all the difference to your survival. Swedish Mora knives and their cousins, the Finnish Puukko knives, are renowned for their wood carving abilities, but they can do even more in skilled hands.

CUT A SAPLING Bend the sapling hard in one spot, and slice into the wood that's on the outside of the bend (and under tension). The knife should easily part the strained wood and cut halfway through a thumb-diameter tree. Now bend the tree the other way (180 degrees from the last bend), and cut on the outside again. This is likely to cut the tree off completely. If not, cut a little more, slicing down on an angle.

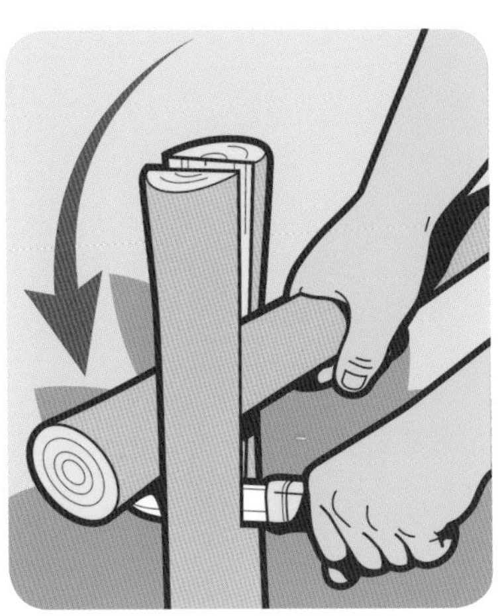

TRY A BATON Since a small knife lacks the weight of a hatchet, it can't normally chop. But by striking the spine of the knife with a small hardwood stick, you can "baton" your way through wood with results that rival a handheld hatchet. You can baton with the grain, to split kindling. Or you can chop through wood, by driving the knife through on a 45-degree angle, to cut off branches or fell saplings.

STRIKE A SPARK ROD Don't ruin your cutting edge! The square spine on most Scandinavian knives is well suited to scrape off sparks from ferrocerium rods. Some knives are designed with this in mind, particularly if they include a ferro rod. If your knife doesn't have crisp square edges on the spine, use a flat file to grind away a little bit of the spine to create these scraping edges.

BUDGET SURVIVAL

THE BASIC MORA KNIFE

These are often considered the best wood carving blade for the money. Both tough and lightweight, blades made by Morakniv are great for survival chores and bushcraft skills (since many survival tasks involve wood carving). The secret is in the "Scandi" grind. The edge geometry has no secondary bevel (seen on most knives today). This flat grind makes the edge extremely thin and exceedingly sharp. If you don't have a Mora knife, get one—or several! Here's why these are such a great deal.

- The blades are razor sharp from the factory.
- They're durable yet easy to sharpen.
- They're at a price anyone can afford.

Worth Every Penny

MORAS WITH SPARK RODS

For just a few dollars more, you can buy a Mora knife with a ferrocerium spark rod, either as a handle insert or as a "sidekick" on the knife sheath. Knife and fire!

HACK HEROES TRASH BAG

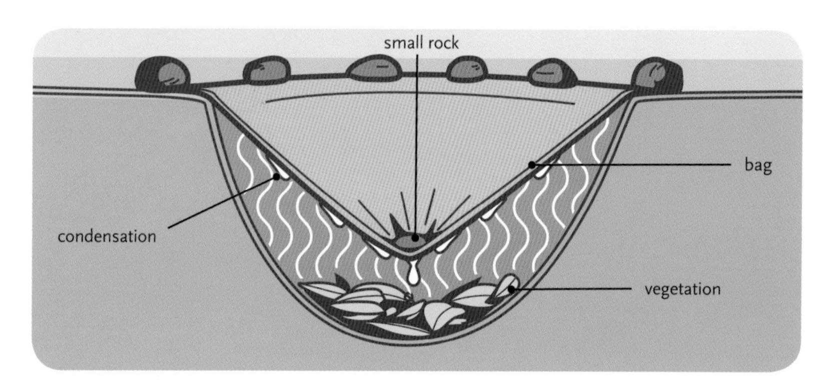

1 BUILD A STILL ▲ A clear or milky plastic trash bag can be cut open lengthwise and placed over a damp or vegetation-filled hole in the ground to create a solar still for collecting drinking water through distillation. Simply put a clean container at the bottom and seal the plastic at the rim with dirt or stones to keep any steam from escaping. Place a small rock on the plastic to make a cone shape. The sun will create a steamy environment under the plastic, and the steam will condense on the underside of the plastic, with water running down into the container. Just manage your expectations appropriately; most solar stills don't produce much water.

2 CATCH RAIN AND MELT SNOW A trash bag's waterproof nature is obviously useful when it comes to catching rain. As the clouds darken over your head, line a hole in the ground with your trash bag and watch it fill up with safe clean rain water. Just one inch (2.5 cm) of rainfall leaves more than a half-gallon (2 L) of water over one square foot (0.09 sq m) of surface area, so your big trash bag can collect a very reasonable amount of water after a good shower. And when you have sunshine after a snowfall,place a dark trash bag in a low spot, put some snow on top of the bag and let the sun's warmth liquefy the snow into drinking water.

3 UPGRADE YOUR SHELTER Regardless of the type of survival shelter you have made, you'll still need weatherproofing. A trash bag can be attached to the top of a door frame to hold in heat. It can even be filled with debris for an insulated door. The bag can also be cut open into a tarp-like piece of plastic and used as a ground cloth to keep the dampness of the ground from seeping into your bedding. And since the typical survival shelter has a roof that leaks like a sieve, place a cut open trash bag into the roof and you'll achieve greater waterproofing. Just make sure you bury it under a little vegetation to keep the wind from blowing it off.

4 CARRY ON For handy storage, cut a trash bag into small or large sections, sized to fit the items you have. Bundle up these plastic sections with string, twist ties, tape, or trash bag cordage. Now you can keep all of your food, clothes, fire making materials, and other supplies clean, dry, and separate. Lacking a backpack? Sling the bag over your shoulder like Santa, and a trash bag will give you a short-term method to transport supplies. Trash bags also make water carriers. Place your bag in a box, backpack, or basket to make a water-proof H2O transport. Make the plastic several layers thick with no contact against sharp points that will poke holes in the bag.

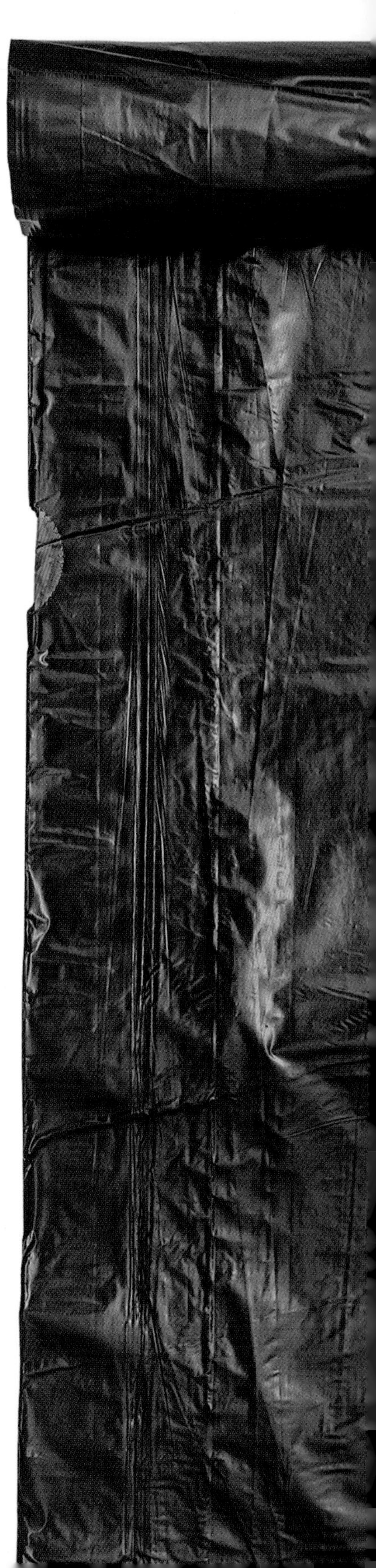

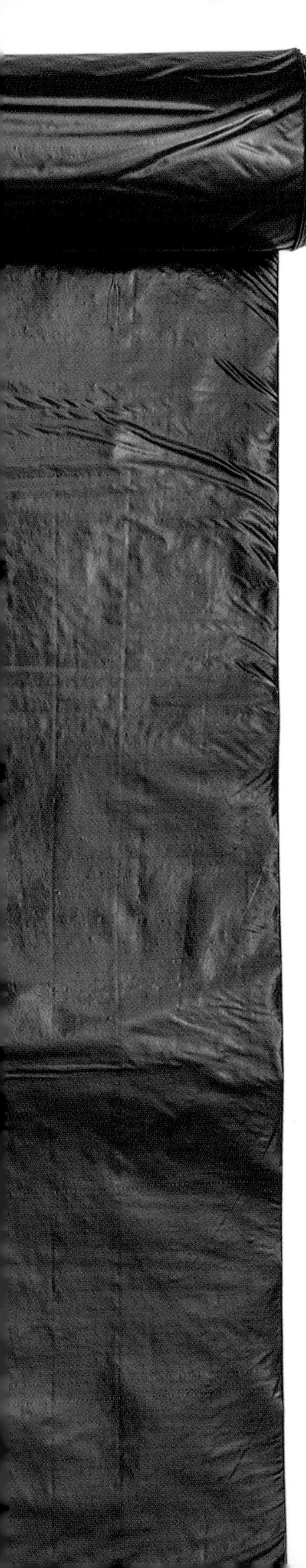

5 MAKE YOUR MARK Need some trail markers? Cut off small strips from a trash bag and tie them to brush at eye level. This can create a trail to help you navigate through thick vegetation or in low light conditions. On a larger scale, make a signal flag by tying the trash bag to a pole like a flag, and stand the pole up in an open area to create a signal for help. For windy conditions, you can even tie the bag opening to the pole in two spots, so that it will act like a wind sock. It's best if you can use orange trash bags or some other colorful choice, so that your signal stands out in contrast to the landscape.

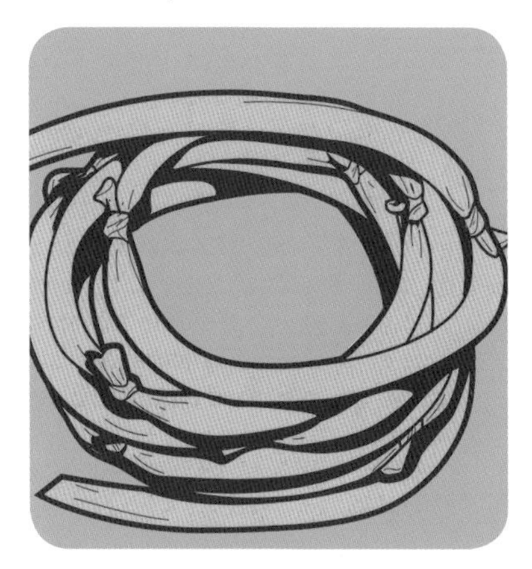

6 CUT UP SOME CORDAGE ▲ For years now, I've carried giant trash bags in survival kits and first aid bags. And while a trash bag is usually thrown away with the trash, that bag is a treasure when you need a versatile piece of strong waterproof material in the backcountry. One of the ways to use them is for improvised cordage. Results will vary, as there are many types of trash bag plastic; but for simple lightweight tying jobs around camp, trash bag plastic can be cut into strips and tied up like ribbons. It can also be tightly twisted into stronger cordage. This is not a load bearing rope, but a light-duty one.

7 FLOAT FOR YOUR LIFE ▲ Next to duct tape, a trash bag may be the most versatile item in your survival kit. That ubiquitous bag could also be much more valuable than you can imagine, especially in an emergency on the water. A trash bag full of air can generate life-saving buoyancy if you find yourself adrift in the ocean or any body of water. Blow some air into a large trash bag, and tie a knot to hold it in. Blow in more air and tie another knot. Repeat this until you have three air chambers in the trash bag, separated by knots. Tie the tightest knot at the end of the bag, to hold the air inside, then place the float under your arms.

8 KEEP IT DRY Trash bags make a great backpack cover, to protect your gear from rain, mud, and dust. And there are two ways that a trash bag can help your firewood to stay dry in a downpour. First, you may want to fill the bag with wood, tinder, and kindling before the clouds release their rain. If you tie the bag shut, you'll have great protection from moisture. And for a larger woodpile, cut the bag open to create a tarp-like rain cover for your pile. Hold it down with a few rocks, so that the wind can't blow it away, and you could store enough dry firewood for the whole evening.

159 USE BARK CORDAGE

You may not expect much from tree bark, but there are hidden virtues in the bark of many tree species, and if you know what to do with them. Tulip poplar, basswood, cedar, willow, elm, mulberry, and several other trees produce fibrous inner bark that can be used as a raw material for cordage. These inner barks can be harvested from dead branches and tree trunks that have rotted to just the right consistency. The bark can also be stripped from live tree trunks and branches, and rotted in water. This process is traditionally called retting (old word for rotting). Place the bark strips under water and leave them there for several days. Then check the fibers every day until they separate from the outer bark in "ribbons". Twist them into cord wet or after drying, or use the ribbons as is for quick tying jobs.

160 TIE SAPLINGS FOR A WIGWAM

Now that you have some bark cordage, it's time to tie together a few little sapling trees into a traditional forest home: the wigwam. This arched dome was once commonly seen as a family home among eastern Native Americans. The name "wigwam" is likely from Eastern Abenaki, and is said to literally mean "their house." To build your own version of this ancient woodland home, cut a dozen tall flexible sapling poles and mark out a circle on the ground. Use a mallet and stake to drive a hole in the dirt around the circle for each pole. Insert the poles into their new holes and bend the poles together. Then, lash all these poles to create a cage like a playground "jungle gym," and cover the dwelling with any available materials. Matts and bark slabs are a classic covering, and today, the tarp will work just as well.

161 BREAK FIREWOOD WITH LEVERAGE

Without a saw or hatchet, it's not always obvious how you will process your evening's firewood. But when you have a fork in a tree, or two trees very close together, you have the perfect place to use leverage to break wood. Insert the piece of wood into the fork, about the height of your hip, if possible. Walk forward, pushing against the wood with your hip and (if it's not too thick) the wood will break at the fulcrum point on the tree closest to you. This doesn't work very well on thick hardwood or short sections of wood (no leverage), but longer pieces of wood should give you all the leverage you need to break them. For a very precise break, use a stone saw or chopper to damage the area you want to break—and make that spot your fulcrum point.

162 LOVE THOSE LEAVES

The forest environment gives us so many gifts, but out of them all, I think that leaves are among the most flexible resources. This foliage is such an abundant material that we'd be foolish to ignore it.

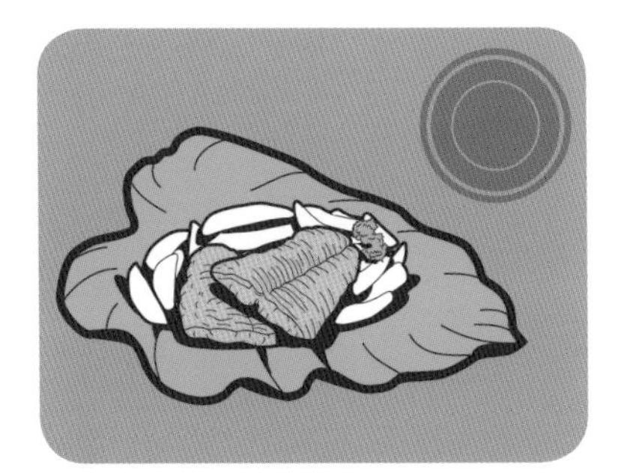

MAKE A PLATE Large non-toxic tree leaves make great containers for forest dining. You can lay one or more leaves on a bark slab to make a nice clean plate. You can line a small basket with a leaf to make a bowl. You can even curl a leaf up into a cone shape to make a drinking cup.

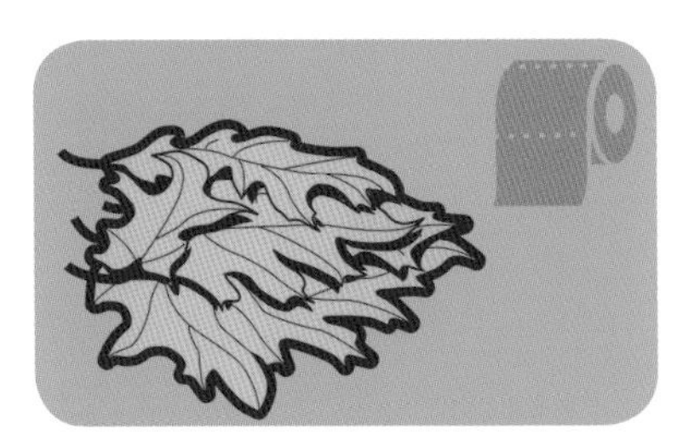

TRY SOME TP Once you've had your leaf-served meal, you'll need some toilet paper, and leaves are there again for your needs. I recommend stacking several dead dry leaves, with a green leaf in the middle for structure.

SLAP ON SOME SHINGLES When huge green leaves are available during the growing season, use them! These can be arranged on your shelter like shingles, and as long as they are intact, they are waterproof.

BRING ON THE TINDER Dead dry leaves make fine tinder for fire starting, especially if they are crumbly. Collect dead ones from trees and bushes, and crush to test them. If they crumble, they are dry enough for tinder.

MAKE SOME TEA The leaves of many plants in woodland areas can become teas. Spicebush leaves make a warm drink with a spicy citrus flavor. Pine or spruce needles can also make a bracing cup full of vitamin C. Consult local experts or regional edible plant guides before drinking any beverages.

163 SKIP THE SHROOMS

I know this is going to get some emails and letters from upset mushroom enthusiasts and experts in mycology (mushroom doctors), and this isn't aimed at you, our wise and cautious experts. This is aimed at everybody else, especially the young people reading this book.

Wild mushrooms may be abundant in forest environments, particularly in spring and fall, but hold on a minute before you start shoveling them down your throat. I can't (in good conscience) recommend mushroom foraging as a wilderness survival strategy (especially not for beginners). Sure, the right mushrooms can make a delicious meal, worthy of fine restaurants. But the wrong mushrooms can be your last meal, or they can put you on the fast track for a liver transplant. In my mind, the meagre nutritional value of wild mushrooms does not justify the risks you are taking. Period.

164 BRING WATER WITH YOU

You may hope, pray, and dream that you'll find some water where you are going, but in a dry environment, these well wishes may leave you without a drop to drink. Creeks may dry up and the rains may not come. This can turn your plan to find water during your travels into a fatal and futile misadventure. The only water you are guaranteed to have in a desert environment is that water which you bring with you. Water filters are great, as are purification tablets, but they're not a complete water solution since neither of them make water out of thin air. Bring plenty of water with you when heading out into dry places, or to places where water is not safe to drink (such as salt water areas). Yes, water is heavy to carry, but I'll wager that those jugs will be lighter before you want them to be.

165 CRAFT A CONTAINER

You might be surprised how well some of these crazy water containers can work.

DRY AN ANIMAL BLADDER Easily the worst and nastiest water container, dried bladders from large animals can be used as water containers. Remove the bladder, drain it, and turn it inside out. Scrape away any membrane, fill it with dry sand, and allow it to dry.

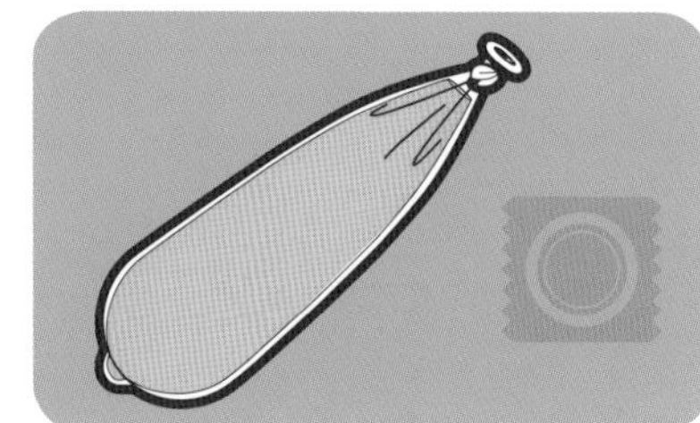

STRETCH A CONDOM Prophylactics are probably the most bizarre water containers, and the average one can hold over a quart (liter) of water. First, stretch it to relax the rubber. Then, quickly drag it through the water to allow it to fill and expand like a balloon.

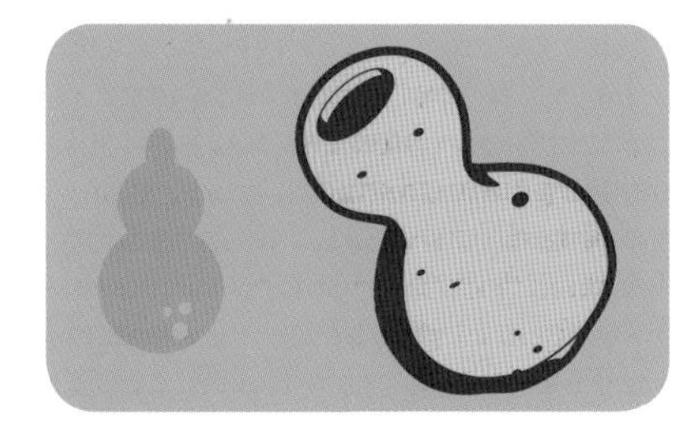

GRAB A GOURD These common plants can be hollowed out and used as lightweight and fairly durable water containers. Saw your way through the top of a dried gourd, and scoop out the innards. Sand the interior smooth, and it's ready for water.

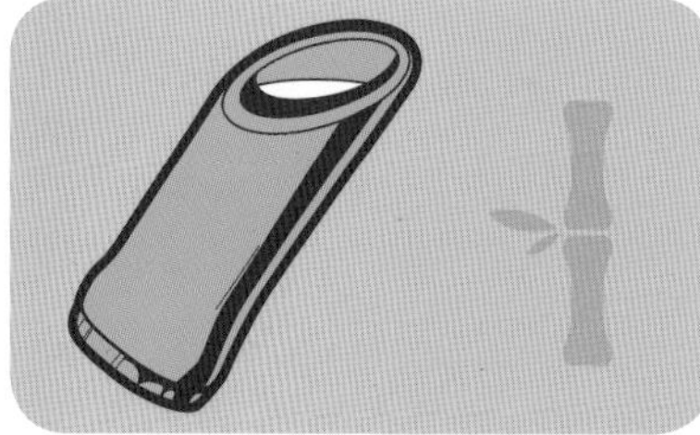

CUT SOME BAMBOO This overgrown grass is full of hollow sections between the nodes. Cut open the bamboo and clean it out. You can make horizontal cuts to make cooking containers, and cut the end of out of bamboo for something more like a canteen.

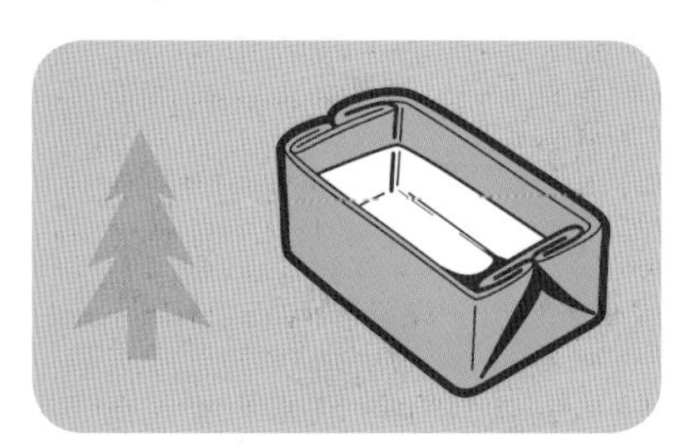

FOLD SOME BARK Fold a container from the same tree bark that you'd peel in the spring for cordage and roofing slabs. Use a stick or small stone to score lines into the freshly peeled bark and fold the container along those lines.

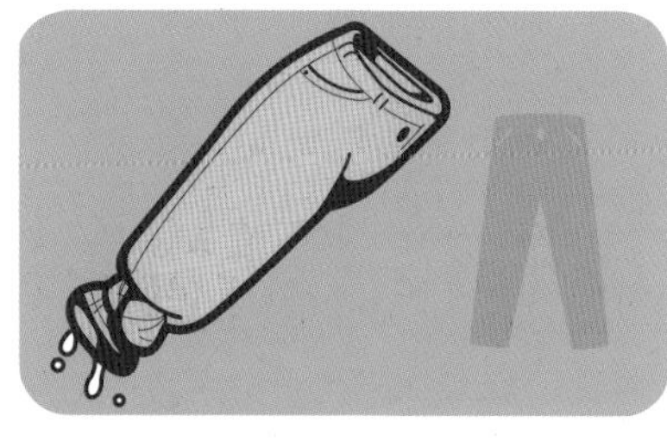

FILL YOUR FABRIC Tightly woven fabrics can swell up when wet; to carry water over short distances, line a basket with cloth or use your hat as a water scoop, or put one pant leg inside the other and tie the bottom shut.

BUDGET SURVIVAL

THE SURPLUS CANTEEN

Sure, they smell a little funny and they can make the water taste weird—but Army-Navy surplus stores can offer you a great deal on old canteens and related gear. Those surplus military-green canteens are rugged, lightweight, and easy to carry with their curved ergonomic design. While you're at the store, treat yourself to a canteen cover, and maybe even a nesting metal canteen cup. Now you can boil water when you run out of purification tablets. If you're concerned that the plastic canteen has been used, maybe by someone with sub-par hygiene, fill the canteen with water and add ten drops of household bleach. Screw on the lid and let it sit a few days. This will thoroughly disinfect the interior.

Quick Tip

In sub-freezing environments, those without a water carrier can simply carry ice. Find some freshwater ice, and a convenient way to carry it. When you're ready for a drink, chip off some ice and boil it for safety.

166 HARNESS THE SUN

A clear plastic or glass bottle with smooth round "shoulders" can be a surprisingly good fire-starting lens, providing a few conditions are met.

GATHER YOUR SUPPLIES First, you'll need bright sunlight that you can focus into a fire-starting dot of white light. Secondly, you'll need to fill the bottle with crystal clear water, capping or corking it as needed. Finally, you'll need good tinder, such as blackened char cloth or tinder fungus powder (like chaga).

SET A FIRE When the sun is low in the sky (in morning or afternoon), lay the bottle on its side in the full sunlight and set your dark-colored tinder on the ground just behind the bottle. Experiment with the bottle's position in the sunlight, and experiment with the tinder placement. If all goes well, you should see your tinder begin to smoke. Add this smoldering ember to a bundle of dry tinder and blow it into flames!

167 WASH A WOUND

Let's say that you've fallen down the slippery rocks of a wilderness hillside. As you skid to a halt, you notice a sharp pain at your calf. You see a jagged wound, oozing blood and speckled with dirt and debris. Your first instinct is to grab your water bottle and pour water across the wound to wash it, but there is a more effective approach. That flimsy plastic water bottle can fire out a jet of cleansing water, after one minor modification. Use the tip of your knife or the awl on a multi-tool to poke a small hole in bottle cap. Turn the bottle upside down and squeeze it. This will cause a pressurized stream of water to squirt out of the cap, gently flushing away the blood, dirt, sand, leaves, and even little rocks that may be stuck in the wound. Flush the wound until all signs of debris and dirt are gone, or you run out of water, whichever comes first. Dress the wound as normal, after flushing it clean.

168 STAY COOL

Heat exhaustion is a common accompaniment to hotter weather, and if left untreated, it can become heat stroke.

KNOW THE SYMPTOMS Heat exhaustion can be identified by clammy moist skin, heavy sweating, cramps, dizziness, tiredness, nausea, vomiting, and a weak but fast pulse. By contrast, heat stroke may be accompanied by other symptoms, such as a pounding headache, weakness, a dizzy or light-headed feeling, a rapid pulse and one of the classic signs: A lack of perspiration. Another key symptom is a high body core temperature (105 °F / 40.5 °C). The dry, hot skin of a heat stroke victim is very different from the clammy and damp skin found on a heat exhaustion patient.

KEEP THEM COOL When you suspect either of these conditions, use water to bring their body temperature down. Wrap a cool wet cloth around their neck, place a cold water bottle under each armpit, and dampen their clothing or wrap the victim in a wet sheet.

169 DROWN YOUR PREY

While drowning would not be the way that I choose to go out, this simple trap can acquire food for you and store the critter underwater (away from scavengers). It requires a snare line with a noose, a heavy rock, a float stick, and a stick to prop up the rock in a precarious position. To make this trap, simply tie the snare line to the rock leaving a length of line free to tie the float. Set the noose in a run or slide that is heading straight down into the water. Prop up the rock so that it will fall into deep water if the noose is tugged, or tie the prop stick in line on the snare line. The animal pulls the rock in after them, is pulled under, and the wooden float lets you see where the rock and animal are located.

170 STEAM CLEAN YOUR BODY

Water is something of a shapeshifter, taking the form of a liquid, solid ice, and also the vapor that we know as steam. This latter form can be used in some very interesting ways, my favorite among them being the sweat lodge. While the sweat lodge can be a deeply religious ceremony for many people, particularly Native Americans, it's a tradition seen around the world. And like a sauna, anyone can have a good sweat for health and cleanliness. It's actually very easy to have a non-ceremonial sweat lodge. Place some hot stones in a small enclosed space (like a tiny hut), dribble water on the rocks, and enjoy the waves of steam. Don't overdo it: If you feel dizzy, open up the lodge for fresh air. Towel off when you're done, drink lots of cool water, and you'll feel squeaky clean and rejuvenated.

HACK HAZARDS

RAW WATER

Drinking raw water is always going to be a gamble. Even in pristine wilderness areas, the water can be contaminated with all kinds of bowel churning pathogens,such as giardia or cholera. Unless you are lucky enough to find a spring that is issuing clean water out of the natural water table, drinking unprocessed water is risky at best. If there's any way to process the water, it should be attempted before you say "bottoms up" to water you find in the wilderness. I will bend the rule with rain water. If I can catch rain in a clean container under an open sky, I'll often use it without fear. But I won't set out my containers under a tree canopy. The rain will wash down bird and bug poop into my water.

- Raw water can carry harmful pathogens and organisms.
- It can introduce parasites into your body, some of which are hard to diagnose or treat.

Worth Every Penny

WATER PURIFIER

Potable Aqua's PURE Water Purifier weighs only 4 ounces (28 g), but it can turn table salt and a few drops of water into a potent chlorine and peroxide solution for water disinfection.

171 DIG A FIRE PIT

Fire is one of our best friends in a wilderness emergency, and we need to plan for fire accordingly. When it's time to set up a fireplace, you'll need to figure out exactly where and how you will build it. Some conditions require a mound underneath your fire, while other circumstances demand that you dig down into the ground. Fire pits are one of the most common places to build and maintain a fire, as they offer safety and efficiency. Most fire pits are circular dish-shaped depressions or holes. They can be almost any size or depth, depending on the size of the fire you need. These depressions cradle the fire, grouping the coals in the center to help them burn longer and hotter. But you don't want to make the hole so deep that it keeps in all the heat, unless you've had to build a fire under very windy conditions.

172 AVOID WATERY STONES

The side of a river or lake may seem like the perfect place to pick up stones for your fireplace, but stop right there! Just because they are washed off and on display, doesn't make those rocks the right choice. When most stones are exposed to water for a long period of time, they tend to absorb it slowly. This can create a real hazard when we decide to place the waterlogged rocks near a hot fire. As the trapped water turns to steam, it expands quickly and forcefully. And since the water can't escape from the stone in the same slow way that it entered, it can only do one thing: Explode! Stones can blow up violently as water turns to steam, and if you happen to be nearby, you can be seriously injured. Always collect your stones from a dry location, well away from the water.

173 BUILD A MOUND

While digging into the ground is the most common approach to building a hearth in the wilderness, the fire mound makes a lot of sense in wetter climates and in areas prone to sudden downpours of rain. Fire pits can easily fill with water after a hard rain or in saturated soil, and either way, the pit will drown your coal bed. When this happens, your fire is doomed. The ancient forebears to the Seminole natives started using simple mounds of sand to keep their fires going in the wet and swampy terrain of the American southeast, and this technique is still in use there today. Fire mounds can be made from almost any non-flammable material. Build the mound as tall as you need.

174 MAKE A FIREWOOD DRYER

If you've ever tried to burn wet firewood, you're probably still coughing. Wet wood doesn't burn well, and it's easy for wood to become wet. It is a hygroscopic material, which means that wood absorbs and releases water in a balancing act with the surrounding environment. When it's been raining for days, the dead wood in a forest is naturally wetter, and of course live wood contains even more water (over 50% of the wood's weight). So, when does it start to burn well?

To call a piece of wood "dry", its weight needs to be less than 20% moisture. And to easily turn wet wood into drier fuel, a simple drying rack is all you need. Cut two poles with stout side branches. Point the bottom ends and drive them into the ground with the side branches extending over your fire. Place your wet wood on this "rack" and watch it dry as you burn your fire. Pull out the sticks that have obviously dried out and add them to the fire. Replace them with wet sticks that need to be dried.

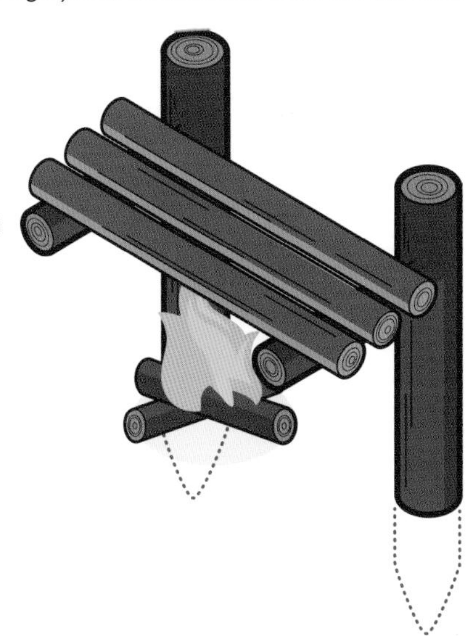

Worth Every Penny

AXE AND SAW

You can drag every type of firewood into your camp, but none of it will burn as well as wood that has been sawn and split into fire-friendly pieces. For those jobs, you'll need a good saw and an axe. These are vital tools for efficient firewood harvesting and processing, and few substitutes will even come close. You'll need a sharp-toothed saw to drop standing dead trees (the best wild source of dry wood), and turn those trunks and branches into short sections. And the axe will finish the job, splitting the pieces open for a better burn.

HACKS THROUGH HISTORY // **STAR FIRE**

With a profound shortage of axe making stones in the region, the people of America's pre-Columbian southeast had a tough time felling and cutting trees. From this challenge, we see a brilliantly simple solution arise: Burning the logs whole. The classic Seminole "star fire" consists of a mound upon which a small fire is built. Logs are then pulled in and arranged around the fire to form the points of a "star." Often, there would be a mix of trunk bottoms and tree top inserted into the fire, as these smaller diameter sections would help the fatter sections burn. These logs can be any length, and small log sections as "rollers" are a great addition can be, placed under the main logs so they can be pushed more easily toward the fire. As the log ends are burned away, just push them toward the center to feed the flames. This will never be a roaring fire, since the fire lay is so flat, but it is an easy to maintain fire with two interesting side benefits. This smoldering fire lay creates a lot of smoke which can keep the mosquitoes and biting flies away. And with so many logs by the fire, there are plenty of places to sit.

175 SHARPEN UP A FIRE

The first thing that a fire needs is tinder, which is some kind of fine flammable plant-based fuel that naturally has (or can be processed to have) a lot of surface area. I often teach this in my fire classes with the "baby food" analogy. Human toddlers can't eat big tough foods; they need little things to eat, and large foods processed into mush. Your baby fire operates much the same way—a fledgling fire needs small things to consume before it can be fed larger pieces of fuel.

When we're lucky, nature will provide us with dead dry leaves and grasses for tinder. And when we're not lucky, we can make our own. A great way to create wood shaving tinder is to twist pencil-diameter sticks in an ordinary sharpener. This gizmo is basic school supply of children around the world, and it's a great fire helper too. For reliability and durability, choose an all-metal pencil sharpener for years of service.

176 MAKE A PJCB

The crown jewel of homemade fire starters, PJCBs (petroleum jelly cotton balls) are able to burn under virtually any conditions. This odd mixture burns exceedingly well for up to 5 minutes, and they're easy to make. You can squish the pasty cold petroleum jelly into some dry cotton balls, or dip the cotton into warm liquefied petroleum jelly for faster absorption. These can light immediately when an open flame is applied. You can also light them with ferrocerium sparks, after pulling them apart to expose shaggy cotton strands. Just store them in a watertight container, so that the jelly doesn't melt and leak all over your gear if your kit gets above 100 °F (38 °C). And keep in mind that these are not a great fit for all ignition methods. For example, a magnifying lens and sunshine won't ignite them; that will just make a melted mess.

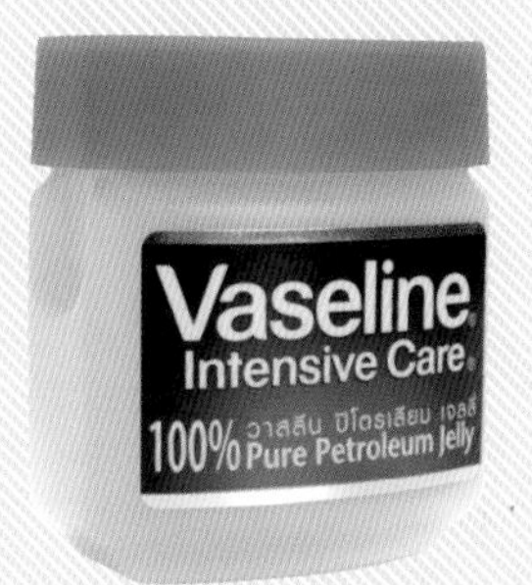

177 BURN A CUBE

WetFire cubes from UST are little chunks of white waxy material that have always delivered impressive results for me. On average, each cube burns for 10 minutes, which is twice the burn time of the homemade alternative (such as PJCBs). The flame is always much taller on these than the petroleum jelly on a cotton ball. I have measured spikes of flame from the WetFire cube that were 10 inches (25 cm) tall, which is twice the height of a greasy cotton ball. You can even chip off part of a cube to assist with fire starting, and then save the rest for later. A few shavings or chips of this material can greatly assist in the lighting of camp stoves and stubborn grills too. Just make sure you use up the product within a few months of opening the package, as the cubes seem to lose some flammability after being exposed to the air for some time.

178 FIND THE FATWOOD

Fatwood may come from several different places in nature, like the heartwood, knots, and old roots of pine trees and several other species of resinous conifers, but it's a great fire starter however you get it. As these pitch-filled trees die, the oils and resin can become concentrated in some parts of the wood, which then become hard and very rot resistant. Once this happens, the center of the stump, the knots in the trunk, and the roots themselves can all be great sources of fatwood.

This strangely fragrant material is prized for many reasons. It lights readily with an open flame. It burns very well, even if it was collected in a damp environment. Finally, it will burn even in wet weather. The resin in the wood makes fatwood almost waterproof and very flammable, which are both great qualities in fire starting. The straight-grained fatwood can be cut and split into small sticks for kindling. Knots can be carved into shavings for tinder.

To find yourself a ready supply of this fire-starting wonder, look through a pine forest until you come across an old stump with only the center remaining. This center (heart wood) should seem solid. You can also find pine knots lying on the forest floor, refusing to decompose. Cut off some pieces of this wood, and give them a look and a sniff. If they look like perfectly good wood (not rotten at all), then smell the pieces. If it really is fatwood, it will smell strongly of pine and resin, with the sharp odor of turpentine. Burn it for your final test. Good fatwood makes thick black smoke. Use strips, shavings, or chunks to get your fire going in good weather and bad.

You can even employ fatwood for "off-label" uses. A large chunk can make an excellent pre-lubricated hand hold block for a bow drill friction fire set. And even bigger chunks can be tossed into campfires to darken the smoke for a better distress signal.

179 GET WEIRD

When conditions aren't favorable for fire, but you need it anyway, you can fall back on some of the common "household" materials for emergency fire starting.

CREATE A FIREBALL Wad up a fistful of toilet paper and drizzle some liquid cooking oil on it to create a shockingly fiery ball of flames, which can be used as the heart of a tipi fire lay or rolled into some other fire building structure.

MAKE A MIXTURE They may be messy, but they're effective: Solid shortening and sawdust can be used in globs or wiped on reluctant firewood for wet weather burning. Just stir some sawdust into solid vegetable shortening, until more than half of the volume of your paste is sawdust. Store it in bags, bottles, tubes, or canisters, and light it with an open flame when you're ready.

BOURBON

1 LIGHT A FIRE ▲ For more than 200 years, a unique style of whiskey has spread out from its birthplace in the mountains of Kentucky. It's popular, easy to drink, and it can even help light a fire! The only trick: Once the alcohol is burnt, all you have left is water. This means that if you dump your booze onto a pile of damp sticks, the alcohol will burn off quickly, leaving the sticks wet. Plan ahead for this by lighting a bourbon soaked rag under your sticks and remove it when it stops burning. Yes, kids! Booze is flammable, and it just might save you on a cold day!

2 DISINFECT A WOUND ▶ With its generous alcoholic content, bourbon can prevent deadly infections when applied to cuts, scrapes and scratches as a disinfectant. Yes, it will sting quite a bit, especially on larger wounds, but few things kill microbes as effectively as liquor. Pour some across the injury as a germicidal wash, or dribble it on a piece of gauze to be left in place. You can also use bourbon to clean out a dirty wound. Add some bourbon to an empty plastic water bottle and screw on the lid. Next, poke a tiny hole in the bottle cap and squeeze the bottle to create a pressurized jet of bourbon to flush debris from jagged wounds and disinfect the injury.

3 SANITIZE YOUR GEAR Need to disinfect dirty knives or clean bloody medical gear? A five-minute soak in bourbon will sterilize your equipment quickly. A shallow pan or tall glass can act as your reservoir for the bourbon, then just add your gear and let it soak. This is best done right before you need to use the items, since there won't be any lingering disinfecting action. Just soak, shake off any droplets, and go to work. You can also sanitize other things, like clothing sprayed with blood or other filth. Soak or spray on bourbon as needed.

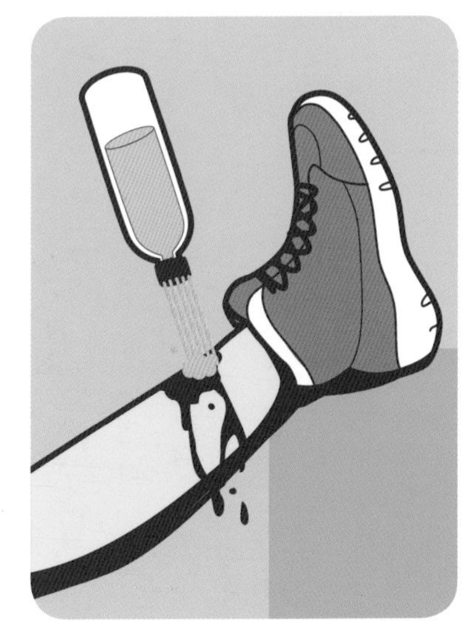

4 THROW A COCKTAIL PARTY ▶ The colorful name "Molotov cocktail" was first used by Finnish soldiers during the Winter War in 1939. Glass bottles were filled with flammable liquid, corked with a rag, lit on fire, and hurled as an improvised grenade. We still see this employed today during times of civil unrest. Stuff a cotton rag into the neck of your bottle, light the rag, and toss it against a hard surface to shatter the bottle—points if you yell something cool as you launch your projectile. Seriously kids, don't try this at home (or anywhere else).

5 RELIEVE YOUR PAIN An injury in an austere environment can leave a person in great pain, with few options for relief. When the OTC analgesics in your med kit aren't killing the pain, consider whether it is safe for your patient to consume bourbon. Soldiers were commonly given American whiskey like this while languishing in Civil War field hospitals, and there are plenty of other historical precedents for giving liquor as a remedy for pain. Just avoid giving hard alcohol to a victim with a head wound (especially a brain injury), or to someone whose wounds keep bleeding, since alcohol also thins the blood.

7 GET SOME SLEEP ▶ In a crisis setting, sleeping may be a challenge. Without restful sleep, your mental, emotional, and physical health will suffer, and you'll be operating at a greatly reduced capacity. Help the sandman along by grabbing a shot or two of bourbon as a nightcap. This nervous system depressant will help relax the muscles and mind, allowing sleep to come easier and helping your worries to drift away. Just make sure you have a reliable team member standing watch over your rest time, and drink plenty of water once you wake up, as liquor has a tendency to leave drinkers dehydrated.

6 REPEL MOSQUITOES ▶ Chikungunya, yellow fever, dengue fever, and malaria are just a few of the diseases that mosquitoes can transmit to humans. So it's a good thing bourbon can temporarily drive them off. Wipe some golden-brown bourbon on your exposed skin or spray it on your clothing to be shielded by evaporating alcohol fumes. Reapply often, as the bourbon will evaporate quickly. And no, you shouldn't try to drink enough bourbon so that it will pour out of your skin.

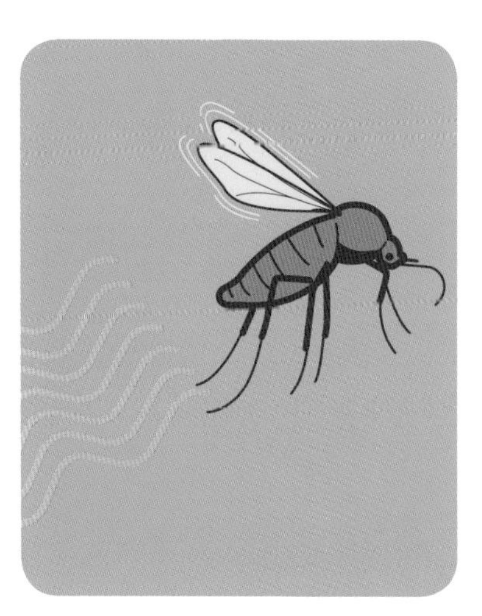

8 MAKE A TRADE Bartering can be traced back to pre-literate cultures at least 6,000 years ago, but could people survive today by bartering? If you were out of cash, money lost its value, or the electronic payment systems were down, you might be able to barter if you had something good to trade (like some top shelf bourbon), and the benefits of bartering booze are plentiful. Even if people don't drink, they might still want it for trade. Trading bourbon for needed supplies makes a lot more sense that trading your ammo, guns, or knives, which an unscrupulous survivor could use against you.

180 USE THE SPARKS

When the butane runs out, the typical disposable lighter may seem like yet another useless bit of junk, but it can still make fire, if you know this trick. Even without flame, you can still create sparks capable of lighting very fine dry tinder.

STEP 1 To bring your dead lighter back to life, place a small fluffy tuft of cattail seed down or some similar fine plant fibers right in the "mouth" of the lighter.

STEP 2 Hold a larger tuft of tinder next to the lighter opening and strike the spark wheel until the fluff ignites.

STEP 3 The tiny flame should be enough to light the small bundle of tinder next to it, which can light your fire. This whole procedure is not as easy as it sounds, especially for the clumsy or cold, but when the chips are down and your lighter is empty, keep trying. That little spark wheel might just save the day.

181 DRY OUT MATCHES

There are four different matches you'll run into when shopping for fire starters. The most common is the "safety" match, which only ignites when struck against a special strip. Then there are "strike anywhere" matches, with a distinctive white tip on their red chemical match head. These can strike on most dry rough surfaces. There are also waterproof matches, which are typically safety matches that have a waterproof varnish. Finally, there are survival matches, which are usually a beefier version of a waterproof match. All are fine fire starters, and I'd recommend waterproof or survival matches for wet climate adventures—though you've still got a shot with safety and strike-anywhere matches that get wet. Allow the match heads and striker strips to dry completely before you attempt to use them. After thorough drying, they should be able to strike unless they've been lying in water which has leached out some of the chemicals.

182 GET ROUGH

When the striking strip has worn thin on your match box, you may think you're screwed since safety match heads don't burn without the striker strip. The match heads contain something called antimony trisulfide, which isn't prone to burning unless it can combine with the red phosphorus in the striker strip. But here's the part that works in our favor when the striker strip is roached out. Any match will flame up, if you can get it hot enough. This can happen with a magnifying glass and sunlight, but if you already had that, there's not much need for the match. Thankfully, friction can also generate enough heat to make safety matches burn. The hard part is finding something with just the right rough texture. Unglazed ceramics, such as the material on the bottom of a mug or bowl, can strike your match about half the time, so give it a try. (Save your attempted match sticks for kindling.) But if you're looking for the best back-up plan for striker strips, cut off some new strips from other match boxes and store them wrapped in plastic as extra strikers.

183 START A FLASHLIGHT FIRE

At the beginning of every cycle of Olympic games, the Olympic torch is lit with the rays from a parabolic mirror. So, too, can your broken flashlight still be useful when you remove the mirror for optical fire starting. With a parabolic mirror from a flashlight, concentrated sunlight forms a blinding white-hot point inside the cup. This means that you'll need to place the tinder where the flashlight bulb once sat when using a reflecting cup. More shallow concave mirrors (like the bottom of a polished aluminum soda can) will also have a focal point like this (a few inches away from the bottom of the curve). Whichever shape you use, this technique will work the same way. Move the mirror so that light focuses on some suitable tinder, and the flammable stuff will start to smolder. The red ember you create can then be blown into flame when combined with more tinder.

184 SAVE A BROKEN SPARK ROD

Whether your ferrocerium rod fire starter was one of the more complex spring loaded models or not, you may yet be able to build a fire even if the tool breaks. Worn down ferro rods will frequently snap in half, especially when they were narrow to begin with and are scraped thin with frequent usage. When this happens, just jam a cracked piece of ferrocerium into the crack of a wooden stick that can act as a handle. Scrape sparks as normal from your re-handled rod. Even very small segments of ferrocerium material will make sparks (there's a tiny piece in your butane lighters, after all). And if your scraper flew the coop, you can still scrape sparks without dulling your knife blade into a butter knife. Just pick up a hard sharp stone and use it just as you would use a metal scraper to scratch off hot sparks.

BUDGET SURVIVAL

HACKSAW BLADES

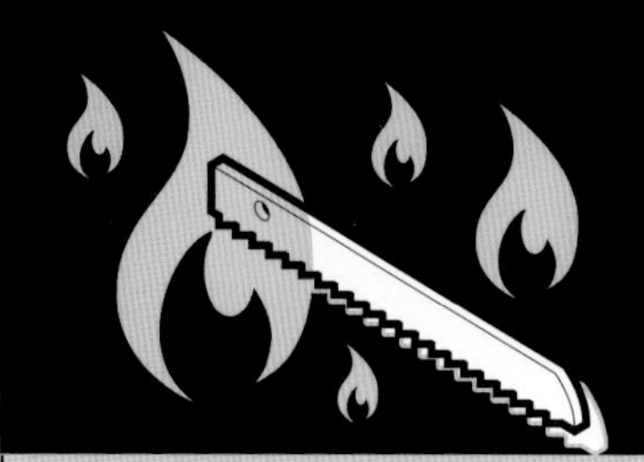

Old, used hacksaw blades may not exactly seem like a great survival resource, but that doesn't mean you should throw them in the metal recycling bin just yet. By cutting them with a grinder or snapping them into short lengths, they can be great ferrocerium and magnesium scrapers. You can use the saw blade teeth (even when dull) to grind away magnesium dust for use as tinder. The thin square spine also makes a great spark rod scraper. They even have a hole at each end, so you can run a piece of cord through each piece for retention.

- They are cheap
- They are light
- They're easy to carry
- They are plentiful
- They are strong

Worth Every Penny

DISPOSABLE LIGHTER

One of the cheapest flame sources, disposables combine spark and fuel. If the spark wheel is broken, but you still have fuel, you just need another spark source to make flame.

185 USE A BOW DRILL

The bow drill is usually the easiest friction fire method; that doesn't mean it's easy, but a firm foundation in the basics will help. Carve a drill along with a fire board, make a bow and lube your handhold, then you're ready. Wind the bow string around your drill, and begin moving the bow back and forth to turn the shaft. Keep the bow level, to prevent the string from creeping up or down the drill. Pin the drill between the handhold and the fireboard, then burn in a hole. Carve a notch in the side of the fire board to collect the dust. The notch should be a 45-degree wedge, just shy of the center. Drill until you fill the notch with dark brown dust, then drill faster to turn it into an ember. Drop the ember in tinder, and blow on it to start a flame. I know that I make it sound easy, and it's not, but with practice, you can do it!

Quick Tip

Your best choices for friction components are fast-growing softwoods. If you want them to work today, they need to be dead and dry, but not rotten.

186 TWEAK YOUR HAND DRILL

The hand drill friction fire method involves a slender drill that is twirled against a wooden board with your bare hands. With this technique, you only need four items: a drill, fire board, tinder, and a knife. Dead weed stalk drills are a practical choice for the drill. Carve soft wood for your fire board. Spin the drill to burn into the board, then carve a notch into the edge. Drill until the notch is full of dust.

If the dust doesn't form a coal, try these techniques.

IMPROVE YOUR GRIP Spit on your hands or apply a little pine pitch to the drill for better grip.

STRING IT UP Tie a long string to the top of the drill, with a loop in each end. Put your thumbs through the loops and use these to help you push downward.

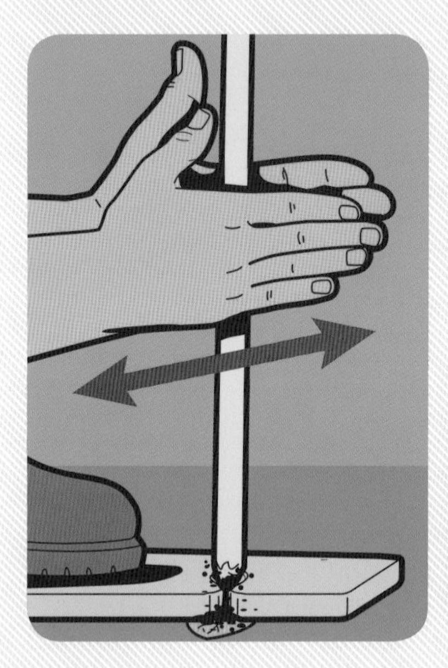

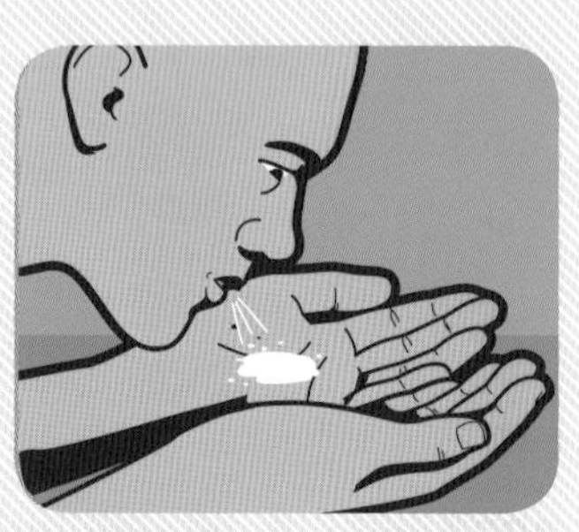

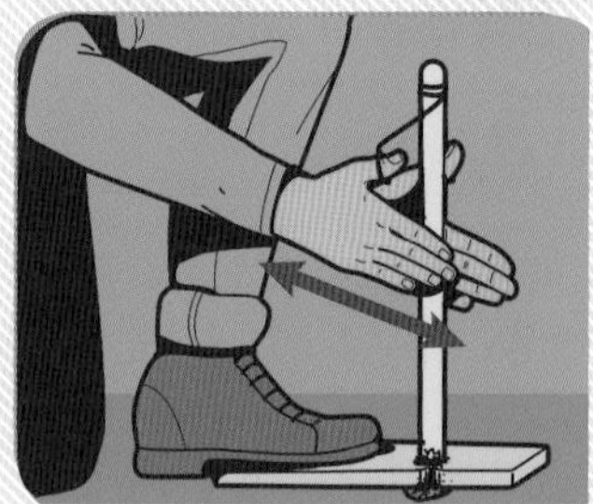

187 MANAGE THE DUST

One of the things that really helps with friction fire making is dust management. With most friction techniques, you'll need a notch full of dust in order to make an ember, but sometimes those embers need a little help. When embers are small and loose, you can make them larger and more stable by adding dust from previous fire making attempts, shavings or dust from chaga (a hard tinder fungus found growing on mountain trees), powdered rotten wood, fluffy down from plants (such as cattail, goldenrod, milkweed, or sycamore balls), and other fine or dusty tinder materials. One additional trick for dust management is blowing on the ember while it's still in the notch. Some dust types don't easily stay lit, but by blowing on the ember as soon as you stop drilling, you can cause the ember to expand and grow. Try this technique with friction woods that make a coarse black dust.

188 BUILD BETTER KITS

Your friction fire kits are only as good as the materials you have chosen and the care you put into their crafting. Grab a bad set of sticks or do a sloppy job carving, and you'll pay the price in blisters and aggravation. Use the following techniques to make your kits great.

ADD A PEBBLE One of the problems with handhold blocks is excess friction. Since lubricant tends to wear away quickly, why not add something slick that won't rub off, such as a smooth little pebble. Search the waterways for a shiny little pebble and embed it into a deep handhold socket. Lube and use as normal, but now your friction will stay where it's supposed to be: at the bottom of the drill.

PAIR UP Take that fancy handhold block you just made and turn your hand drill into a two-user operation. One person spinning the drill, and another holding a handhold block on top of the hand drill, means greater stability and increased downward pressure—and likely a fire built faster.

ADD CHAGA Birch tinder fungus, also known as chaga, is a woody type of fungus that grows on a variety birch trees. You'll find this crusty, black growth primarily on yellow birch and white birch trees, often at higher elevations. And if you are looking for something raw from the wild that catches sparks like char cloth, you've found it. Use powdered chaga for a friction fire dust additive, or strike sparks from flint and steel directly into the dust; no charring needed!

UPGRADE YOUR CORDAGE Bow drill cord slipping a lot? Many people use paracord, but it's slender and slippery. Try something twice as thick, with a grippy texture, for your next friction fire bow string. A thick rough piece of cordage may not seem like the right choice for bow drill, but it is!

HACKS THROUGH HISTORY // CRACKED CAP POLYPORE

Chaga isn't the only fungal friend we can use for fire building. One Eastern American shelf fungus had been used as a tinder additive and even used as a fireboard since ancient times. There are stories of Cherokee medicine people in former days, making fire with this fungus while it was still attached to the tree! The cracked cap polypore is a woody shelf fungus which can be found on dying or dead black locust trees. Dry pieces of this fire fungus can be ground into powder to add to your embers, flatter ones can make a bow drill fire board, and slender bits can make for nice long matches. Just grab a dead cracked cap polypore, get one edge of the shelf fungus smoldering with a coal from your fire, and carry it to your new campfire location (big ones burn for a few hours).

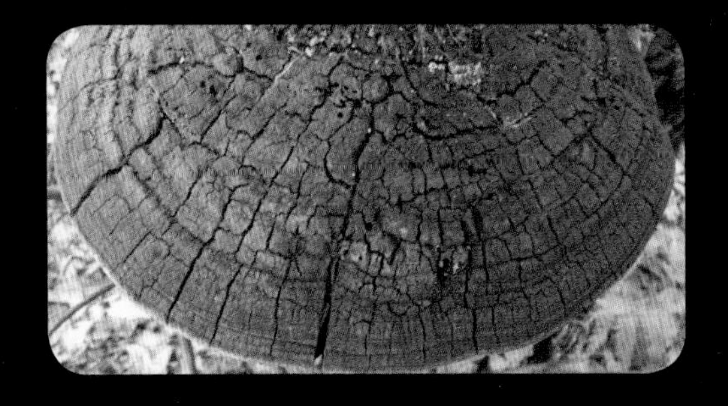

189 USE A CRYSTAL

In days gone by, the U.S. military issued a little bottle of potassium permanganate crystals in first aid kits. This was meant to be sprinkled on wounds as a disinfectant (and you can still use it that way). It also disinfects water, and can make a fire when used with other materials. One simple way is to make a friction fire with these dark colored crystals and ordinary table sugar. Just blend a little of each on a dry slab of bark and grind them together with a blunt stick. Have tinder right next to the crystals, and then nudge it over into the crystals when your grinding starts to make a fire. The other way to go is to make a small pile of potassium permanganate with a dent in the middle. Pour a little glycerin into the dent, and wait for it to flame up. Add your tinder quickly and build your fire as normal.

Worth Every Penny

TORCH IGNITER

Cheap, lightweight, and also reusable, a machine-shop flint striker used to light welding torches can create a generous burst of sparks for your tinder, with each squeeze of the handle.

190 ROLL A COTTON BALL INTO A FLAME

No wooden drills spinning or bamboo strips sawing back and forth. This is friction fire, done in a whole new way. Survivalist, author, and TV personality Creek Stewart first showed this technique on his acclaimed show Fat Guys in the Woods, and the skill has since swept the country and the internet. Cotton balls and wood ash can make a friction fire, when aggressively rolled between two boards. Try it yourself with these steps.

STEP 1 Rip open a cotton ball to create a square shape, and drop a few pinches of white wood ash on one end of the cotton.

STEP 2 Hand roll the cotton into a "cigar" shape as tightly as possible, then start rolling it between two wooden boards. After about 30 seconds, lift the top board and check for smoke.

STEP 3 Repeat the rolling of your cotton cigar back and forth, periodically checking for smoke. Once you have smoke from the cotton, blow on it gently and transfer it into a tinder bundle.

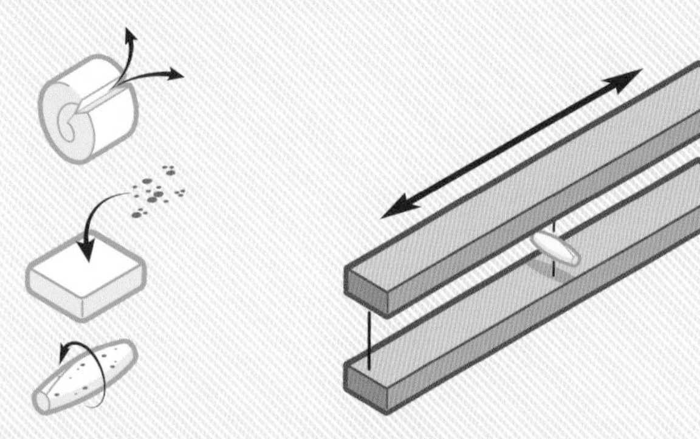

191 SET A FIRE WITH STEEL WOOL

You won't find steel wool growing in the woods, but if you plan ahead by bringing some with you, it can make a fire when combined with a battery. Hit your local hardware store for some fine steel wool—the more zeros on the package, the better. You'll also need a battery that's 3 volts or higher, with the positive and negative terminals close together. A 9-volt or 6-volt battery is great for this; just touch a ball of steel wool to both terminals and it will start burning. A 3.7-volt cell phone battery can also do the trick. You can even use two batteries that are 1.5 volts each. Just align them side by side, with the positive and negative terminals head to tail. (For this last configuration, you'll need to place a ball of steel wool at both ends of the battery stack to create the closed circuit which ignites it.

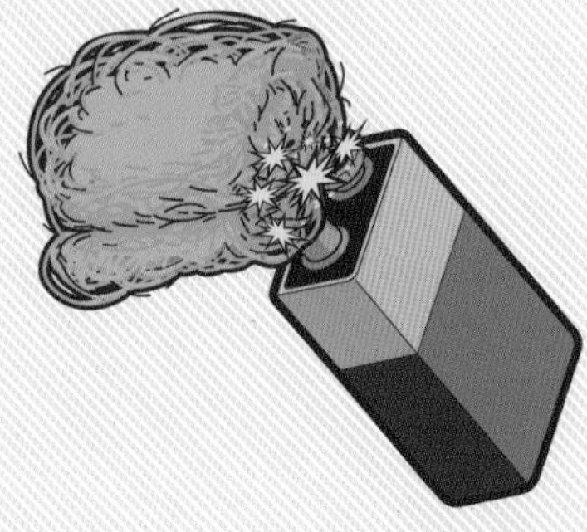

192 FIRE UP A BATTERY

Making fire with just a battery and a gum wrapper isn't that farfetched. All you need is a single D-cell battery, a paper-lined foil gum wrapper, and of course, dry tinder and fuel.

PREPARE YOUR PAPER Cut or tear the wrapper to make a thin "bridge" of foil and paper in the center of the paper strip. The easiest way to try this at home is to fold the wrapper in half lengthwise, and use scissors to snip out a triangle from it. Let the triangle point come within 1/16th-inch (1.5 mm) of clipping the wrapper in two. If you do accidentally clip it, bring the ends into contact.

MAKE A SPARK When you're ready to create fire, hold the wrapper's ends tightly against both ends of the battery. The foil will create a circuit, and the paper may flame up for a second or two. For the best chance of success with this technique, the paper liner of the foil gum wrapper should be bone dry.

GET A GRIP You'll also need to have nimble fingers if you're doing this by yourself. Holding the ends of the wrapper against the ends of the battery and manipulating the "bridge" and the tinder will require some dexterity.

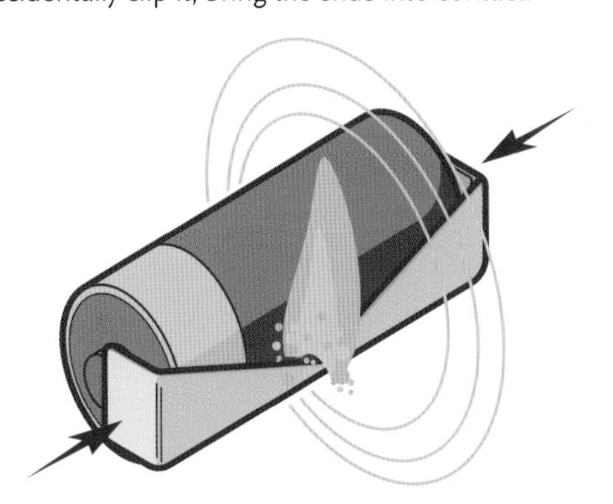

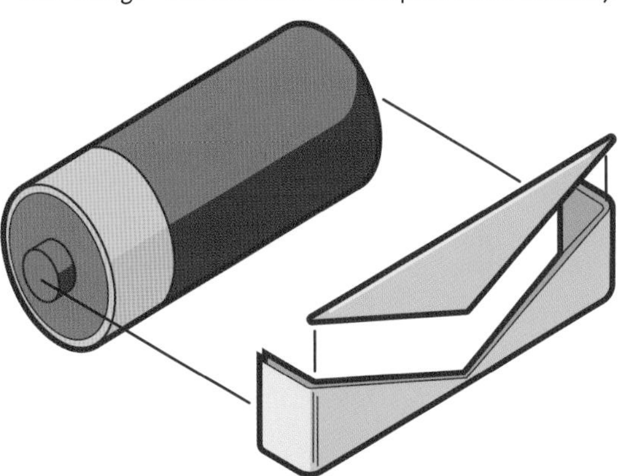

HACKS THROUGH HISTORY // MOUTH DRILL

Our cousins above the Arctic Circle figured out a fire making method that is almost as tough as they are. It's the "mouth drill" and you hold part of it with your teeth! Carve a friction fire drill and board, similar to a bow drill set, but with a longer board and taller drill (at least 12 inches (30 cm) high). Carve a bearing block with a smooth socket, and whittle a ledge that you can bite. You'll turn the drill with a bow that is similar to bow drill, or with a short rope that has a toggle at each end. When you're lubricated the socket of the bearing block and gathered your tinder and kindling, you're ready to give it a try. Bite on the bearing block plate, wind the bow cord around the drill, and pin the drill in place between your block and fire board. Using your neck and head to push down on the drill, begin to spin the drill and keep it up until you have a notch full of dark dust and you believe you have an ember. This will hurt your teeth and give you a sore neck, but it's a traditional method that everyone should at least try once. With a bow and a bite plate bearing block, you could make a bow drill fire one-handed.

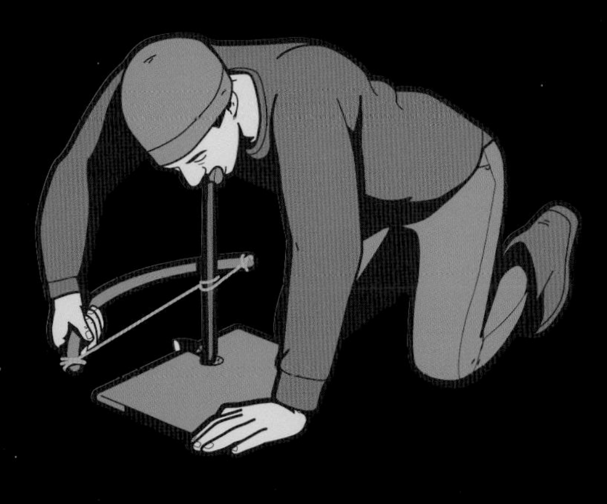

193 APPLY WAX

While butane lighters are a top choice to start a campfire, you shouldn't ignore matches. These common little fire starters work just fine, unless they get wet. But there is a way around the soggy match problem.

STEP 1 Start by melting down a few ounces (20 g) of candle wax in a disposable container (such as a tuna can) near a fire or on a low stove setting. Dip the head and a half-inch (1 cm) of the matchstick into the wax as quickly as possible.

STEP 2 Blow on it to cool the wax so that it won't soak into the match head and ruin it. Let them cool down, then store them someplace dry and cool until they're ready to use.

STEP 3 To use the wax coated matches, scrape off the wax down to the match's chemical head and strike it! Give your creation a test at home before taking it into the wilderness. You don't want bad matches when you're out in the field.

194 POLISH IT OFF

Once you've mastered making the wax coated match, it's time to try the nail polish method of DIY waterproofing. Get a bottle of quick-dry nail polish—bright colors like red or orange definitely add to the survival look.

STEP 1 Paint one side of the head and a half-inch (1 cm) of the stick on a wood match. Blow on the fresh paint to dry it. Then paint a neighboring stripe and blow to dry.

STEP 2 Repeat this until the entire match head is encased in quick dry nail polish. If you don't blow to dry the polish, it will soak into the chemical head on the match and ruin it just like wax.

STEP 3 To use a polish-coated match, use your knife or something rough to scratch off some of the polish on the side that you will strike. And just like wax-coated matches, definitely test them before heading out into the wild.

195 GRIND A MATCH

We've already talked two options for igniting your safety matches: a magnifying glass, and a rough ceramic surface. But what if you don't have either of those items with you? There's one more way to strike safety matches. Locate a dry piece of wood, at least a foot long (35 cm). This could be a dry log in the sun or chunk of firewood. Find a smooth flat section, and put your index finger just behind the match head to support it, and make a long strike with the match (8–10 inches). Try again with a little more pressure, if it didn't light. Move your index finger out of the way quickly at the end of the strike, as the match will light if enough friction is generated. For even better results, rub a stick against the wood to heat it up before your strike the match. This will make it light even easier!

196 CARVE IT UP

If you don't mind a quicker burn time and you need more flame, consider carving a "fuzz stick" from your matches. A fuzz stick is any piece of wood that has been carved so that thin wood shavings stay attached to the main piece. This technique provides much more surface area to burn. It also exposes dry wood from the interior of a piece that may be damp on the surface. To carve a fuzz stick match, carefully hold a thick kitchen match at the end (without the chemical head) and carve little slices of wood so that they are long, but still attached. It's easiest to start with the four corners of the match, then make slices on the spaces in between. To turn this match into a tiny torch with a longer burn, drip a few drops of oil on the fuzzy section, making sure you don't drip oil on the match head (which could prevent it from lighting).

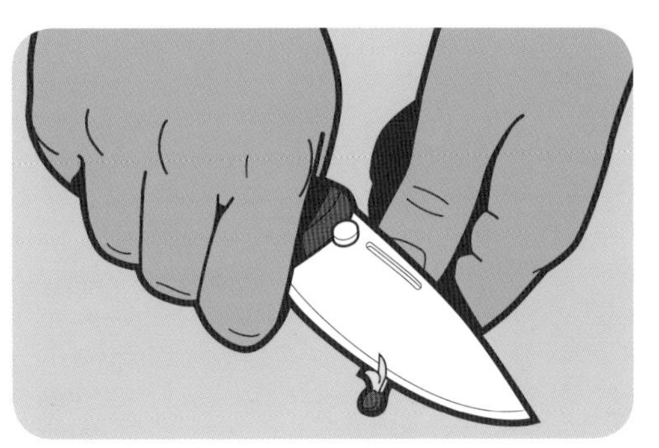

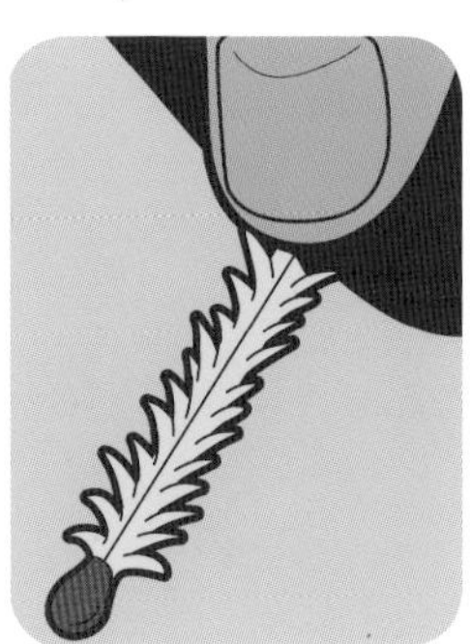

197 GET TWO FIRES

You can double your supply of matches, if you learn to split them. The paper book match is the easiest to split. Tear one free from the book, and gently start to peel the paper in half, starting at the torn end of the match. Make sure the split gives you equal paper on each side. When your split reaches the chemical head, it should pop into two pieces. These only have half the burn time of a regular paper match, but if you strike them carefully, each one will work and be capable of starting dry fluffy tinder ablaze. Another handy split match opportunity comes with stick matches. I would not try to split small stick matches, as they usually break, but large kitchen matches can be split with a razor blade or sharp knife. Pierce the wooden stick, just below the chemical head on the match. Rock the blade a little and shear the match in half.

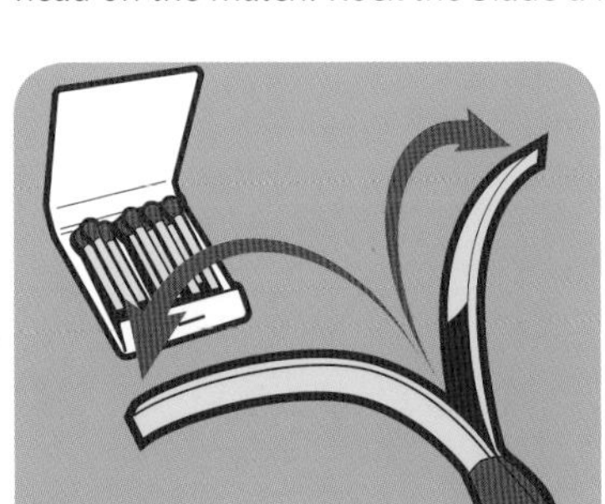

BUDGET SURVIVAL

SUPER MATCHES

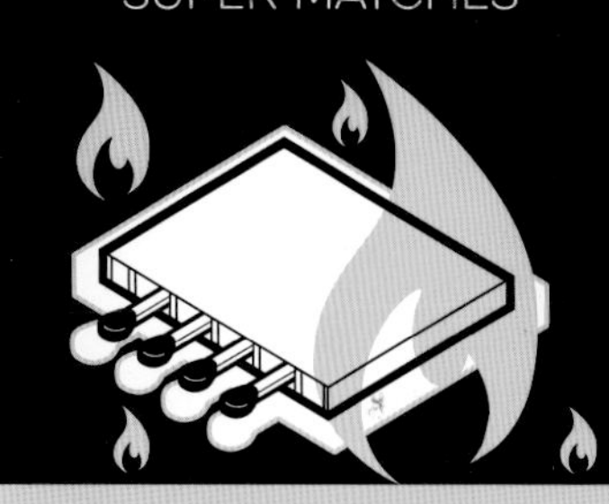

Wet weather, cold climates, and windy conditions can be a challenge for even the best fire maker. So why not stack the deck in your favor by building a "super match"? Cut a small square of cardboard and dip it in melted wax. Let it drain so that the open slots inside the cardboard stay empty. Once the wax has hardened, insert several matches into the cardboard slots. Carry this "super match" along with a separately packaged striker strip, or use strike-anywhere matches.

- Each one can burn for more than a minute.
- They are flat and easy to carry.
- Super matches are fun to make!
- If kept dry, they never go bad.

Quick Tip

Candle wick too short? Poke a hole into the wax with a hot piece of metal and insert a burnt match stick. Light the match at the base, and it will begin burning the wax just like a candle wick.

198 TRY A DANDELION

The lowly dandelion is familiar lawn weed with a basal rosette of leaves. The flower stems are smooth, hollow, and each one bears a solitary yellow head consisting solely of ray flowers, which later produces a puff-ball seed cluster of numerous single-seeded "parachutes." The plant has a deep taproot. The leaves are highly variable and may be nearly smooth-edged, toothed, or deeply cut. Dandelion grows wild in most of the world, typically in full sun conditions; and it is also completely edible. The young leaves of dandelion can be eaten raw before they become too bitter. The blooming flowers can be peeled of their down-pointing green sepals to be eaten in salads or fried as fritters. The leaves and flowers pack a massive dose of Vitamins A and C, as well as a strong flavor. The larger leaves, along with buds and roots, can be cooked in many ways to become tastier. The roots can even be roasted to create a coffee-like beverage.

199 PICK A BERRY

Raspberries and blackberries are close kin, both being in the genus Rubus. These tasty berries are like sweet little gems from the wild. They are a delicious and nutritious source of food that we can forage almost anywhere, since they are found around the Northern Hemisphere. The berries are high in minerals, including potassium. But there's more to these berries than just a snack. While the ripe berries are edible raw or cooked, the leaves of blackberries and raspberries can be dried to produce a mild tasting herbal tea. When consumed in larger amounts, this tea can help to relieve the symptoms of diarrhea. And if the leaf tea isn't getting the job done, steep one ounce (28 g) of fresh blackberry root in a cup (240 mL) of hot water and drink half of a cup per hour. The fragrant white flower petals can be added to salads and other dishes. They don't contain many calories, but they can make those bitter wild greens taste much better.

200 CRACK A HICKORY

The trees of the genus Carya are deciduous hardwood trees found in North America and Asia. The leaves are alternate compound and the nuts have a "double" nut shell. There's a husk that peels off, revealing a nut shell underneath—but make sure you don't get a buckeye! They have a double-layered nut shell like hickory, but buckeye nuts are poisonous. Hickory nuts have a multi-chambered inner nutshell like a walnut, while the toxic buckeyes have a solid nutmeat like an almond. Hickory nuts are the most calorie dense wild plant food. One ounce (28 g) of shelled out hickory nut meats packs a whopping 193 calories, with most coming from fat. These sweet and fatty nut meats can be used as a raw food, picked right out of the shell. You can also make a traditional Native American dish (from which hickory derives its name) by cooking the nut meat in water until it becomes a fatty porridge.

201 PUT PINE ON THE MENU

There are many pine species throughout the world, and all of them have something to offer a survivor in the wilderness. The inner layer of bark can be stripped, dried, and ground into meal to provide emergency calories, even in the dead of winter. The green needles can be steeped in hot water to make a pleasant tea that contains four times your daily allowance of vitamin C. The flammable pitch is the thing that makes so many parts of pine into an excellent fire starter. The dead brown needles of pine are great tinder, and the brittle dead twigs are fine kindling, especially when you are making a wet-weather fire. If any pitch is present, oozing from wounds on the tree, swab it up with tinder to make an even more flammable fuel source. Even the wood is helpful, particularly when it has aged and become fatwood. You can also use pine boughs to cover improvised shelters.

202 GRAB A CATTAIL

Cattail has been called the "Walmart of the waterways" (since it's a one-stop shopping trip). It grows in wet areas and resembles a tall grass with a burnt "corn dog" at the top. With uses throughout each season, the cattail freely offers us a variety of foods, as well as tinder and cordage material. The rootstocks of the swamp-loving cattail will start to swell in late summer and can provide us with a great starch source. Dig them up, wash, and peel them; once cleaned, crush them in water to separate out the starch. The young shoots can be boiled in springtime and the pollen can be collected in early summer, to add to flour as a protein supplement. The horn-shaped sprouts at the base of the stalk also make a nice cooked vegetable. The green leaves can be dried, moistened, and twisted into a light duty rope. And for starting fires with sparks or embers, few things rival the flammability of cattail seed down. Collect this fluffy stuff as soon as it starts to peel from the seed head and expand into a fuzzy mass.

HACK HEROES ACORNS

1 LEACH IN A CREEK Ancient peoples used acorns for carbohydrate-rich staple food, similar to bread. Today, we can use them the same, and in other ways—but first, we have to remove the tannic acid. Luckily, it's water soluble and easy to extract. Crush acorns to remove the shells and break the pieces up. Soak the pieces in a pot of warm water and dump the water off when it turns brownish, repeating until palatable. Alternatively, put crushed nut pieces in basket, and set them in a flowing creek with a flat rock on top (to keep them from washing away). The running water will strip away the tannic acid in one to three days of soaking.

2 GRIND ACORN FLOUR ▲ Acorns are a wild food powerhouse, containing about 2,000 calories per pound (0.45 kg), and they can be found across the Northern Hemisphere. Once you have leached out the tannic acid, you can convert the nut chunks into many foods. Nut pieces can be eaten as-is, if you soaked them in potable water. If it was a creek soak, the water could be tainted, so a cooked acorn food will be safer. Roast the nut chunks to eat them as a snack. You can also let them dry out for a few hours, then grind them to make acorn flour. You can add this flour to existing recipes, or try your hand at making acorn porridge.

3 BREW NUT COFFEE ▲ Acorns don't have caffeine, but you could use them to make a coffee-like brew. Take some leached chunks of acorn nut meat and place them in a cast iron skillet, in the oven at 350 °F (180 °F) for half an hour or until the pieces almost burn. In camp, set the skillet in a bed of coals and stir the acorn chunks often. Once they are roasted to a dark brown color, use 1 or 2 tablespoons (14–28 g) of roasted nut chunks in one cup (240 mL) of scalding hot water, then sweeten, and enjoy. You can mix in your normal additives, or drink it black.

4 BAIT A TRAP Any trapper worth their weight in groundhog pelts will be able to tell you: "Don't bait with acorns under the oak tree." They're absolutely right—when you're trapping, you never want to use food baits that the animals can have with easy access. They are never going to nibble on the acorn that you touched with your human scent and placed next to a noose or deadfall that smells like you, not when they have hundreds of other acorns to eat that don't smell funny and aren't in a weird place. So, minimize the human scent on your skin before collecting them, and take them to an area without abundant acorns. Now animals will find your bait more appealing, and hopefully, irresistible.

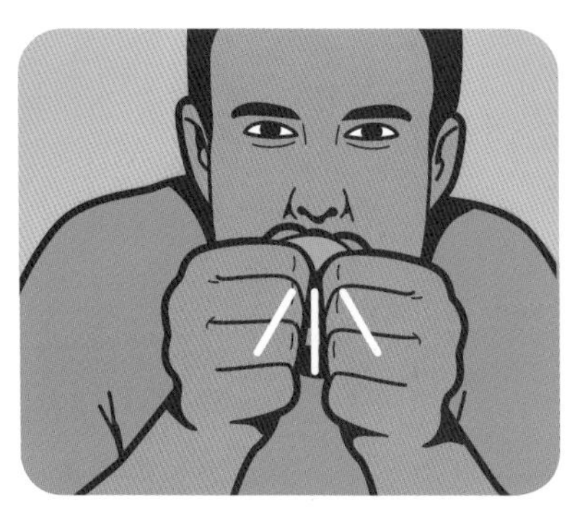

5 BLOW A WHISTLE ▲ Acorn caps come in a range of sizes and shapes, and plenty can be used as whistles. Larger ones have a deeper tone, and smaller caps can be deafeningly shrill. Test them by holding the cap in both hands, with your thumbs over the open side. Make a V-shaped gap between your thumbnails, put your lips to your knuckles, and blow hard! When the jet of air hits the top edge of the cap, you'll hear it whistle. Acorn caps with different sizes will even make different sounds.

6 TAN YOUR HIDE ▶ Crushed acorns, along with fresh oak bark, can be added to hot water to draw out tannic acid for hide tanning. This solution can be added to other mixtures or used on its own. For brain tanning, you mix animal brains and water to make a conditioning solution. If you use tannic acid water, you'll have an even better chance of turning out a soft yet durable hide. You could also use tannic acid alone for vegetable-tanned leather. Soak hides in batches of strong tannic acid for several months and move them around in the fluid regularly, to soak up an even amount of tannin.

7 USE THE ACID It seems like we're brewing up some medieval potion, but crushed acorns and hot water can provide a tannic acid remedy for many ills. You can use the first water you pour off from soaking acorns, or make a more concentrated liquid by boiling crushed acorns (shells and all) in a pot of water. A handful of crushed acorns in one pint (470 mL) of water makes a small batch of strong solution. Soak a clean cloth in this fluid, and apply to rashes, ingrown toenails, hemorrhoids, and any other inflamed skin ailment. Leave the cloth in place, and repeat this treatment as needed. For tooth troubles, simply swish the bitter water in your mouth for toothache.

8 STORE FOOD ▼ There are many different ways to store acorns and their resulting nut meat. Our ancestors found the best ways to suit each climate. Some left the nuts in their shell and stored them as is, though this is a good feeding ground for acorn grubs which could devastate your food storage plans. Other predecessors broke up the shells and nut meat, disrupting the grubs' life cycle. The acorns were then stored in chunks, with all of their natural tannic acid in place, as a good preservative. Other ancestors clearly completely processed the acorns and stored them as flour. With electricity as an option, the easiest way to store acorns is in the freezer.

203 CAMP ON THE SIDE

Mountains have many hazardous features and they often make their own unique weather patterns. So when it comes time to set up camp in mountainous terrain, there are a number of points to consider. The first thing is always safety. You don't want to camp below a rockslide area or in any other risky spot. But being at the tip top of the summit doesn't eliminate your risks either. You're more prone to lightning strikes and fierce winds from storms hitting the pinnacles of mountains. And if you're thinking that the bottom of the mountain is safest, think again. Even small storms can generate flooding, causing raging creeks and rivers at the bottom of the mountain. It's also colder there in the morning, since cold air falls during the night. So where do we camp? The safest and most practical spot is on the side of the mountain, preferably the sunny side. In the Northern Hemisphere, this is the south side, which receives more sun light and is naturally warmer.

204 ENJOY BIG BENEFITS

Mountain terrain can be as unforgiving as it is beautiful. The amazing views and the chance for solitude draw many people to these giant land features throughout the year—unfortunately, the mountains are also often the setting for many outdoor emergencies. But there's a bright side. This very same environment also has certain advantages in the game of survival.

DRINK DEEP It's quite common to find many springs in the mountains, and these are often safe to drink as-is. Depending on the local geology, there may be pockets of water trapped on high ground. These "kettles" may hold water for a long time on mountaintops and ridges.

FIND A CAVE Caves, rock overhangs, and stone ledges all have long been favorite shelters by our ancestors, and we can use still use them today as ready-made shelters.

BEAT BUGS Not every pest likes the thin mountain air. While there are certain species of ticks and other hazardous creature that only live at great heights, many of our day-to-day troublemakers are absent once you reach certain elevations. Enjoy it!

BUILD WITH ROCK Quite often, mountain terrain is strewn with loose rock. This can be a hazard, in areas prone to rockslides. But elsewhere, it gives us plenty of building material. Loose rocks can be used to build fire hearths and heat reflectors. You could also build shelters from rock, if you're skilled at stone work. Rocks can even help the unskilled builder, by acting as anchors for tent ropes and tarp lines.

USE THE COLD Thanks to their elevation, it's often colder in the mountains, so make use of that chilly air and water. Keep food and drinks cold in frosty mountain streams, just watch the contamination of surfaces by potentially dirty water.

SIGNAL FOR MILES No one may see your signal fire in a dense jungle, but they're a lot less likely to miss it if it's been set on a high-altitude mountaintop. When you have to signal for help, do it from high points.

HACK HAZARDS

MOUNTAIN LIGHTNING

From the first roll of thunder or flash of lightning, every mountaineer should be worried about lightning and taking steps to avoid getting struck. Lightning causes 55 to 60 deaths and 400 injuries each year in the United States, and this bolt from the sky accompanies every single thunderstorm. Do your best to safely descend the mountain when you see or hear a storm approaching. If you're caught above the treeline, stay away from ridges and summits, since these are likely to attract lightning. In the forest, move to an area with shorter trees. Stay separate from other group members, squat down with only your feet touching the ground. Cover your ears with your hands (for hearing protection), and pray you are spared the jolt of a lightning strike! If someone is struck by lightning, seek immediate medical help.

Quick Tip

Gear up before you head up. Take extra clothing, food and supplies for your mountain adventures. It's better to have it and not need it, than the other way around. (I've learned that the hard way.)

205 WRANGLE WORMS

There are scores of different species of earthworm and all are considered safe for human consumption, but they should be purged of their "dirt" before you eat them. An easy way to clean them out is to place them in a container of damp grass. After a few hours, the critters will be void of the dirt and sand they normally hold. Worms can be dug with a shovel, or located by quickly flipping over rocks and rotten logs. You can also "thump" for worms, pounding a mallet, club or staff against the ground to vibrate the soil. Many species of worms will respond to this by crawling up to the surface. You can even cut notches into the side of a stick, brace it against the ground and scrape the notches with another stick to vibrate up worms. Like all animal foods, worms should be cooked before eating. I recommend frying. The good news is that fried worms taste a little like jerky. The bad news is that average sized worms are only about 1 calorie per gram (not counting any fat used for frying).

206 POACH WILD EGGS

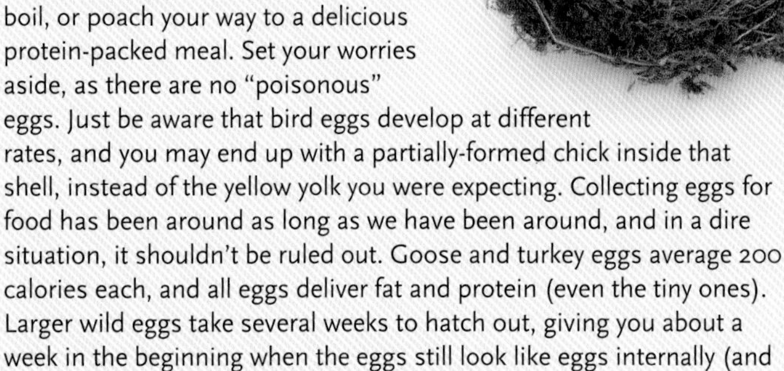

The act of stealing songbird and game bird eggs is illegal in most areas, but you've got to do what needs to be done in an emergency. When you're lost and hungry in the mid-spring wilderness—and you find a nest full of fresh eggs—you can fry, hard boil, or poach your way to a delicious protein-packed meal. Set your worries aside, as there are no "poisonous" eggs. Just be aware that bird eggs develop at different rates, and you may end up with a partially-formed chick inside that shell, instead of the yellow yolk you were expecting. Collecting eggs for food has been around as long as we have been around, and in a dire situation, it shouldn't be ruled out. Goose and turkey eggs average 200 calories each, and all eggs deliver fat and protein (even the tiny ones). Larger wild eggs take several weeks to hatch out, giving you about a week in the beginning when the eggs still look like eggs internally (and they don't look like a mutant chick yet).

207 SEEK SHELLFISH

Shellfish are found around the world, and many are good for eating. There are two kinds of shellfish: crustaceans (such as shrimp, crab, and lobster) and mollusks (such as clams, mussels, oysters, and scallops). Clams, mussels, and similar shelled creatures are often buried in sand or mud, so you'll need to dig quickly to find them. In tidal saltwater areas, be there at low tide. The right time to go clamming is at the lowest tides. A clam's neck near the surface of the sand will produce a distinct "show." Shows are found most commonly by one of two methods: Looking for small holes, round dimples, or indentations in dry sand, or by pounding your clam-digging shovel handle in receding surf. If you are lucky, a pounding of the shovel handle will reveal a show and if you are really lucky, your efforts may reveal multiple shows. And if the clams are absent, slower crustaceans can be hand-caught.

208 EAT BUGS

With so many bug species in the world, how do you figure out which ones are edible? They're not all safe for people food, but there are quite a few that can be eaten.

TRY TERMITES These are the highest calorie bug in this section. These pale colored, ant-looking insects provide about 6 calories per gram. You'll have to work to get it, though. These little guys go scurrying for cover anytime you damage the wood they reside in. Roast them in a dry pan, and some species take on a shrimp flavor.

CRUNCH CICADAS Your prep work for these noisy bugs is easy, just harvest the slow-witted and slow-moving things in the early hours of the morning. They should be blanched (boiled for 4–5 minutes) soon after collection and before eating. Not only will this make their insides solidify a bit, but will kill any bacteria and parasites. Remove the wings and legs. At this point, you can either freeze them for later use, or cook them immediately. These fatty bugs pack a ton of protein, have a mild flavor, and can be cooked in many ways.

GRAB A GRASSHOPPER Crickets, katydids, and grasshoppers are a very diverse group of bugs that are generally safe to eat, if you avoid the colorful members of these families. Red, orange, yellow, and blue are usually warnings. The heads and small legs should be removed, and the bugs should always be cooked thoroughly. Bugs with crunchy shells (exoskeletons) are often the most parasite-laden. Hunt for them in the early morning, when they are less active from the colder temperatures. This group yields approximately 4 to 5 calories per gram.

SNATCH A SNAIL Terrestrial slugs and snails (found on land, not the sea) are generally safe for human consumption, always after a thorough cooking. In addition, their nutritional value certainly justifies the effort of collecting and cooking them. These critters have about 90 calories per 100 grams of "meat," which is high in protein (12 to 16 percent) and rich in minerals. Determine if there are any toxic species in your area. And remember that snails are usually served in garlic butter to hide their strong flavor, so season them well.

209 COOK OFFAL

Beggars can't be choosers, so when times get tough, you may have to eat some foods that you would not prefer. For many of us, offal is on that list. It turns out that edible animals have edible organs inside them—with a few exceptions. Hearts can be cut up and prepared in the same ways as meat, since they're a muscle. Liver can be fried with bacon and onions, if you have them. Lungs are an odd flavor and texture, but edible. Stomachs can be emptied, rinsed, scraped and cut up into pieces as tripe, often used in spicy acidic soups, where their natural flavor is camouflaged. Intestines can be thoroughly flushed out, and prepared into chitterlings or processed a little further into sausage casings. Kidneys are best slow cooked until tender. All the bones can be used as soup bones, which provide minerals that are vital to your health. Just skip any organs that look diseased, and avoid the livers of arctic mammals, as they carry toxic levels of vitamin A.

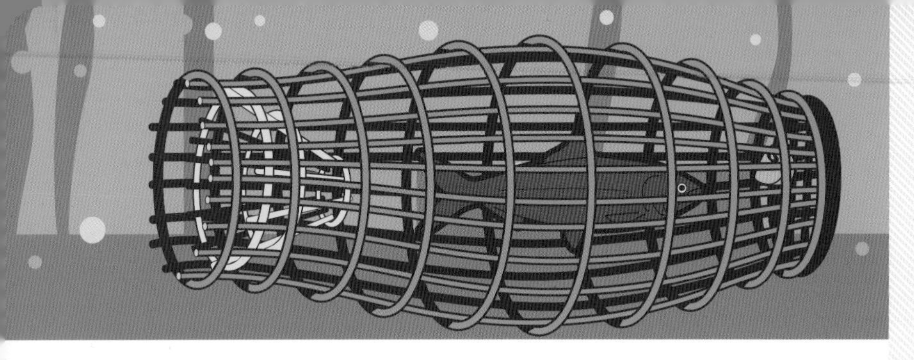

210 TRAP A FISH

Trapping underwater has many of the same benefits as terrestrial trapping. The trap can be placed, and left working to collect food for you while you're somewhere else. Almost all fish traps work off the same principals. Animals are lured into the trap by bait, or because it looks like an inviting shelter. The entrance is a constricting space, typically funnel-shaped, leading from outside the trap to the center of the trap's interior. Animals work their way around the outside of the trap, until they find the entrance. Once inside, their behavior causes them to repeatedly try to seek exit at the edges, corners, and perimeter of the trap. Rarely, will they go back to the center of the trap to find the only exit. The animals are trapped, unless they are small enough to fit through the gaps in the trap wall (a great trick for eliminating undersized animals). A cool addition on these traps is an interior bait cage, to keep the bait from being eaten by the trapped animals, and let the bait keep working.

211 LIFT YOUR QUARRY

For this trap, you'll need a spring pole, a peg in the ground, a snare line with noose, a trigger peg, and maybe some bait (if you're making a bait-driven trap).

BUILD YOUR TRAP Drive your peg deep into the soil, and carve a hook near the top. If you have a saw of some kind, you can also saw off the top of an existing bush or sapling. This woody plant and its extensive root system will provide an exceptional anchor for your trap.

MAKE YOUR PEGS Carve your trigger peg with a matching hook which will grab onto your peg in the ground. Tie your snare line to the spring pole, and tie the trigger peg onto the line. Make sure you tie the knot on the trigger peg on the side of the peg you have cut the hook into. Tying the line on any other side of the peg will pull the trigger at an odd angle, and you'll never set the trap.

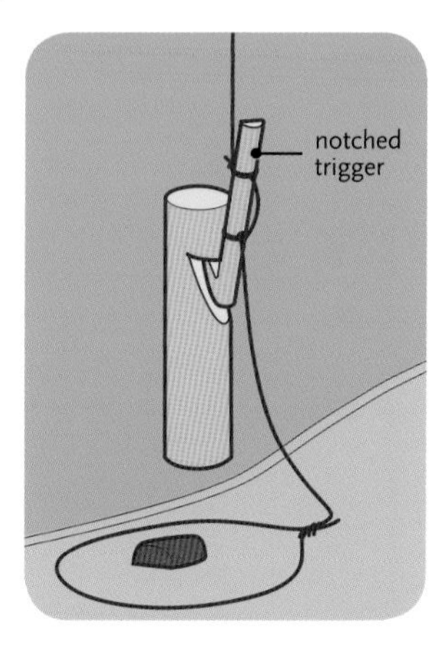

SET YOUR TRAP Attach bait to the trigger peg with the noose set around the bait, or set the noose in a trail near the peg trigger.

212 DROP A CAGE

Mammals would have no trouble chewing their way out of this trap, lifting it up or burrowing out from under it. Small birds, however, lack the strength, skill, claws and teeth needed to escape this basic "drop trap." There isn't that much meat on their hollow little bones, but small birds can be plucked, cleaned, and boiled whole to create a nourishing broth or soup. Start assembling this trap by creating a cage. Build a square or pyramidal box out of sticks and string. Leave few sticks moveable on the top. This way, you can move them to the side to create an opening you can reach into to grab the bird. Carve a vertical post with a "chisel" top to support the trap. Add a forked stick with a side notch to act as a lever on top of this post. Use two long thin sticks to brace between the bottom "rung" of the trap and the end of the lever. Scatter bait under the trap and wait. When one or more birds hop onto one of the long slender sticks, the lever will move out of place and the cage will drop. That was complicated, but wait for the finale: getting the bird out of the cage without it flying away! May I recommend putting a snake in it, then eating the bird-filled reptile?

213 GET A MONKEY

Stuck on an island full of coconuts, and you've worked up a hankering for some tender monkey meat? A hollow coconut can help. You'll need one large coconut, a tool to cut openings into it, a rope, and some irresistible solid bait. Drill a small hole in the coconut, the diameter of your rope. Drill a slightly larger hole, a little bigger than the imagined diameter of monkey's wrist. Thread your rope through the small hole, knot it, and secure the free end of the rope to a tree or root. Get a piece of bait that barely fits in the larger hole. This could be a chunk of coconut, a tree nut, or some other hard bait. Finally, crumble more of the bait around the coconut and retreat to watch your trap. Most monkeys will want every single piece of the food. When they figure out that there is a piece inside the coconut, they'll reach in for it. They generally won't let go, and their own closed fist keeps their hand stuck inside the coconut on a rope. You run up and dispatch them.

214 FIX A SNARE

Often made from wire or cable, the fixed snare is connected to an immobile object, like a tree or a stake in the ground. This trap doesn't usually kill. It merely restrains an animal until you come around to dispatch it. The fixed loop snare is easy to make, using metal for its odd combination of strength, rigidity and flexibility; but it's not perfect. These are usually single use traps, as the animals often bend and kink the wire making it vulnerable to future breakage, or they actually break or chew through the wire. To make one from solid wire, find a twig that is about 1/8 inch (0.25 cm) in diameter that is breakable. Wind one end of your wire around the twig two or three times. Then twist the twig like a little propeller, which will twist the end of the wire closed. Break the twig, and remove it to reveal an eye which you can use to make your noose. Place these snares over burrows, in small game trails, or attach them to spring pole snares for a more secure snare line. You'll need about 2 feet (20 cm) of wire to form one wire snare for medium-sized small game animals (like rabbits, opossum and smaller raccoons). You'll need one yard (1 m) of heavy wire for slightly larger animals. And of course, you could use a shorter and thinner wire for the smallest of game animals (like squirrels).

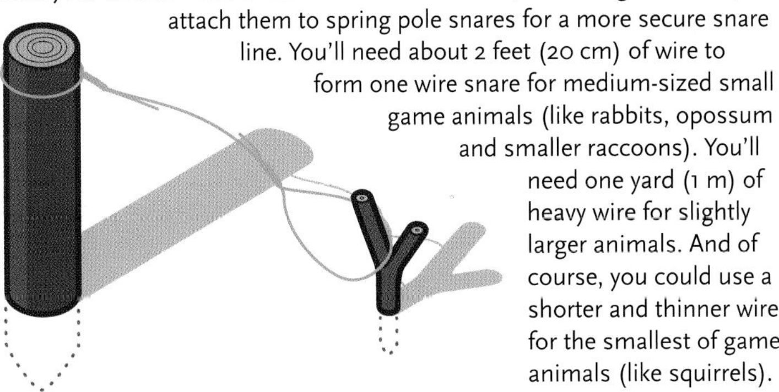

HACK HAZARDS

IT'S A TRAP!

By design, a trap is a machine that cause bodily harm. So, we shouldn't ever forget that fact when we are working with them. For one example, never handle the noose of a lifting snare with your hands, once the trap trigger is engaged. If the trap goes off unexpectedly, the snare noose can grab your hand or a finger, and tear off skin and muscle! Use a stick if you need to adjust the snare noose after the trigger is set. Similarly, don't try to set giant deadfall traps. This group of traps is best reserved for small animals, since the weight is typically five times the animal's body weight. If you decide to try to set a deadfall for a 40-pound (18-kg) beaver, that means you'll have to wrestle a 200-pound (90-kg) rock into position, and set a trigger under it, placing your hands and other parts at risk. Traps cause harm, often to the quarry and sometimes to the trapper as well.

Worth Every Penny

CABLE SNARES

Steel cable snares can be found in many sizes. Often manufactured from aircraft-grade steel, these braided cables will hold your prey securely, and preventing escape.

215 SURVIVE BY BOW

When we craft a bow, we're trying to modify a sapling, branch, or section of tree trunk so that it will bend easily, snap back quickly, and hold onto our bow string.

STEP 1 Select the proper materials. Black locust and hickory are two of my favorites, though most hardwoods will work. Start with a relatively straight section of sapling or branch that is free of knots, branches, and twists—about 6 feet (2 m) long and about 2 inches (5 cm) wide.

STEP 2 Stand the bow stave upright, hold the top loosely, and then push outward lightly on the middle of the prospective bow. The stave should swivel to show you which way it is slightly curved or naturally more bendable. The outside bend of this curve is called the "back," and the inside bend of the curve is the "belly." Leave the back alone; you'll only be carving the belly.

STEP 3 Begin removing wood from the stiff parts of the belly, while leaving the areas that already bend. The goal at this step in the process is to get the limbs to bend in an even curve. Take off material slowly and recheck the bend of the limbs frequently.

STEP 4 Carve small notches on the both sides of each tip, being careful not to carve into the back of the bow. They only need to be deep enough to keep a bow string in place. Don't fully draw the bow yet (doing so can break the bow).

STEP 5 Hang the bow up horizontally on a branch by the handhold. Now pull down a few inches (10 cm) on the string while observing how the limbs bend. You want each limb to bend evenly throughout its length. Shave, scrape, sand, or carve the belly of each limb until both limbs bend equally and evenly.

STEP 6 The tillering process is complete once both limbs flex equally and evenly, and the draw weight (pressure required to pull the string back to a full draw) is at your desired poundage. Wipe some oil on the bow as a sealant, and start shooting.

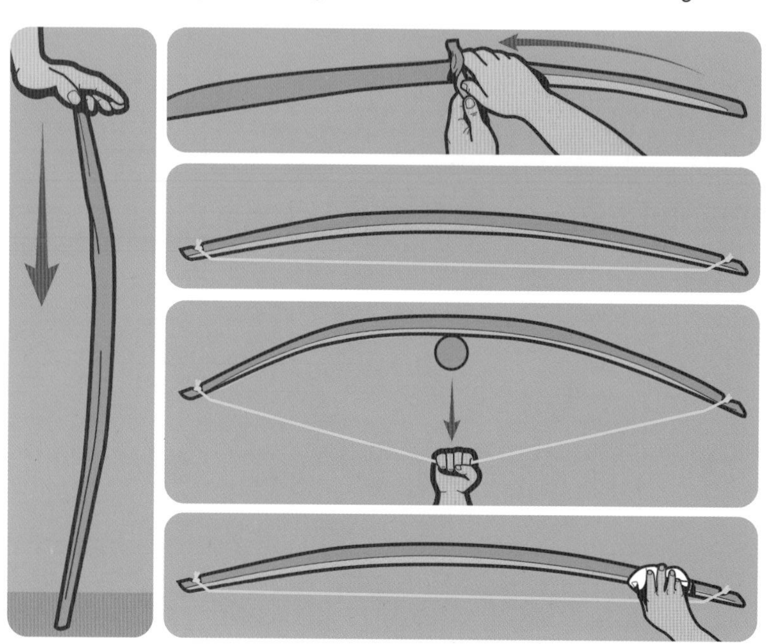

BUDGET SURVIVAL

550 CORD BOWSTRING

550 cord is great for a bow string, except for one trait: It stretches. Imagine using a rubber band; it would stretch lengthwise as you drew the arrow back, then compress lengthwise when the arrow is released. The energy wouldn't all go into the projectile. But there is a way to get rid of the stretchiness of 550 cord. Determine the length of cord you'll need for your bow, cut the cord, and tie a loop in each end. Loop one end onto your bow and place a thin stick through the other end. Turn the small stick to place a tight twist on the 550 cord. Once it's as tight as you can manage, place one of the loops onto your bow, twist the cord tightly to remove the elasticity, and secure the end of the line.

Quick Tip

Sometimes you can't find a single quill or feather to make fletchings for your arrows. When that happens, you can use strips of duct tape cut to shape, instead of feathers, for a quick yet effective arrow fletching.

216 BREAK IT UP

Each arrow can require up to two notches, one for the bow string and one to haft the arrow head. These notches can be tricky to cut, if you lack a saw and a vice to hold the shaft. That's why the broken notch technique is a valuable skill to learn if you need to make arrows in the field. Near the end of an over-length arrow shaft, carve a pair of shallow grooves on opposite sides of the shaft. Then come down a half-inch (1.25 cm) and carve another pair of grooves on opposing sides of the shaft (and opposite to the other grooves). To explain it a different way, if the first grooves were north and south, the second pair are east and west, with 3/4-inch (2 cm) of distance between the pairs. Now start to wiggle the end of the shaft, to crack the wood between the first pair of grooves and the second pair. Wiggle the piece front to back, and side to side. When it feels ready to break, move the breaking piece so that it slides out of the newly formed notch and break it out completely. Now you have your notch!

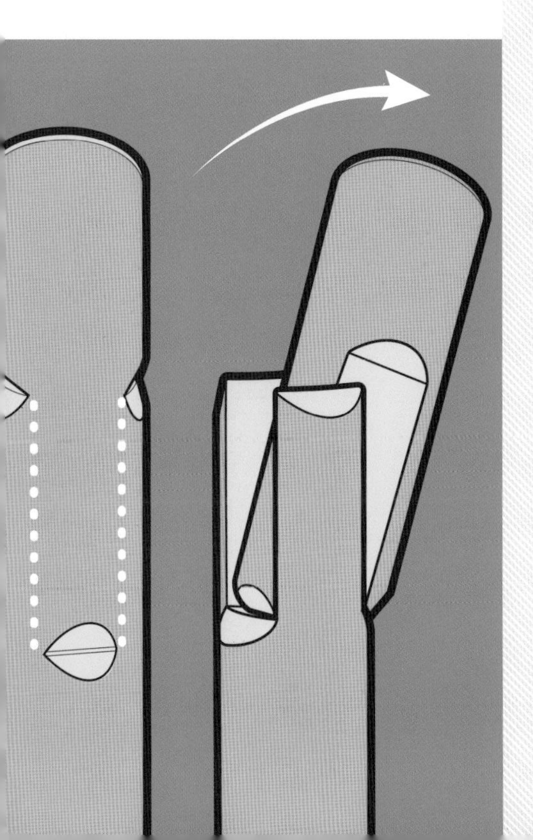

217 BE BLUNT

Blunt points on arrows are commonly used to hunt rabbits, birds, and other small game animals. They won't slash or pierce, but the blunt point can kill through impact. And when shooting at tree dwellers, the blunt point won't get stuck in a tree top. It will bounce off branches and fall down. To make a blunt in the field, you'll have to do a lot of carving. Select a thicker sapling than you'd normally use for an arrow shaft, and carve the majority of it down, leaving just the tip of the arrow thick. At home with your woodworking tools, you could drill an arrow-shaft-diameter hole in a round block of hardwood, and glue in the arrow. Achieve your final shape by rasping and sanding. The use of blunt arrows reaches back into ancient England. After William the Conqueror established the first "game preserves," Saxons were allowed to shoot birds and small game with blunt arrows. But if an archer were found with a sharp arrowhead, it was assumed that he was after the king's deer and that archer was hanged.

218 FIRE A FLU-FLU

This twisted fletching looks different because it is different. Rather than attaching feathers parallel to the arrow shaft, this style of fletching uses several long feathers (or many pieces) around the arrow shaft. This won't offer the flight stabilization of a normal fletching, but it does straighten out the arrow's flight in the beginning, and then opens up to create drag, acting as a drag-chute after a certain distance. This can prevent arrow loss when hunting quarry like birds in trees. The arrow will travel about 30 yards (27 m) very quickly, then slow down dramatically. If you shot a normal arrow upward and missed your mark, it would continue in an arc that would take it out of sight in a forest environment. The flu-flu is also used in grasslands, to keep it from becoming lost in the grass. To aid your retrieval further, it's best if flu flus are brightly colored.

HACK HEROES DENTAL FLOSS

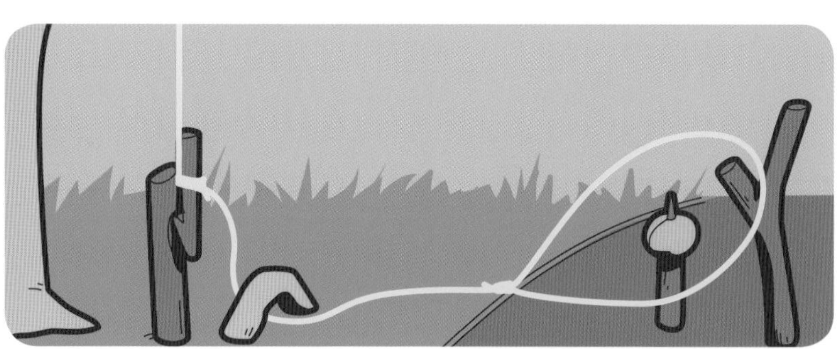

1 FISH WITH IT ▲ Besides cleaning your teeth, dental floss is naturally suited to many other tasks which require a thin, strong line. One of the handiest uses in a survival setting is using dental floss as an improvised fishing line. Sure, keeping a spool of monofilament fishing line in your survival gear is a great idea, but floss is a decent runner-up. Being so thin, fish don't seem to mind biting the line; and being so strong, this line (and a baited hook) can help you land a whopper of a fish. Use the floss tied to a long flexible sapling tree or long tree branch as a traditional fishing pole. You can also use perform hand-line fishing by simply holding the line and casting it out into the water.

2 MAKE ARROWS ▶ Floss can lie flat when tied around hard objects, so it's a great substitute for cord you'd use to haft an arrowhead or affix feathers as fletching. I like to tie the line around the arrow shaft, leaving a tail that's a few inches (10 cm) long, so I can secure the other end of the line when I'm done tying on the point or feathers. Your best choice for these jobs is un-waxed floss. This dry nylon line can absorb glue, which can reinforce knots and help to secure points and fletchings. You won't have much color choice in floss, but once the line has been secured, it will readily accept color from paint and ink.

3 SNARE YOUR DINNER ▲ For very small game animals, one or several strands of floss can be used as a snare line. The only real trick between using this material and proper snare line is that it's much easier for animals to chew through the floss. That's why snares that have a thin line like this should be designed around a choke point, something I typically call the "constrictor." As a simple example, let's say that you have set a snare that can lift a rabbit off the ground. By running the snare line under an exposed tree root, the snare is pulled tight against the root and the ground, choking out the animal more quickly than if it were dangling by its own weight.

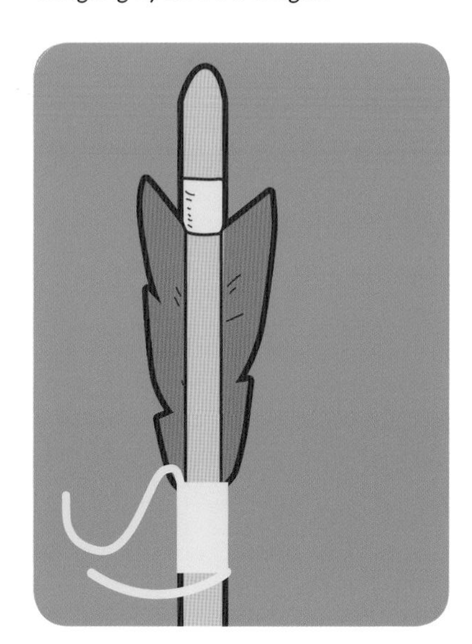

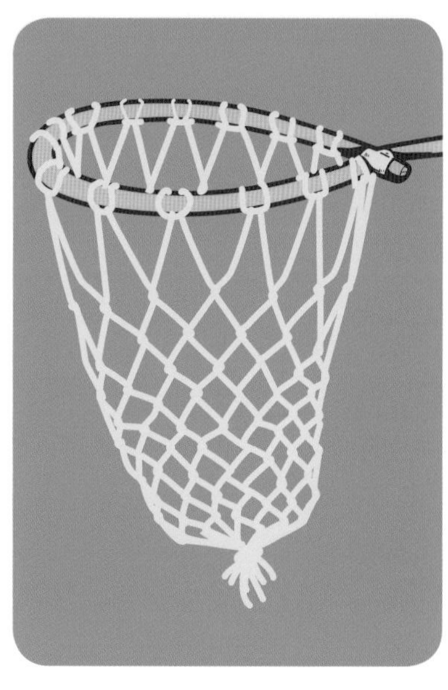

4 WEAVE A NET ▲ I don't expect anyone to have enough patience (or floss) to weave a large fishing net out of dental floss, but there are other kinds of nets. By bending a forked tree branch into a hoop, you now have a frame to build a dip net to assist in fishing. Just tie numerous long strands of floss around the hoop, then begin tying the strands to their neighbors. Use a fat stick as a spacing gauge to keep the mesh size consistent. Tie the ends of the floss strands together at the bottom of the dip net and it's ready to use. When trying to catch a fish with a line or some other methods, you can work the net underneath the fish and scoop it out of the water.

5 MEND YOUR GEAR Did a sleeve rip off your coat during your fight with a bear? Or did you split your pants scrambling down a cliff? Our outdoor clothing and gear can really take a beating, and floss can help you put the pieces back together. Replace a boot lace with a few twisted strands. Stitch up torn clothing with a needle and some floss for thread. Sew up the feather-spewing hole in your down sleeping bag. The list goes on and on for floss repairs. Just keep in mind that this strong material will melt, so keep your repairs away from the fire, if you want them to last. Other than that, the floss may just outlast the garment you are trying to repair.

6 TWIST A ROPE ▼ When you need a line that's thicker than floss, you can add several additional strands (and even put a twist on them) to start making simple rope. Use two dozen long strands to make a bow string for your survival bow. Use three dozen shorter strands to make a cord for your bow drill fire set. Most floss products have plenty of strength, since they are made of nylon fibers. You can give them the thickness they need for specific tasks by adding more strands to thicken it up. Floss can be braided, reverse wrapped, or simply twisted and tied in place to become light duty rope.

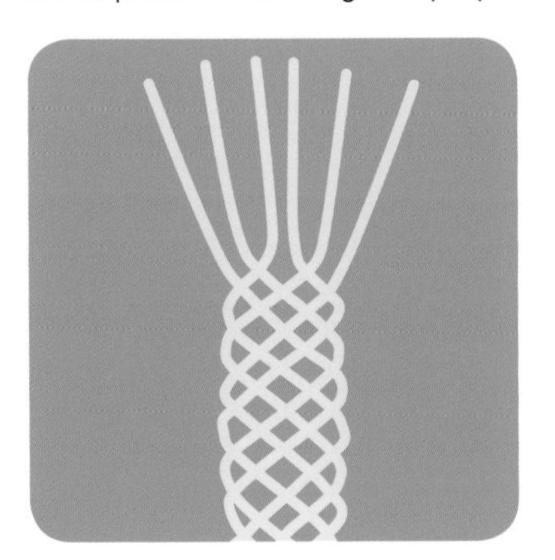

7 BURN IT UP ▶ By this point in the book, it shouldn't shock you that so many common household items are potential fire starters. Being made of plastic and wax, some brands of ordinary dental floss can ignite from an open flame. Of course, this shouldn't be your first choice for tinder. Strong line can be hard to come by. Burn any of the leaves, grass, or paper that you may have first, since the value of cordage may outweigh that of fuel. But this is a great terminal use for floss which you have used for other projects. Whether you flossed your teeth with it or used it to lash together a hut, waxy floss is one more fuel to add to your bag of fire-building tricks.

8 SUTURE A CUT It's rarely a good idea to suture a wound in a survival setting. However you or your patient were injured, the cut or tear is likely to be full of dirt and bacteria. Stitching it closed will only seal in those seeds of infection. Even with aggressive wound irrigation, stitching somebody up is probably going to result in infection. That being said, if the injury were in a place with a lot of skin movement (hand, foot, elbow, or knee, for example), you may need to suture the wound so that you can keep working in order to better your situation before more medical care. If that is the case, sew up the irrigated wound with a needle and floss that have been soaked in alcohol for at least two minutes. It's not as good as real suture material, but it will work in a pinch

219 PAY HEED

Jungles are some of the most biodiverse and life-dense environments on earth, and with all those life forms fighting for space, some magnificent defenses have emerged. These armaments and accoutrements work well for the plants and animals, as they are able to defend themselves, but it bodes ill for unfamiliar travelers who are lost in the jungle's embrace. Pay attention to these details, and you'll stay a little safer out there.

AVOID NIGHT TRAVEL When it gets dark in a rainforest, the more hazardous creatures often come out, and you won't be able to see them very well.

BRING A MACHETE Use it to chop or part the vegetation rather than moving vegetation out of the way with your hands. This protects you from bites, stings, and thorns.

CROSS WATER CAREFULLY Only cross shallow waterways and go slowly. Check thoroughly for leaches when you emerge.

AVOID ENTANGLEMENT If you get tangled in vegetation, step backwards to get out of it—don't push ahead or move to the side; you may get stuck even worse.

SECURE YOUR CLOTHING Keep your gloves, boots, and all garments in a tent or a sealed bag overnight. Spiders and other dangerous creatures love to crawl into them.

SIDESTEP SNAKES When you encounter a snake, go around it. You're more likely to get bitten trying to move it, kill it, or go past it. If it turns out to be an aggressive species, trying to move toward you, run away!

MENTAL HACK // LEARN THE PLANTS

I've said it for years, if you want to be a serious survivalist, you have to learn your plants. There's no other way around it. How will you know which plants to eat and which ones will poison you if you can't tell them apart? How will you know which sticks can make a friction fire if you can't tell a hardwood from a soft wood tree? The jungle is the best example of the necessity for this "native knowledge." With an abundance of plants that shouldn't even be touched, you'd need to know which plants to avoid. You'll also need to learn about the plants that will benefit you. Water vines, also known as Linnaeus vines, are named after the famous 17th century botanist Carl Linnaeus (often called the Father of Taxonomy). You can get clean safe drinking water by cutting into vines of certain Linnaeus vine species, but you can't just run through the jungle hacking at vines with your machete and drinking whatever fluid seeps out. You'll have to make a positive identification of that vine, and you'll want to avoid touching or drinking the sap from any vines that have a milky or colored sap. These can cause severe reactions, including poisoning.

220 FIGHT OFF ROT

Immersion foot (often called foot rot) is a condition caused by constantly wet feet, a frequent issue in the jungle. When the skin on your feet (or other extremities) is subject to days of uninterrupted moisture, the tissue can swell up, shrivel, and even die. This damage is similar to frostbite injuries, though immersion foot tends to sneak up on its victims, as opposed to the rapid harm and obvious surface symptoms of frostbite. The tissues do not freeze in immersion foot, but the circulatory, nerve, and skin damage can still be significant. How do you avoid this malady? Foremost, keep your feet as dry as possible. Waterproof footwear is key. If you don't have that, then dry your feet and warm them periodically. This may mean spending time drying your feet near a small fire or changing footwear and socks. Finally, inspect your feet often. Feet that are swollen, mottled in color, or have a waxy appearance are probably suffering from this ailment to some degree.

221 BLOCK OUT BUGS

A hammock is a great place to sleep in the jungle, keeping you off the ground, but it isn't a fortress. The last thing you want to find in your jungle hammock is a sampling of the local wildlife, especially if it bites!

KEEP COVERED Things have a tendency to drop out of the trees in the rainforest, and when strung up, your hammock hangs there like a mid-air catch basin. Hang a rain fly over the hammock, even in the dry season.

LIMIT ACCESS Keep to a minimum the number of access points that pests and dangerous creatures could use to join you in your hammock. Don't tie six lines to your rain fly when four will do the job.

REPEL PESTS Tie a kerosene-soaked rag on each hammock line to keep spiders, snakes, ants, and other creepers from scuttling down the lines. Because of the scent and the feel of this fuel, most creatures won't go near it (let alone crawl over it).

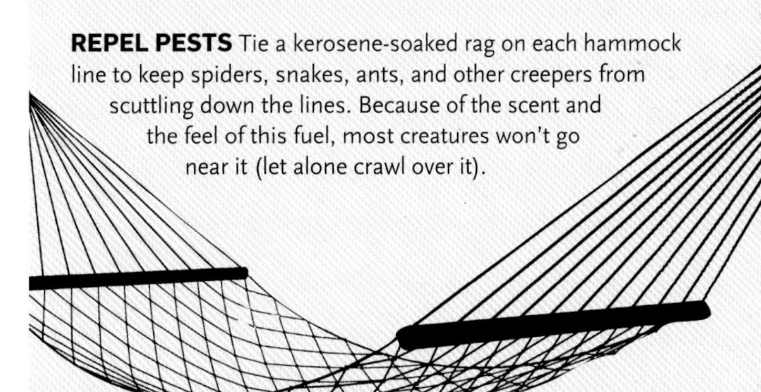

222 USE A NET

Mosquito nets are a true lifesaver, blocking the disease-carrying bites of mosquitos and other nasty insects. It's also useful for a few other things in the jungle environment. Don't forget your bug netting!

MINNOW NET If you can spare a small section of a large mosquito net, you can use a remnant of it around the water to catch minnows, leeches, water bugs, and other aquatic animals for fish bait.

BLANKET By folding a large bug net several times, you'll get a multi-layer blanket to keep you warmer on those damp chilly jungle nights.

WATER FILTER It's pretty obvious, but worth mentioning: Multiple layers of mosquito net will act as a crude water filter. It won't remove any pathogens, or even strip out silt or mud, but it will remove debris in the water, which will certainly plug up your water filter.

CAMOUFLAGE Wipe some mud on a bug net and poke a few leaves through the mesh. Now you have a jungle-ready Ghillie net, which is practically a cloak of invisibility.

223 MAKE YOUR TACKLE

When you don't have the right tackle to catch fish, make your own fishing supplies from whatever you have at hand!

FISH WITH A CAN While a soft, malleable fish hook is just about the worst fish hook you could ask for, you can catch fish by using a gorge hook fishing technique, and an aluminum can, by breaking off an aluminum can's pull tab, and cutting out a section of so that it looks like a fish hook. Sharpen the hook tip to a point, attach it to your line, and bait it appropriately. Instead of trying to set the hook in the fish's mouth when it bites, give it some line and let the fish swallow the hook. The pull-tab hook will hang up on the soft stomach or esophagus a lot better it would pierce the fish's jaw.

BOB WITH EARPLUGS Those little foam disposable ear plugs are great at protecting our hearing when we preform noisy tasks. They're also great bobbers for still-water fishing. Set up your hook line and weight as normal, and tightly tie an ear plug into the fishing line. These plugs are often brightly colored, making them very visible in the water. You might even try them on a hook as a colorful bait.

USE ANOTHER CAN The old hobo fishing reel can be almost anything, but a beer can makes a fine spool for storing the fishing line. It's even possible to cast the line right off the can. To make your fishing kit, tie the monofilament to the can's pull tab, or better yet, tie the line through a small hole that you have pierced through the can (you might have used the pull tab for a fish hook). Wind up the line around the can, trying not to overlap the mono too much. For storage, put a rubber band or tie a string around the can and fishing line, to keep it from unraveling. The aluminum-can fishing rig casts a bit like an open-face reel, so be patient and cautious, to avoid tangling the line.

224 MELT THE ICE

Ice fishing can provide much needed nutrition, if you can make a hole through the ice. This can be done with no special tools—just a hot rock. With a large fire on the shore, heat up a large stone in the blaze. Make sure you collect the rock from a dry location, as waterlogged stones tend to explode violently in high heat. After an hour of heating, use a shovel to carry the dangerously hot stone to your fishing spot, and set it on the ice. It will begin to melt through the ice immediately and work its way downward. Soon the rock will melt an opening in the ice cover, and drop into the dark water below. Your ice-fishing hole will be open, smooth, and ready to fish.

You can even use this trick on thin ice. Without setting a single foot on the ice, you can use a shovel or stick to skate a hot rock out onto the ice with a hard shove. When it stops sliding, it will melt a hole. From the safety of shore, cast your line over the hole and then pull it across the opening so that the line drops into the water.

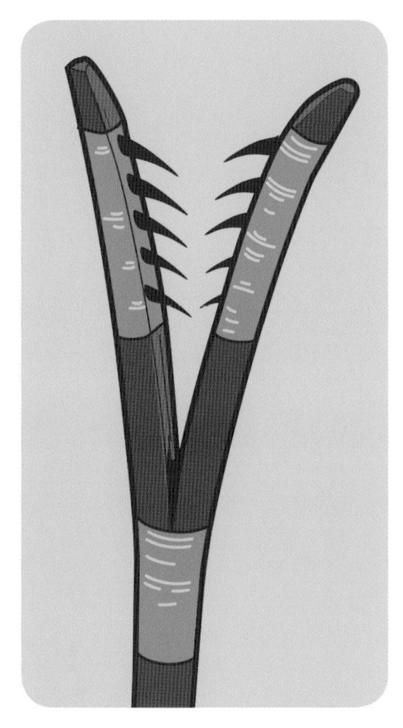

225 SPEAR A FISH

It's not easy to pierce the slippery scales or defeat the slender profile of most fish, but spear fishing is still a worthwhile activity in survival situations near ponds, lakes, and rivers. By cutting a straight sapling tree and splitting the end into four sections, you can sharpen each of the four "tines" by carving them to a point. This is the quickest spear to make, though it's the least effective to use. You'll have better luck by taking the same sapling with the same split, spreading it to make a V-shape, and tying two rows of thorns on each side. Use strong thin cord to tie these thorns in place, as they need to withstand a thrashing fish. Aim the thorn points inward and backward as you tie them. Now you're ready to stalk through the water. Keep in mind that the fish is not quite where it appears to be; because of the way that water bends light, your aquatic target is lower in the water than it appears. Compensate for this refraction by aiming a little below the fish.

226 SCRAPE AWAY

Scales are protective structures for the fish, guarding them against all kinds of injuries. And since scales are so tough, this also makes them tough to eat. You could certainly fillet the fish to remove the skin, but removing only the scales will allow you to cook and eat the skin—a valuable calorie resource. Keeping the skin on the fish for both cooking and eating helps to preserve the fat contained in the fish, which is important for flavor and for food value. Simple fish scaling tools can be purchased, improvised from existing gear, or made on the spot. A knife can be used to scale the fish. So can a sharp stone flake. Shells work too. And some people will screw bottle caps to a stick or strip of wood to create a toothed fish scaler. Whatever you use, just scrape the fish from tail to head to begin removing scales. Do this all around the fish, preferably before gutting. When you don't feel or see any more scales coming off, drag your fingernails from tail to head to check for stragglers. Scale the fish at the water's edge, once you have dispatched them, to rinse off the skin, and keep smelly scales out of camp (important in bear country).

227 CLEAN IT UP

You've got fish! Whether by spear, by hook, or by hand, you now have caught one or more fish to satisfy your hunger. Now you need to clean the animals, and prepare them for cooking. Fish are the easiest animal to process, but there are still a few finer points that make the process smoother. Now for the part you've been waiting for: gutting the fish. It's a very easy task, especially with a sharp blade. Use these steps to reach fishy tasting success.

STEP 1 Begin by cutting into the fish's underside, starting between the gills and slicing down to the anal vent. It's okay if your knife tip slices through a few organs; fish aren't that germy.

STEP 2 Use one or two fingers to swipe out the innards, and you're basically done for head-still-on cleaning. You can also use your thumbnail to scrape the body cavity of blood and leftover entrails.

STEP 3 Rinse the fish quickly in cold water and then keep it out dry for firmer flesh. Store the fish on ice or cook immediately. Don't waste the organs you remove, as these make great fish bait and trap bait. Don't discard the head either; use it for soup stock to make a broth full of minerals.

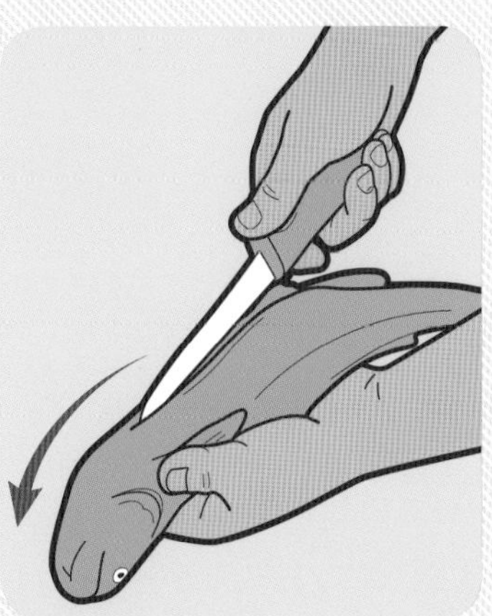

228 DRY SOME MEAT

The only guarantee of eating in the wilderness is when you bring your own food along for the journey. From antiquity until today, jerky is one of the most popular and universal trail foods you can find. You can even make it yourself, just like our ancestors did.

START FRESH Cooked meat is not suitable for jerky. Red meat is the best choice, though any mammal, bird, fish, or larger reptile meat will also work.

TRIM AND SALT Cut the meat thin and across the grain. Slice your pieces less than 1/4 inch (0.5 cm) thick, and cut perpendicular to the grain of the meat. Also, trim off all visible fat, as it will go rancid in the dried meat. While the meat is still juicy, sprinkle on a little salt or spices. Salt will create a less hospitable environment for bacteria.

SMOKE IT Dry the meat by hanging your jerky slices on an improvised rack near a small, smoky fire. Don't leave it unattended or cook it. Just dry the meat until it becomes brittle, and then store it in a dry place until you are ready to eat it.

229 MAKE HARDTACK

This rock hard cracker isn't just cowboy food in the Wild West. It dates back to ancient Egypt, and has been eaten by travelers and soldiers for thousands of years. The recipe is fast and easy.

STEP 1 Blend 5 cups (600 g) of wheat flour (all-purpose flour is perfect) with 2 cups (480 mL) of water and 3 teaspoons (40 g) of salt. That's all you need! Mix the wet and dry ingredients thoroughly until you have a stiff dry bread dough.

STEP 2 Try a rolling pin to create a flat sheet of dough, or pat it flat with your hands, until you have a half-inch (1.25-cm) thick sheet of dough.

STEP 3 Cut your dough into small squares and poke each piece several times with a fork, on both sides. Bake them on a dry cookie sheet 30 minutes per side at 375°F (190°C), for a total of one hour baking time.

STEP 4 Once cool, store your hardtack somewhere dry. It can be a bit tough on the teeth when it comes time to eat; soften it in water, coffee, soup, or—the sailor's choice—rum. Hardtack takes getting used to, but it's a way to store flour for years, and you can grind it back into a coarse flour-like substance to use for thickening soups and stews. You can also mix it with fresh flour to bulk up your supplies if they're running low.

230 PARCH YOUR CORN

This unusual Native American food was once a common snack among first Nation peoples, and later copied by settlers, mountain men and trappers. This rudimentary form of popcorn is easy to make, tasty, filling, and lightweight—perfect for trail food. You can also grind parched corn into a rough cornmeal and then boil it to make a traditional corn soup. To make your own, you'll need a skillet, fine salt, some animal fat (pig fat is a colonial tradition), and you'll need some dried sweet corn. This last item is the only tricky ingredient to get, but it's the best type of corn for this food. Melt a little fat in your skillet over a medium heat (over the campfire, or your home cooktop), dump in enough dried corn to barely cover the bottom of the skillet, and start stirring. Keep it up, stirring the greasy corn until it starts to swell up and make little popping noises. Stir until all of the corn kernels are golden brown. Add salt to the corn and you're done! Parched corn can last for months in a cloth or paper bag.

231 BAKE A FRUIT CAKE

Fruit cake usually makes people think more about the holidays, but this trail-ready food has been helping people survive for centuries. These cakes have typically been made from flour, honey, spices, and fruit—a recipe hailing from Roman times—but here's a more modern version.

STEP 1 Gather together 4 cups (1 L) mixed dried fruit (the majority should be golden raisins for the classic taste), 1 cup (240 mL) self-rising flour, 1 tin (400 g) sweetened condensed milk, 1/2 cup (120 mL) water, one egg, and a dash of rum.

STEP 2 Place the fruit and water in a pot, and bring to a boil. Simmer uncovered for 2 minutes. Cover and cool to room temperature.

STEP 3 While the fruit cools, line a deep square or round baking tin with parchment paper (made for baking), bring the paper 1/2-inch (1.25 cm) above the edge of the tin, and preheat the oven to 300 °F (150 °C).

STEP 4 Add the condensed milk, egg, and then the flour (and rum, if using) into the pot of fruit. Mix thoroughly, spoon the batter into the prepared tin, and bake for 2 hours.

232 LEARN THE ABCS

How can you tell if someone has merely fainted, or they are having a heart attack? When it comes to first aid, you have to know your ABC's. These aren't the letters you learned in kindergarten—these stand for Airway, Breathing, and Circulation, and they can help you determine whether you are facing a minor medical event or a major issue. In a deadly medical emergency, there's no time to flip back and forth in your pocket medical guide. You have to know this information. A problem with the victim's airway can kill them quickly. If they're not breathing, you'll have to perform CPR. And major bleed can be a life threatening condition, too. The ABCs are simple, but still too involved to explain in one paragraph. There's just no substitute for hands-on medical training and continuing education in first aid and first responder skills. This type of training gives you the knowledge and experience to assess situations and make the right move.

233 STOCK A KIT

Buying a ready-made medical kit off the shelf can be an instant way to prepare for wilderness emergencies, but building your own kit will allow you to tailor it to your specialized needs. So what goes in a wilderness medical kit? The supply list we provided for the disaster medical kit (see item 031) will also suit you well in the outdoors. The only major stumbling blocks are weight and space. The disaster medical kit can be organized in a bin or box, with plenty of room and redundant items. Since it has to fit in a pocket or backpack, the wilderness med kit will have to be packed tighter, without much room for extras. You don't want to cut corners on life-saving equipment, but you probably don't need large quantities of anything (unless you're far removed from modern medical care). You may also be able to find smaller items that do the job. Mini EMT shears can cut almost as well as the full sized version. Compressed gauze will take up a lot less room than bulky gauze rolls.

234 REPURPOSE SUPPLIES

Medical kits are stuffed with items that can be used in creative ways, far beyond their intended usage. These are some of the most common adaptations, and the handiest.

START A FIRE From cottony gauze to the paper wrappers, many wound care products and their packaging can act as tinder if you have nothing else to start your campfire. You can also use alcohol swabs and wipes as your fire helpers in wet weather.

BLAZE A TRAIL Tape, gauze, and other basic medical supplies can be used to mark trails, to lead search and rescue crews to your location, or to keep you from getting lost (again). Stick tape around twigs and branches, and tie little strips of gauze at eye level to make a trail through the wild.

FILTER YOUR WATER Triangle bandages, gauze, and dressing pads can filter debris, mud, and sediment from your water, improving your luck with other disinfection methods like chemical tablets and water filters.

235 PLAN AHEAD

You'll need gauze, bandages, and pain relievers everywhere you go, since the injuries that require those supplies are likely to happen anywhere. But you probably won't need malaria pills in your wilderness medical kit, if you're only trekking through cold climates. Your med kit should match the climate and terrain, so give your kit a tune-up before every outing. Toss another space blanket (or two) in there when you're heading for places that are cold and wet. Add a bottle of rehydration salt tablets when you're going someplace hot and dry. Take the time to research the most common injuries and ailments for the area you're traveling through, and make sure you have the medical supplies to treat these problems. You already planning ahead by having a medical kit, so why not plan ahead accurately by including specialized supplies? There aren't many drug stores in the wild, so the only supplies you're sure to have are the ones you brought along for the trip.

HACKS THROUGH HISTORY // TOURNIQUET

Modern versions of this life-saving tool have plenty of features for a rapid and effective application, though the concept dates back centuries. The first recorded use of a tourniquet was at the battle of Flanders in 1674. At that time, doctors were applying tight bands around limbs to prepare them for amputation. These were strips of cloth or leather, tightened by twisting a sturdy stick or, later, a screw. From the beginning up until the 20th century, the application of a tourniquet meant saving the life, but losing the limb. Today, both lives and limbs are being saved with speedy and correct use of tourniquets and more advanced medical care. So, when someone is bleeding hard and fast, soaking through your pressure dressings, it's time to take a page out of history. Commercially-made tourniquets should be in every medical bag, but if you didn't have one, or you needed several, you can improvise.

Field-made tourniquets should be strong, broad, flexible objects, such as a rolled-up shirt, thick cord, rope, or belt. Wrap the tourniquet around the limb as high as possible. With improvised tourniquets, you can tie them around the limb in a loose loop, then insert a handle such as a short, strong stick inside the knot of the loop. Turn the handle until you stop the blood flow and pulse on the limb, no matter how much they scream. Secure the handle and write the time of application on their body with a marker.

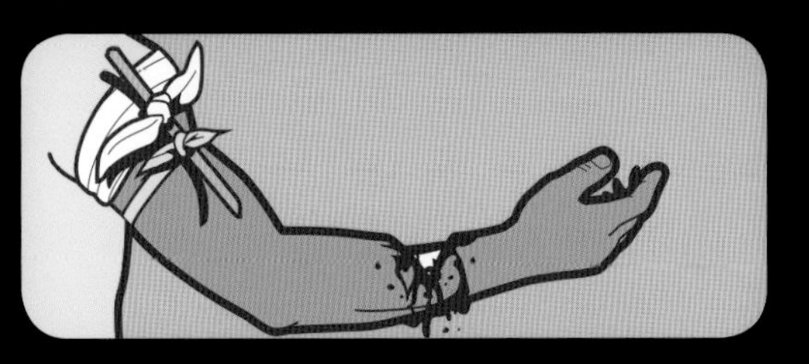

236 SOOTHE A STING

Before the corner drug store existed, our forebears would have made use of helpful medicinal compounds from the neighboring plants around them. Since store shelves are stocked with medicines of every kind today, it's easy to forget that many of those medicines were first discovered in wild plants. Take bee stings for example. These can be treated with a very ubiquitous plant. Fresh plantain leaves are a great remedy when crushed into a wet green paste and applied to bee stings and other venomous bites. There's no shortage of it, either. This common little lawn weed is found in pretty much every yard across America. (Just for clarification, the banana-looking fruit called "plantain" at the grocery store is not the same thing as the lawn weed plantain.) Plantain can also be applied to promote the healing of cuts, scrapes, scratches, and burns, thanks to the tannic acid and other medicinal compounds.

237 CURE AN ACHE

The common and abundant willow trees that cover this continent are good for more things than just looking at. Willow wood can be an outstanding choice for friction-fire equipment. The flexible twigs can be used in basketry. The leaves and twig bark can even be used for medicines when you are all out of options in the wilderness. Black willow has been used since at least 400 BCE to treat inflammation and pain, and it only takes one teaspoon (5 mL) of dried black willow twig bark shavings to provide you with the recommended dose of 100 mg of salicin to treat pain and fever. Salicin is an anti-inflammatory and pain relieving agent produced from willow bark and other plant parts. It was once common for people to chew directly on the shaved bark for pain and fever relief. Not all willows can be used in the same ways, so you'll want to consult with a local plant expert to find the best local species to use.

238 STOP DIARRHEA

Maybe you got some bad food or water, or you caught a gut-churning virus. Loose bowels are uncomfortable under most circumstances, and they can be downright dangerous when in a survival setting. Luckily, there is a way to control the symptoms with a wild plant medicine. Blackberry leaves are a common herbal tea ingredient (particularly for the Celestial Seasonings company). Steep one teaspoon (5 mL) of dried leaf in a cup (240 mL) of hot water for 10 minutes to make a pleasant herbal tea. This can boost morale, warm the belly, and hide the taste of an "off" water source. The leaf tea can also be drunk repeatedly to help diminish the symptoms of diarrhea. Steep two teaspoons (10 mL) of dried leaf per cup of hot water. Start with half a cup every hour, and continue until the ailment improves. And if the leaf tea isn't getting the job done, steep one ounce (7 g) of fresh blackberry root in a cup of hot water and drink slowly.

239 HEAL WITH YARROW

If you're looking for a natural counterpart to antibiotic wound cream, this is it! Yarrow was originally from Europe, but brought here by European settlers. The fern-like leaves can be found all year in the lower half of the country, but the biggest leaves will be found in summer. The plant blooms at the height of summer, with a stalk that is about two feet tall and bearing a flat topped cluster of white flowers. This flower cluster resembles Queen Anne's Lace, but Yarrow has a triangular flower cluster, while Queen Anne's lace is a round cluster of tiny white flowers.

The yarrow plant also has a long history as a powerful healing herb used topically for wounds, cuts and abrasions. The genus name Achillea is derived from Greek character Achilles, who reportedly carried yarrow with his army to treat battle wounds. This medicinal action is also reflected in some of the common names, such as staunchweed and soldier's woundwort. These are just a few things it can do. (Warning: Make sure it really is yarrow. Fool's Parsley and Poison Hemlock resemble yarrow and are very poisonous and fatal if eaten.)

STYPTIC Yarrow can stop bleeding quickly, due to its astringent and vasoconstricting compounds.

ANTI-BACTERIAL Whether fresh or dried, crushed yarrow leaves contain compounds that have an anti-bacterial action. Leaves can be applied directly to wounds as a poultice, or soaked in water to make a tea which can be employed as a hot compress.

DIAPHORETIC Strong yarrow tea can increase perspiration, helping to break a fever.

ANAESTHETIC Crushed fresh yarrow leaves can result in a numbing action when applied topically, similar to using a lidocaine patch—although yarrow does not have this particular effect for everybody.

240 HAVE A MINT

There's a practical reason many restaurants provide tasty little mints after your meal: the mint oil in the candy will sooth your stomach in cases of overindulgence or indigestion. People have been using mint for thousands of years. The special ingredient is menthol, an organic compound with counterirritant qualities. It is widely used to relieve minor throat irritation and nausea. Peppermint is an excellent choice for a soothing tea to calm an upset stomach. It isn't native to North America, though it can be found growing wild now from coast to coast. Add a little over 2 ounces (15 g) of dried leaf, or 4 ounces (30 g) of fresh leaf to a cup (240 mL) of hot water, cover, and steep for 10 to 15 minutes. This tea also helps with hangovers. There is a warning that comes with it, so keep in mind that pregnant or nursing women; anyone with gastroesophageal reflux disease (GERD); or anyone with liver disease should avoid ingesting strong peppermint teas (or mint oils) on a regular basis.

241 BUILD BY DIGGING

You don't have to know how to build an igloo to survive in the arctic (although it would be nice). With a snow shovel and a saw, you can build a much simpler snow shelter. Start out by determining how big it needs to be. Don't build a huge one for just one person. It should be just big enough for one or two people, as a maximum. Dig out a trench in the snow, roughly 1 yard (1 m) each in width, depth, and length. This can be narrower for one inhabitant, or a little wider for two. Using the saw, cut blocks of snow that will fit together as a roof, and compact the snow to create a step down into the trench. Cut bevels on the snow blocks, so they fit together well. Block the end of the shelter, on the opposite side of the doorway. If possible, cover the floor with a very thick layer of vegetation. Sculpt a door area that can be covered by a blanket or plugged by your backpack. Leave a tiny air gap somewhere for ventilation.

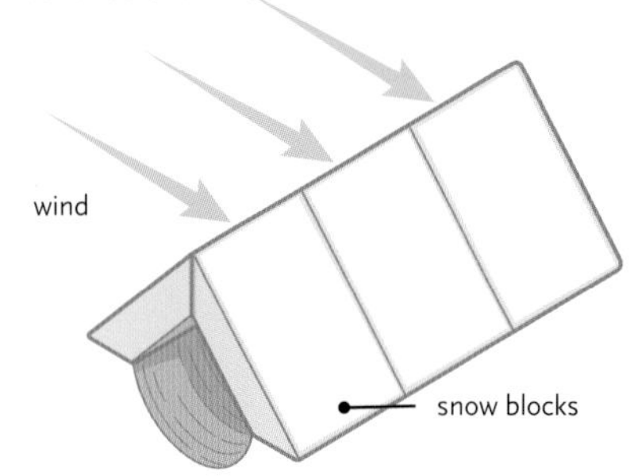

242 MAKE SNOWSHOES

Walking through deep snow without any snow shoes is a massive drain on your energy, but making a pair of snow shoes is easier than you might think.

STEP 1 Collect ten fresh cut sticks, just under 2 yards (2 m) long, some shorter sticks and some cordage.

STEP 2 Make two bundles of five sticks and lash together one end of each. Mark a point halfway down each bundle, and lash on a cross piece that is roughly 10 inches (25 cm) long across each bundle. This is where the ball of your foot will pivot. Lash a similar stick in front of each of the cross pieces, about 2 inches (5 cm) in front of it.

STEP 3 Now, step onto the shoe, with the ball of your foot on the first stick you tied. Make a mark where your heel will fall. Lash another crosspiece (or two) where your heel will fall on each shoe. Tie the free ends of the long sticks together. Using more cordage, tie a snow shoe to each foot and try them out.

243 USE A PROBE

The wind can build drifts over deep holes in the snow, effectively hiding them from view, but a simple pole can act as a lifesaving probe in deep and uneven snowpack. The probe can also be used as a walking stick, a staff for self-defense, and even a pole for ice fishing. Before you're above the tree line, cut a sapling tree that is strong and straight, with a sturdy section the same height as you. One end can be sharpened, though it's not necessary. Use the probe by sticking it into the snow to test prospective places to step. If you feel a void or place of less resistance under the snow, don't step there! A probing tool like this can be vital when crossing glaciers and other terrain which commonly have holes, crevasses, water under the snow, and other hazardous features. Make a probe pole from whatever materials you can find (naturally growing or scavenged from manmade materials). Carry it with you through the snow, since you never know when you'll need it.

244 WORK WITH ICE

Ice is abundant resource in the colder places and seasons, so why not use it for survival tasks? Clear ice can make an outstanding window in your snow shelter. It blocks the cold air and allows light to enter the structure. It doesn't insulate the shelter, so keep your window small. You can also cover it at night to block bright moonlight and to preserve warmth in the shelter. Ice can also shelter your food when your follow our ancestors by freezing the food in an outdoor ice cache. Pick someplace near your dwelling and on the north side of a large structure. This northern orientation will keep the southerly sun from warming up that spot, and your ice will last much longer. Lay out some ice blocks to create a small ice platform. Place your food on top of this. Then, using blocks of uniform thickness, build an ice wall around the foundation and carve an ice lid. If you need something to fill gaps, apply slush to freeze into a solid enclosure.

245 ENJOY THE SNOW

Snow can often place people in deadly situations, but that same snow is also a versatile and useful substance that can help you to get out of trouble. Here are a few ways to use snow for survival.

MAKE SIGNALS Stamp out a giant SOS or "V" in a snowy clearing. Use powdered charcoal or other substances to write on the snow.

MARK TRAILS Create temporary trail markers with pylons of snow. Use colorants, if possible, to help you spot the white pillars against the white background.

STORE FOOD Use snow to keep your foods from spoiling. Pack snow into coolers or simply bury your food in the snow. Just make sure to mark it for easy retrieval.

MAKE COLD PACKS Snow makes a great cold pack for injuries. Fill a plastic bag with snow, wrap it in cloth, and apply to sprains or strains.

BUILD TRAPS Build excellent funnels and fencing out of snow at your trap sites. These walls, holes, paths and other structures will direct your prey to just the right spot.

TRACK WITH EASE Even a novice can see the secret lives of animals laid bare in the white stuff. Learn which species are present, find out their numbers and follow their wanderings by tracking them in snow.

SUBSTITUTE FOR TP Snow that packs into a good snowball is great for wiping—no kidding! It's brisk, but nothing else in the wild cleans so well with only moisture as residue.

BUDGET SURVIVAL

OVERSIZED BOOTS

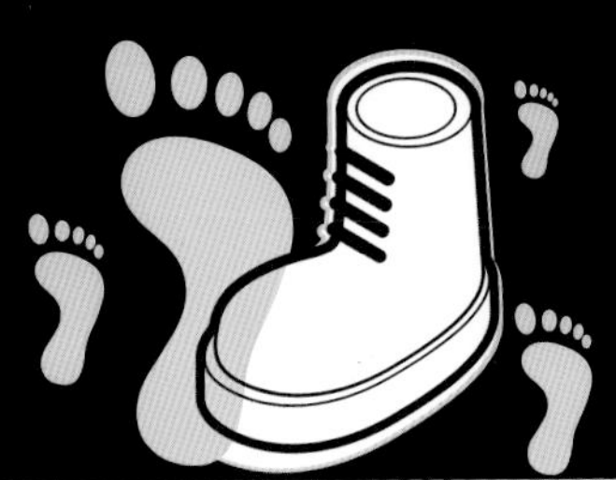

Those giant "Mickey Mouse" boots you often see worn by folks in the far north can be expensive. A cheaper way to keep all ten of your toes from turning black is to buy boots that are a size or two bigger than you normally wear. Inside these oversized boots, wear two or three pairs of thick warm socks to insulate your feet. Since the boots have extra room, the loft of the socks will remain and the extra layers won't cause any constriction on your toes, feet, or ankles.

- Bigger boots don't usually cost any more.
- With the extra sock padding, they can be quite comfortable.
- Your small booted friends will be envious.

Worth Every Penny

SNOW GOGGLES

Snow goggles may be a little pricey, but a pair of wraparound glasses can block the harmful UV rays that bounce off the snow. You can't afford to go blind in an emergency.

246 DON'T DRY OUT

Dehydration is one of the most common issues in wilderness medicine, especially in dry climates. This lack of water can cause headaches, diminished strength and energy, constipation, cramps, and a host of other symptoms. The treatment of dehydration is painfully obvious: Hydrate your patient! But are you giving them enough water? How can you gauge dehydration in yourself and others? The best way to keep track of your hydration level is to keep track of your water intake and urine output. You should be taking in more than 2 quarts (2 L) every day, and urinating at least 1.5 quarts (1.5 L) each day. This volume of output factors in your exertion level, stress, health, weather, caffeine consumption, and other issues; as long as you are peeing every few hours, your body won't have to shift into the water thrifty setting. You can keep more water in your body by keeping skin covered, breathing through the nose (not the mouth), and avoiding heavy work in the heat.

247 DEAL WITH EXTREMES

Don't let a trip into the great outdoors become your final adventure! Learn to deal with the extremes that nature can throw at you.

HYPOTHERMIA Low body heat can manifest in shivering, confusion, slurred speech, clumsiness, pale skin, and blue-colored lips, ears, fingers, and toes. When it's very bad, you'll have trouble speaking, amnesia, extreme tiredness, and irrational behavior (like clothing removal and burrowing into snow). Rewarming is the main method of treatment for hypothermia victims. Get them into some properly insulated dry clothing and a warm environment. Give a little high-calorie food and sips of a hot beverage, if they are conscious. Place hot water bottles under their armpits and at the groin for more help.

FROSTBITE Frostbite occurs when ice forms in your skin and tissues. The treatment is usually a painful process that involves slowly rewarming the skin and tissues. This can be done both in the field and in the hospital, but should only be attempted if there is no danger of re-freezing.

HEAT EXHAUSTION Identified by clammy moist skin, heavy sweating, cramps, dizziness, tiredness, nausea, vomiting, and a weak but fast pulse, heat exhaustion, if left untreated, can easily turn into heat stroke, especially if you remain in hot environments.

HEAT STROKE The key symptom of this is a high body core temperature (105 °F / 41 °C). Heat stroke may be accompanied by other symptoms, such as a pounding headache, weakness, a dizzy or light-headed feeling, a rapid pulse, and one of the classic signs, the lack of perspiration. With any heat illness, get the victim into the shade, apply wet cloths, and provide fluids to hydrate them.

ELECTROLYTE IMBALANCE When a person has been sweating profusely, been ill, or drunk too much water, their electrolytes can become dangerously out of balance, resulting in many of the symptoms of heat illness. If intravenous treatment isn't an option, the next best thing is oral rehydration salts, as a drink mix power or tablet. Alternatively, mix a handful of sugar and a pinch of salt in a gallon (4 L) of water and have them sip on it until they recover.

STARVATION Eat something! Don't be picky, as long as it is prepared safely and has digestible calories. Toast some bugs in a pan. Make a soup from birds. Bring in the calories, and avoid work that wastes energy.

HACK HAZARDS

HYPOTHERMIA MISTAKES

There are many things that you don't want to do to a hypothermia victim, though some of them may like the right move (like a hot tub dunking). Here are three major things that you should never do.

DON'T DROP THEM If you lose your grip while lifting or carrying a victim, watch out! A sudden jolt to the chest when the body is deeply chilled can cause lethal heart arrhythmia.

DON'T COOK THEM Never place your hypo victim in a hot tub or sauna! They do need heat—but it's too much too fast, and can cause heart issues.

DON'T WRAP THEM Space blankets reflect body heat, but they don't provide warmth. If your patient has ice-cold skin, they are no longer radiating heat. Give them an extra heat source, such as warm water bottles, or another person.

Quick Tip

Don't cut and suck on a snake bite! It's a bad idea constantly shown in television and movies. You won't be able to extract any real amount of venom, and your cutting may end up doing more harm than good.

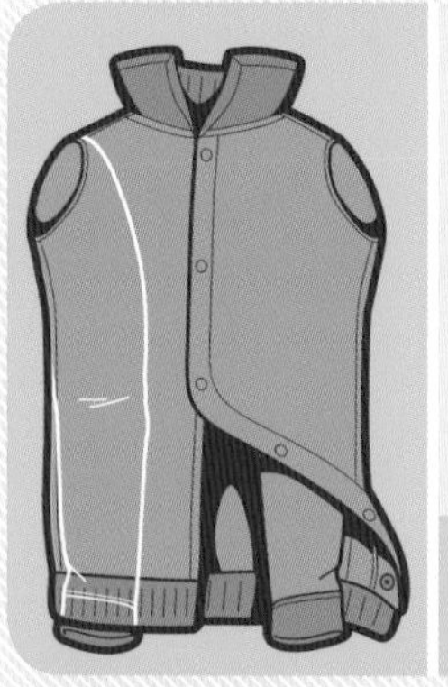

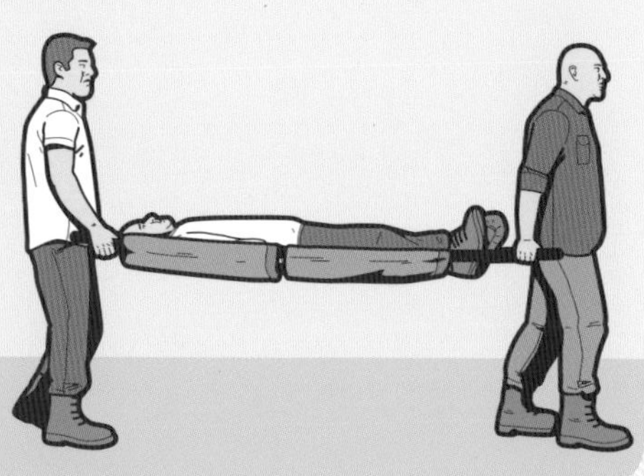

248 BUILD A JACKET LITTER

When someone can't hobble on their own with a crutch, you may need to carry them to a safer location. You can make a great litter with two 8-foot (2.4-m) poles and two sturdy jackets. Just follow these simple steps.

STEP 1 Cut or scavenge two poles that are longer than your patient. These can be tree limbs, saplings, or other long rigid objects.

STEP 2 Turn the jackets inside-out, while leaving the sleeves on the inside. You could just pull the sleeves inside a jacket, but turning the garment inside-out means the zippers and buttons are on the inside, so they're not caught on rocks or bushes (and they're not poking your patient). Thick shirts, coats, or other clothing can be used too.

STEP 3 Slide the poles through the jacket sleeves, load up your patient, and carry them to safety. Just be very careful not to drop them!

249 MAKE A CRUTCH

Sticks and branches are available in most places on Earth. Deserts and grasslands have woody shrubs and trees growing throughout them or along the local waterways—even the arctic has driftwood. And whether your wood is dead or it's a green branch, if it has a fork at the top, you can make a fully functional crutch with only a little bit of work! Your crutch should be about 4 feet (1.2 m) tall, for most folks of average height. The fork should be heavily padded with clothing or some other soft material. A little duct tape and a bit of foam sleeping pad can work, too. The broader the angle on the fork, the more comfortable the crutch. And if the crutch starts to hurt, just add more padding. Now, you're all set to hobble your way back to civilization!

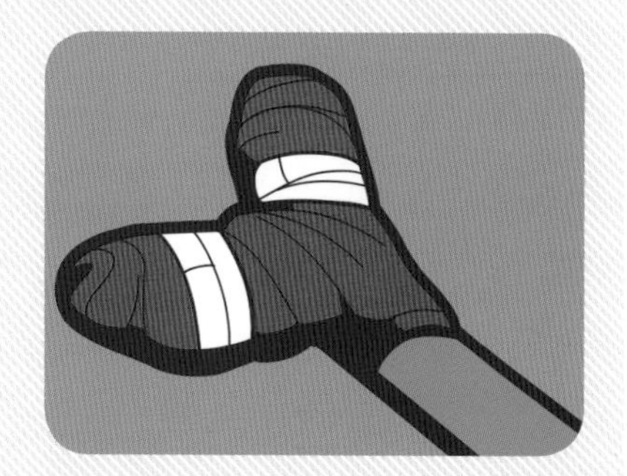

250 TRY A TARP

Similar to the jacket litter, you can make a different kind of improvised litter using two poles and a tarp (a large blanket will also work). The best part: When your patient is placed on the litter, it's their own body weight that keeps everything bound together. Start by laying your tarp out on the ground and placing a long stout pole in the middle (A). Fold the tarp over the pole so that it is doubled up and then add the second pole so that it divides the tarp in half again(B). Flip the tarp edge over the second pole, and the litter now has four layers of material (C). Have your patient lie down, and have two or four people lift the litter simultaneously. Both the jacket litter and this one can fit into an urban survival setting, since metal pipes or pieces of lumber can be used instead of the tree poles. Whatever you use, make sure the combined strength of these two poles and tarp are more than adequate to carry your patient, with no risk of breaking or dropping them.

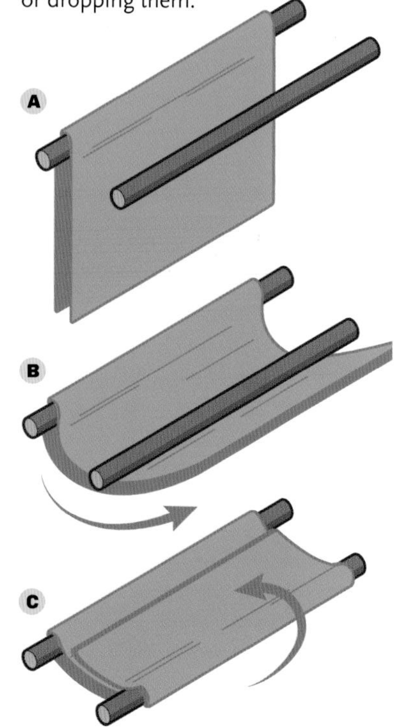

251 WRAP YOUR PATIENT

In cold-weather emergencies, your injured friend may need special care. This style of litter will keep them warm as you carry them out of the wild. Gather two long poles, a 50-foot (15-m) rope, a sleeping pad, and a sleeping bag. Start building the litter by laying out the rope in a zig-zag pattern. Static rope used in tech rescue is your best choice, but any line can work. Make the rope wide enough to go around the person and their padding. Tie a loop in the end of the rope that will be at the foot of the litter. Now, lay sticks, branches or poles on top of the rope, and spread the sleeping pad on top of that. You can use two pads, if you have multiple pads in your group. This helps if the pads are thin. Add the sleeping bag next, and zip your patient up inside of it. If your patient is hypothermic and you have a long trek ahead of you, wrap them in a space blanket inside the sleeping bag. This adds warmth and acts as a vapor barrier. You may also want to improvise a "diaper" on your patient, as hypothermia can cause a greater need to urinate. Once bundled, start lacing the first loop at the foot of the sleeping bag through the loop on the opposite side, continue lacing the loops in a "daisy chain," pulling them tight. Secure the end of the rope, making sure your patient can breathe well, and their head and neck are supported. This litter works best with four to six people carrying it. Short sticks can be threaded under the ropes to act as handles for each carrier.

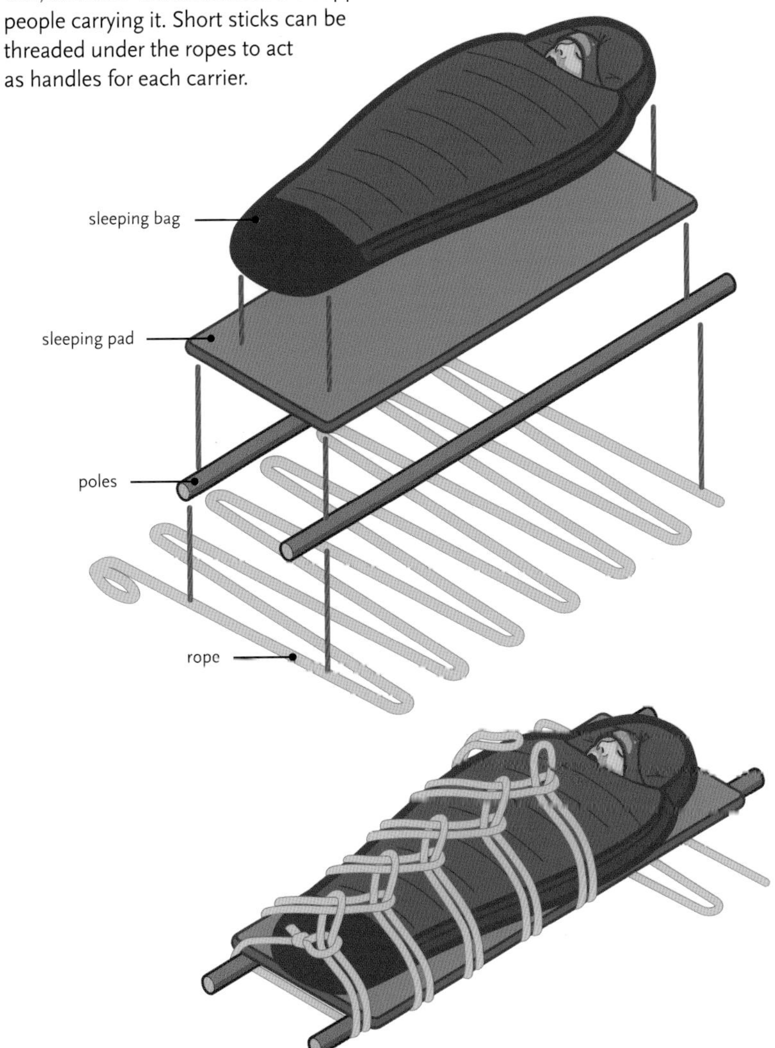

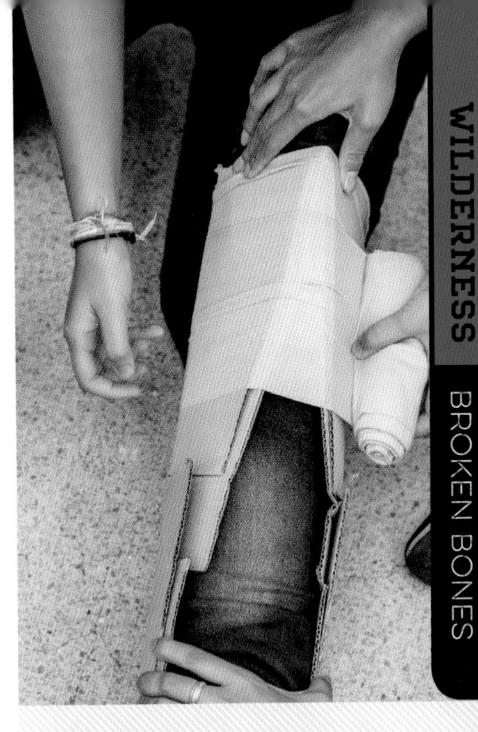

252 FORM A SPLINT

Outdoor injuries can cause sprains, strains, and breaks with relative ease, but thankfully it's also easy to splint those injuries. The first part of splinting is immobilizing the moving parts. It's always best to immobilize the next joint up from the injury, if possible. If a foot seems broken, splint all the way up to the ankle. If an ankle seems sprained, splint up to the knee. If the knee is tweaked, splint up to the hip. Padding is another chief concern. Ample padding helps to stabilize the injury, and provides pressure to keep any swelling in check. Wrap the limb or joint in any bandages or padding that you have available. Don't allow any hollow spots under the rigid splint material that is coming next. For the stiff part of the splint, you'll need to find some bark strips, sticks, or any other rigid material. Tape or tie them around the splint padding on the injured limb. Make sure that you don't tie the splint or any of the wrappings so tightly that you cut off circulation.

253 PICK A PLAN

Signaling is the skill that gets you rescued, and it should be taken as seriously as your other skills, just like shelter and fire making. But when exactly are you going to start signaling, which method will you use, and how often will you signal? You should start signaling as soon as you realize you are in trouble, and with as many methods as you can muster (while still allowing time for shelter, water, fire, and food procurement). Then, you should keep signaling as you work on survival tasks, and keep going until you've encountered a helpful party. There are three main groups of emergency signal methods: auditory, visual, and electronic. The first two groups include many different items and techniques. And I'd like to think that most of us would be carrying some kind of electronic signal equipment such as a mobile phone and flashlight; this group can also include PLBs (personal locator beacons, essentially satellite rescue systems) or other gadgets.

254 DRAW SIGNS

Charcoal chunks and partially burned sticks make great charcoal "pencils" to write messages and draw arrows on trees, rocks, and other materials. These messages can be simple words like "help" or "SOS", or you can leave more detailed messages. Arrows can also be drawn to point toward your camp. These can be done in a circle around your survival camp and even set up in concentric rings around your campsite. These marks are long lasting, but do not harm the trees or leave a permanent scar on the landscape. In clearings and on trails, you can bring the charcoal arrow concept into three-dimensional reality by assembling stick and log arrows to point searchers toward your camp or your trail. Set these up where you know they will be seen, and make them obviously unnatural. Symmetrical shapes and patterns aren't usually seen in fallen limbs and logs, and if you have it, use a charcoal chunk to scribe your name and predicament on a smooth log.

255 STACK ROCKS

In a survival scenario where you are short on signaling supplies, one of the best tips is to use the environment around you as a resource. Since most areas have stone, rock cairns can be a useful navigational tool and signaling mechanism. A cairn is a stack or tower of rocks that is clearly man-made. These simple structures are often used in rocky treeless terrain to mark trails and provide landmarks for navigation. The same rock stack can be a signpost to search and rescue crews, especially if you incorporate an arrow to lead them in the right direction. Cairns can be easy to make if flat rocks are available, but even with chunky rocks you can still build this pathfinding pillar. When any rocks are unstable, mix a bit of mud and dry grass to make mortar to secure the stones into place. With simple stonework techniques like this, you can use primitive signaling methods to become an active participant in your own salvation.

256 SIGNAL WITH A MIRROR

A signal mirror is one of the furthest reaching, non-electronic signal methods. Properly aimed, a signal mirror can shine a beam of daylight up to 10 miles (16 km), creating a flash of light that can catch the attention of distant aircraft, water craft, vehicles, or persons on foot. Any shiny flat object can work as a mirror, and practice makes perfect. Practice signaling with a friend in a large open area. If you both have mirrors, you could even make a game of your practice time. Try a game like "who can blind the other guy the most," or something similar, for immediate feedback that your aim is true. If you get caught with a mirror that doesn't have the aforementioned sighting lens, then hold the mirror under your eye, direct the beam of light onto the tip of an outstretched finger, and then place that illuminated finger just below your target. Sweep the mirror very slowly side to side, and up and down. This should sweep the beam across your target and hopefully they will notice it.

HACKS THROUGH HISTORY // SIGNAL FIRES

Fire can be used as a very effective signal for help, with many documented successes over the past centuries. Your fire should be in a prominent place, so that both the smoke and light are visible. Deep forest or jungle can really hinder signal fires, especially when the smoke is diffused through the canopy. If you cannot find an open place or can't move, then you'll need a thick column of smoke to do the work without the benefit of the fire light.

257 GO BIG

Ground-to-air signals can be your salvation when aircraft are searching for you. Create a large "V" shape, which is an international signal that means "we require assistance." It's easy to build with logs, or other long materials, though it can resemble a natural occurring shape. You can also consider making a giant "X" which means "we require medical assistance" or "unable to proceed," depending on the pilot's training. (This is legitimate for any situation, I think, as dying in the wilds would be a medical event and you wouldn't be able to proceed anymore.) The "X" is also a less frequently seen shape in nature. Build your "X" with wood, rock, dig the shape into soft ground, or anything else you can do, so long as it's big and visible. You can use string lines to make it straight, or drive a stake at each end of each line to "eyeball" for straight lines. If you have the energy and materials, try something more creative like spelling out "SOS" or "HELP." These will surely get some attention if they are big enough. If your signal isn't massive, no one is going to see it. Make it at least several dozen yards (meters) across—going even bigger could be even better.

Quick Tip

If the day is cloudy or foggy, no one will notice white smoke from a signal fire, so create some contrast: Pour a generous splash of motor oil, brake fluid, or any other petroleum substance into the fire to produce thick black smoke. This will have a greater contrast against a pale sky and will be easier to see.

HOMESTEAD

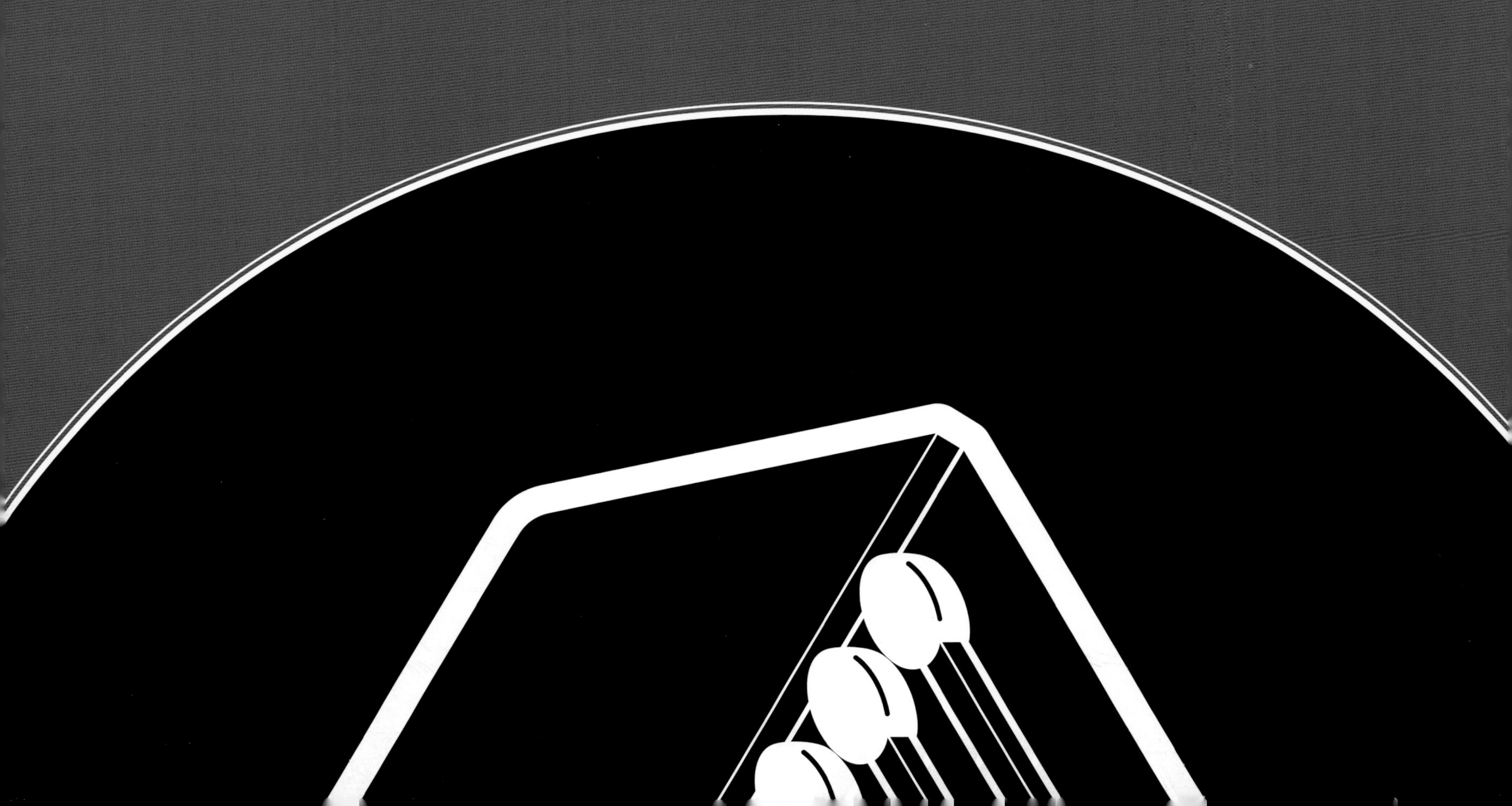

WE'RE NOT DONE YET! THIS FINAL CHAPTER IS ALL ABOUT THE LONG SHOTS, THE LIFE-ALTERING SITUATIONS, AND THE SYSTEM REBOOTS.

It's about the events and situations that would reset the game that you and I know as life. But make no mistake: This is not a video game. When you get killed, you can't just start the game over again. You only get one chance in this life, and this is it, right now. Some of these grim scenarios deal with major emergencies and catastrophic events which could happen anywhere and at any time. Some of the weirder situations, while possible, make for an outlandish palate cleanser to lighten the mood of this final chapter. And even through the most troubling scenes, there is still a thread of hope: These situations can be survivable. With the right combination of skill, preparation, and luck, you may just make it through one of these dire emergencies. You might even be better off for hard-learned lessons. Change is the only constant in nature, and while it doesn't benefit all, it often benefits survivors.

258 PLAN TO BUG OUT

You've probably heard the term "bug out" a thousand times, but what does it really mean? It's a military term from the 1950s, synonymous with evacuation, and the term has now been adopted by the preparedness community to encompass any situation where you'd leave your home or workplace in a hurry. You can certainly bug out without any planning, but a far better approach is to have a plan with numerous contingencies and backups. An easy framework to use is the "Five W's", which are commonly used today in journalism and other investigations. This stands for Who, What, Where, When and Why. A common sixth question works well here too, and that is, "How?" So, let's break down your plan: Who is going to bug out with you (or rendezvous at your destination)? What are you taking with you? Where are you going? When will you leave? Why are you leaving? How will you get there? Answer these questions, and you'll have a big part of your planning complete.

259 GET THE DETAILS

We just asked a lot of questions, but if you're going to make a plan, you might as well be serious about it. Let's fill in the details of your bug out plan.

WHO IS GOING? Immediate family members and close friends are the usual suspects in plans like these. Take into account any mobility issues for the very young, the old and those who are disabled. Determine who else you may want on your "team" and who you will not allow to go.

WHAT ARE YOU TAKING? This refers to the supplies that you'll be carrying. You'll need bug out bags, in case you have to walk or hike to get there. If you can take a vehicle for part of the way, determine what supplies you'll carry in there too.

WHERE WILL YOU GO? Bugging out without a destination makes you a refugee. If you have an off-the-grid property that you have been developing into a homestead, you already have a great BOL (bug out location). But what if you don't? Or what if you had to leave that self-sufficient property? The wise will consider having a "Site B" as a back-up plan. The site needs to have water and natural resources, be off the beaten path, be defensible, and it should have a cache of supplies hidden on it.

WHEN DO YOU LEAVE? Are you leaving at the first sign of danger? Or will you wait to see what happens? This can be the toughest decision of them all.

WHY ARE YOU GOING? What set off your "bug out alarm"? Are you following evacuation orders or did you decide to leave on your own? Decide which events would cause you to shelter in place and which ones would cause you to bug out.

HOW WILL YOU GET THERE? Determine several routes to get to your bug out location. Also consider how you will maintain security, which vehicles you'll take, and what rules you'll all try to abide by during the trip.

HACK HAZARDS

OVERSHARING

Imagine how much more your apocalypse will suck with this complication. Your former spouses, ex-friends, and creepy neighbors show up at your bug out location, with a bunch of their deadbeat friends—all expecting you to feed them and take care of them with your limited supplies. They know you have stuff, and they're showing no intention to leave. They're getting irate that you don't want to share. This is an alarming situation, and a preventable one. Loose lips sink ships, and you don't want the wrong people to know about your emergency plans. Your homestead, cabin, or camp would be very tempting target for desperate people. Anyone can justify any brutal action if they're scared enough or hungry enough. So limit your risks by keeping your mouth shut about your bug out plans and emergency supplies. You can still help others; just be careful.

Quick Tip

For your safety, your bug out gear shouldn't stand out in a crowd. Don't call attention to yourself by having tools and weapons within view. Choose clothing and backpacks that look sporty rather than tactical.

260 GET THE POINT

What you would need to survive if you had to flee your home with no guarantee of shelter, food, or water during an emergency? A bug out bag (BOB) is your survival insurance policy for any disaster or mayhem. There may not be one perfect, universal set of equipment, but with a core set of items, you can put together a BOB suited for a wide variety of situations. Most people use either a backpack or a duffle bag as the container for their goods, which should include basic survival essentials and a few irreplaceable items. If you're looking for a role model, long distance backpackers have it right. The thru-hikers that roam the wilderness walking hundreds (or even thousands) of miles understand what you need to survive and they've got the right recipe for a BOB. Ultra-lightweight tents, sleeping bags, and pads give you great shelter from the elements. Dehydrated food and super-light water filters give you food and drink. They've got living out of a backpack down to a science.

261 STOCK IT WELL

Fill your BOB with a minimum of the following, with most items sealed in zip-top bags or dry bags to prevent water damage.

- ☐ Security items, such as a firearm, large knife, pepper spray, and/or stun gun.
- ☐ Shelter: an ultralight tent, pad, and sleeping bag, with a space blanket for backup.
- ☐ Water (at least 2 quarts, in a sturdy container), with a water filter to help with refills.
- ☐ Food; pick ready-to-eat meals that you can eat while traveling, and carry a LOT!
- ☐ Walking shoes and seasonally appropriate clothes and outerwear
- ☐ Digital backups of important documents, such as a thumb drive with your bank info, insurance documents, wills, and family photos and videos.
- ☐ A few tools such as duct tape, trash bags, a head lamp with spare batteries, and a multi-tool
- ☐ Also carry some cash in small bills; waterproof matches; a lighter; hand sanitizer; a compass; a local map; and one of your old cell phones which is fully charged (it can still dial 911)

262 AVOID MISTAKES

Building a bug out bag is a great survival strategy for a variety of emergency situations, but for those who haven't done much backpacking or gone on any bug-out campouts (practice drills), little mistakes and miscalculations can pile up quickly. With that in mind, here are five things that a lot of people get wrong when packing their own bug out bag.

GET MORE HYGIENE SUPPLIES I know, you're planning to wipe with leaves—but have you lived like that for days? Toilet paper may just be the crown jewel of your bug out hygiene collection, but you'll need soap, a toothbrush, and feminine hygiene products too (for yourself, others, or the many off-label uses).

KEEP UP THE CALORIES The survival rations you packed may last for 5 years, but how long can you last by eating them? Your BOB should be stuffed with high-calorie food, since there's no guarantee of finding things to eat. Forget about the fluffy stuff that has no calories (bye-bye, rice cakes!) and don't bother with the heavy stuff that doesn't earn its keep (even though a case of canned peaches would be delicious). Bring a couple jars of peanut butter instead.

263 GET A GHB

In some situations, you won't need a full bug out bag—you'll just need enough supplies to "get out of Dodge". This kit (AKA GHB, or Get Home Bag) is much leaner and meaner than the average bug out bag, and its purpose is clear: getting you home. This bag isn't for people who are fleeing into the wilderness, it's for people who are planning on camping out at their own house. Some preppers will have a get home bag in their car and a separate one at the office. The supplies are simple and affordable, so multiple bags won't empty your bank account. Just modify the bug out bag list to make the kit smaller, lighter, and cheaper (just in case it gets stolen out of your car or at work). Shelter could be just a bare bones tarp and fleece blanket, or a space blanket if funds and storage room are limited. The water can just be store-bought bottles, with a pack of disinfection tablets so you can refill your them as needed. Remember, this kit is just to keep you safe until you reach your better gear at home.

MENTAL HACK // GREY MAN PRINCIPLE

The "grey man" principal is a very interesting psychological tool. It's a tactic often used in the intelligence community for movement and observation—but it isn't exactly the art of hiding. Being the grey man is about being noticed and then immediately dismissed. You've tried this already. Remember back to your school days, when you didn't want the teacher to call on you. If you had your hand up or you slumped down in your chair to hide, you had a good chance of being called on. If you had only known to look toward with a furrowed brow, imitating the stupider students who were trying to remember what the question was, you'd rarely get called to answer that question. (You're welcome, kids.) Now, let's apply this tool to the bug out scenario. Let's say that the streets are full of abandoned cars, and you have to walk to your bug out location with a backpack full of gear. If you march down the side of the road with your tactical-looking backpack (strapped with weapons), how far do you think you'll get before some desperate person tries to mug you, grovels at your feet for supplies, or starts following you? But costumed like a homeless person, muttering angrily to yourself, with your BOB in a garbage bag over your shoulder or hidden in a shopping cart, people won't give you a second look.

264 IMAGINE AN EMP

Few survival scenarios have captured the imagination (and spawned fear) like the electromagnetic pulse, or EMP. This event is a short burst of electromagnetic energy which can disrupt or even destroy electronic devices and systems, potentially even the electrical power grid. An EMP can be naturally occurring, such as the pulse from a massive solar flare. EMPs are also created by technological devices, typically nuclear weapons. The most frightening scenario is the detonation of several high-energy EMPs over an unsuspecting nation. According to some models, just a few of these devices detonated at a high altitude could wipe out all of the unshielded electronics and all power grids in the continental United States. Commonly used as fodder for apocalyptic novels and TV shows, these weapons have become a fixture of pop culture. And in the event that this threat becomes reality, here are some things that you'd wish you had.

265 BUILD A CAGE

One possible way to protect your valuable electronics is to construct a Faraday cage. Named for the 19th-century inventor Michael Faraday, this is any conductive structure that protects its contents from electrical and magnetic pulses. This may not protect every piece of electronic equipment, but it's a cheap way to prepare for this threat.

STEP 1 Gather up everything you want to shield. Likely items include shortwave radios, walkie-talkies, electronic medical equipment, night vision optical equipment, and spare electronic parts for your car. Batteries are not affected by an EMP, so they don't need to be included in the "cage."

STEP 2 Grab a metal garbage can with a tight-fitting lid and line the inside with cardboard or packing paper. Wrap each electronic item in paper, then in aluminum foil, and pack it in the can with more cardboard as insulation.

STEP 3 Close the garbage can lid, tape the lid edge with metallic tape, and pray this prep is unnecessary.

266 ARRANGE TRANSPORT

Modern vehicles may or may not operate in the wake of an EMP. Some experts believe that car and truck electronics will be fried in a weaponized EMP strike, while others believe that modern vehicle shielding (like the kind that keeps your engine from making your radio crackle) will be enough to protect normal vehicles. Certain types of pulse may shut your car off, but unhooking and re-hooking your battery may allow it to start again. The bottom line is that we just don't know what is going to happen, or what the results will be, so it's wise to arrange alternate forms of transportation. Get a bicycle or, better yet, a dirt bike that is purely mechanical (not a single electronic system). Buy some hiking boots and a backpack if you don't have them already. Learn to ride a horse. Restore that old antique car in the barn—you know, the one that was built before computers existed. There are plenty of ways to get around, so explore your options.

267 BE SELF SUFFICIENT

When the power is gone, you'll need to provide for yourself.

MAKE SOME LIGHT Chemical light sticks are a good non-electric light source, but what about something with a longer "burn" time? Candles are EMP-proof, but they are dim, messy, and vulnerable to the wind. This is where oil lamps come in; these old-fashioned lamps work indoors and outdoors, through wind and rain, and they're cheap! These lamps usually cost less than $20 USD and operate on a few pennies of lamp oil per hour. Never use gasoline, stove fuel, alcohol, or other creative fuels—use only approved fuels for oil lamps, such as non-dyed (clear) kerosene, clean-heat kerosene substitute, standard clear lamp oil, Citronella oil (outdoor use only), or liquid paraffin.

COLLECT AND DISINFECT WATER Water filters and disinfection tablets can be key players in providing you and your family with safe water, but you have to get the water first. Find a creek and collect some rain, or put your water well back into use with a well sleeve or well bucket. Instead of an old-fashioned wooden bucket and an above-ground stone well, this is a metal cylinder fitted with a couple hundred feet of cord, and lowered down slender modern wells to draw up water. This is a cheaper option than a hand pump for your well, but much more work.

GROW YOUR OWN FOOD Let's face it, your hoard of MREs will only last so long. There would come a day when you'd be out of food, if an event like an EMP occurred. It could take years to restore power to a handful of regions; in the meantime, people would have to find ways to provide food for their families other than the local grocery store. Having the knowledge, means, and location to grow food crops and raise livestock might just keep you alive during a multi year blackout. Of course, you'd need the seeds, livestock, and tools to jump start the system, along with the knowledge of seed saving and livestock breeding, but a little experience and a few good books can set you on the right path.

268 PLAN WELL

No power to operate your fancy electric can opener? Good! (Shame on you for owning one.) Choose manually-operated devices and gizmos, which are capable of working perfectly under any conditions (EMP or not). Check out camping catalogs and companies that sell non-electric household devices; there are a surprising number of choices in the non-electric marketplace.

KEEP YOUR KITCHEN READY
With a solar oven, as long as the sun shines, food can be cooked and water disinfected. Manual can openers won't run out of power; the P38 is a military classic, and it even fits on a keychain. A hand-powered grinder for grains and meats will let you make flour from whole grains, or "hamburger" from available livestock and other critters.

GEAR UP IN THE GARAGE
People have gotten along fine for millennia without plug-in or battery-powered hand tools—in a power-out situation, hand tools including saws, hammers, shovels, axes, even drills, and more besides, will all be useful. Add in a hand-powered water pump, to get water out of a shallow well.

269 GET A CLUE

Bugging out will not actually be a cool adventure. There's no theme music playing in the background and you're not walking down a road with a big explosion behind you. If you had to bug out, it would be one of the worst days of your entire life, so let's kill this action movie trope right now. Worst day of your life, got it?

Now, let's talk about the situations that could cause you to bug out. Natural disasters, terrorist attacks, and industrial accidents are the most likely issues that would cause you to run to the hills. These are all local or regional issues, and if you travel far enough, you'll be out of harm's way. Some of these situations give you warning, and some don't. If a hurricane and flooding are predicted for your low-lying home, bug out before the storm hits. If terrorists set off a dirty bomb in your home city, then you'll be fleeing along with tens of thousands of other evacuees. In either case, quick response is the best response. You'll need to have your supplies and plan ready to go.

270 SCOUT A SITE

If you had to bug out, someplace nice would obviously be your first choice. Your rich uncle's house or a posh hotel would be great, if they were outside of the disaster radius. Just keep in mind that bugging out without a destination makes you a refugee, and that's not a desirable condition. You could certainly travel blindly to an unknown destination, but wouldn't it be better to have a location in mind? One that you'd seen before? When deciding to head into the wild to avoid the aftermath of a disaster, you can significantly reduce your variables by heading toward a site you have previously scouted. With firsthand inspections of possible bug out locations, you'll know what resources are available and how long it would take to get there. You'll want a bug out site to have water and be away from the masses, while being a realistic distance from your home and work. A bug out camp location that is a hundred-day march from your home might as well be on the moon.

271 DIG A CRAPPER

Once the first fleet-footed souls in your party reach the BOL, it's time to set up a latrine (if you haven't done this already). Dig a fairly deep but slender hole in the ground, situated both downwind and downhill from your camp. Choose a spot at least 50 yards (50 m) away from your water source, whether it's a spring, stream, or pond. The bottom of the latrine should also be at least 6 feet (2 m) above the water table. If security and camouflage are no concern, you could build a privacy screen with tarps or other materials. But I'd keep the latrine (and every other aspect of your camp) stealthy, by situating it in a cluster of bushes or boulders. Keep the latrine hole covered with a board or a flat rock, when it's not in use. Stock some toilet paper in a waterproof container at the latrine (coffee cans are great). A pile of dirt and a small spade can allow you to cover the waste after each latrine use. Also keep some hand sanitizer nearby, to limit the spread of bacteria in camp. If you are unable to build anything over the hole, use boards or plywood around the edge of the hole. This will keep the footing drier and more stable.

272 ASSEMBLE A KITCHEN

"An army moves on its stomach," and so will your camp. You'll need a food preparation and cooking area, upwind from your latrine and away from your camp in bear country. This area should have a fire pit and rigs to suspend pots over the fire. Create a makeshift table for food prep and serving. The area could also have a food cache and some cooking equipment pre-positioned. You certainly wouldn't want to backpack a heavy Dutch oven that's big enough to serve a group, but you could drop it off ahead of time. Your camp kitchen should also have a dish washing station. This could be buckets of hot soapy water, and bucket of bleach water, and a rack to dry dishes in the sun (for UV disinfection). Inevitably, you'll run out of some kind of supply that requires replenishment. When it's something locally available, like firewood or water, this supply run could be a welcomed diversion for a few group members. But never send out one group member alone, whatever the task.

273 SET UP SECURITY

How will you defend your camp from man and beast? Not setting up camp on the side of the highway is a good place to start, but keep in mind that the most remote corner of the earth isn't perfect either. Getting away from the masses will likely mean that you'll be on your own for self-defense. When planning your camp site, consider spots that offer natural obstacles to hold off unfriendly interlopers. Ravines, cliffs, rivers, embankments, and even briar patches can slow or halt intruders, or funnel them toward your sentries. It's also helpful if your site provides a vantage point to see oncoming friends or foes (while keeping you hidden). As a final consideration, choose a path to retreat from your camp and a location to regroup, should your camp be overrun. Grim stuff, I know, but it should still be considered. And in a prolonged emergency, it's quite possible that your group would need someone or several people to stand watch against outsiders.

BUDGET SURVIVAL

AIR HORN ALARM

With an air horn, a rock, a stick, and a little fishing line, you'll know if your camp has a nighttime prowler! Bury the canister of the air horn, leaving the horn and the top button exposed. Position a flat rock to fall on the air horn button and prop it up with a small stick. Tie your mono filament to the small stick, and run it out as a trip wire across a trail. When an interloper hits the tripwire, it pulls the stick out of its position holding up the rock. Then the rock is free to drop onto the button of the air horn. It blasts a shrill honk until the air horn runs out of air or the rock slips out of position. And whether the blast is long or short, it will likely cause someone to jump out of their skin.

Quick Tip

Avoid drawing attention to your camp. Keep quiet, during the day and night. Minimize fires and bright flashlights after dusk, or make no light at all from dusk 'til dawn. Better to be off the radar than a target.

274 HIDE IN A GHILLIE

Ghillie is an old Scottish word for a special kind of game warden. Ghillies were tasked with protecting the game on their lord's lands from poachers, and they employed a unique style of camouflage to do their job. Commonly used today by elite military, ghillie suits allow the wearer to disappear into the local vegetation. We can borrow this technique for our own safety and defense, buy purchasing ready-made ghillie suits and netting, or make our own. A 5-by-5-foot (5x5-meter) section of heavy fishing net (available at craft stores) will make a fine ghillie cloak for a person, or as a drape to cover gear. Cut strips of burlap or other rough fabric that matches your target environment. Tie them into the net and shred the edges, and tie in local vegetation as well. Once covered with well-matched fabric, rags, and natural materials, your ghillie net will provide the colors, textures, patterns, shapes, and blurred edges you'd need for a great camouflage system that's adaptable for different environments.

275 CREATE A CACHE

Have you ever thought about making a stash of supplies at a remote site? It makes sense for a number of scenarios, and people have been caching valuable things for ages. (Pirate treasure, anyone?) But what should you cache? Top items stored by modern preppers include food, ammo, hand tools, communication equipment, and medical supplies. We need to consider the "what" part of your cache storage, and just as importantly, we need to get a handle on the "how" part of our cache storage plan. Any cache container should be able to withstand the environment it is located in, and protect against the natural enemies of storage, which include moisture, rodents, insects, freezing, heat, and theft, at the very least. Purchasing waterproof containers and boxes are a great choice for wet conditions. These are ready to use, though they can be expensive. For a thriftier approach, you can make your own home-made vaults from large diameter PVC pipe, some glue and a few fittings. Here's how to make your own weathertight storage containers.

STEP 1 Get a length of PVC sewer line, primer, glue, end caps, and spray paint. Choose a screw-out plug for one or both end caps, and buy pipe joint compound to prevent leaks.

STEP 2 Wipe primer on the surfaces that will be glued, then glue the caps (but not the threads) in place.

STEP 3 Let the glue dry for a few minutes (or a few days, if you're putting food in there).

STEP 4 Load up your cache, wipe joint compound on any threads, and screw then down tight.

STEP 5 Spray-paint or otherwise camouflage the tube so that the color matches your area.

STEP 6 Conceal or bury the cache in an out-of-the-way location. Mark it in an inconspicuous way for retrieval.

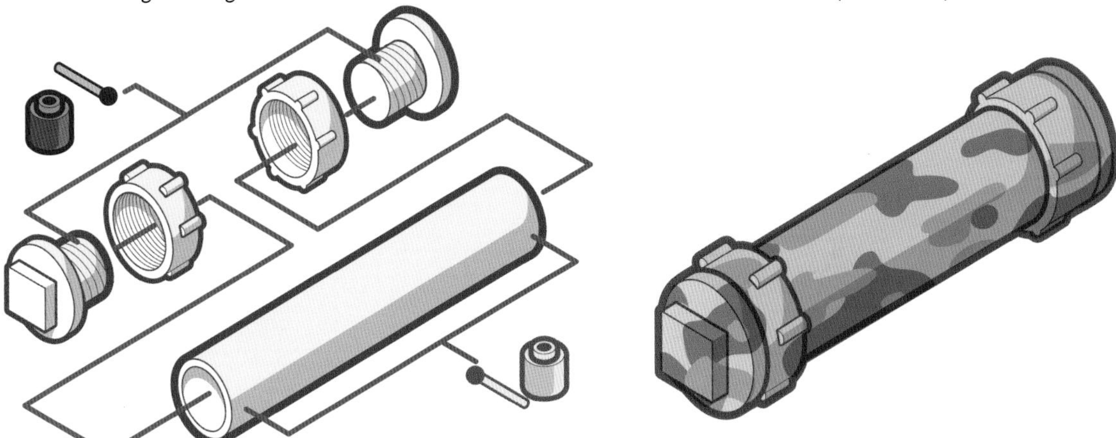

HACKS THROUGH HISTORY // MUD SUIT

Want to disappear? If you need to hide in the wild and you don't have a ghillie suit or net, then you can make the next best thing: a mud suit. We've seen versions of it in action flicks (Stallone and Schwarzenegger covered in mud), and from tribal hunters across the planet, it's a legitimate and effective camouflage technique. The first step is to wallow in some mud, coating every part of your body—clothing optional. Next, you can use crushed black charcoal from a campfire to "paint" dots and stripes here and there overtop the mud. Darken the high spots, leave the low spots, and don't make symmetrical patterns. Keep it random. Then, while the mud is still wet, roll on the ground to pick up leaves, moss, and other debris. Whether crouched in the bushes, lying flat on the ground, or just kneeling there pretending to be a stump, this highly effective camouflage will allow you to completely disappear. You're perfectly mirroring the local landscape because you're covered in it!

276 WASTE NOT

When we successfully take a game animal, we receive the gift of survival in the form of meat, but do we use those animals as thoroughly as your forefathers would have? When it comes to eating an animal, many hunters start and stop with the meat. A few intrepid diners may fry up the liver with onions, but it doesn't need to stop there. The heart, lungs, kidneys, eyes, tongue, brain, stomach, and intestines can also be cleaned, cooked, and eaten. For deer, we do want to be aware of deer illnesses (such as chronic wasting disease). When this is a possibility in your area, don't eat the brain and spinal tissue. Use these parts, along with unwanted meat trim, to bait traps for weasels, coyotes, raccoons, and other scavengers. And even though many cultures and faiths don't use blood as a food item, it could be treated as "liquid meat" and added to stews for additional protein or mixed with ground meat to make the famous British dish, blood sausage.

277 TAN YOUR HIDE

Mammal skins, particularly deer hides, can be tanned into soft and stretchy buckskin with a very strange tanning agent: animal brains! For centuries, this coveted alternative to cloth has been a favored material by many cultures, for many uses. Buckskin is made by introducing the fine oils of the brain into the prepared deer skin, then stretching it until soft.

STEP 1 Scrape all possible meat and fat from the animal skin you plan to tan. Stretch it out flat and dry it completely (in the shade). Scrape off the hair and sand both sides.

STEP 2 Prepare the brains by mashing them, boiling them in water to kill any pathogens, then smearing the paste or soup of brain all over both sides of a dry scraped hide. Then mix some brains and two quarts (2 L) or so of warm water, and submerge the hide in this brain solution.

STEP 3 After soaking the hide overnight in brains, wring it out and commence stretching the deer hide. It may take many hours, but once the hide is dry and soft, smoke it lightly for color. Now you have brain-tanned buckskin!

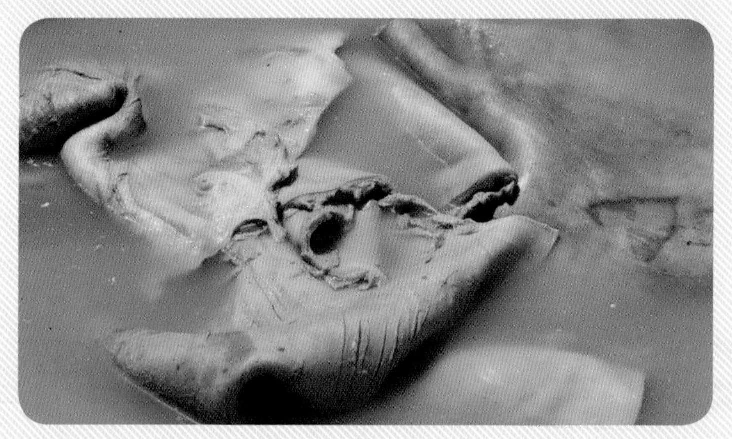

278 CRAFT CORDAGE

For thread, string, and rope, we can make surprisingly strong cordage from dried sinew and intestine. To make sinew cord, dry out some strips of back strap or leg sinew. This is the tough whitish-grey tissue found on the outside of the deer's tenderloin and running up and down the lower leg bones. Cut them free, scrape off any meat clinging to the tissue, and dry them for several days. The dried material can be pounded with a hard smooth object (like a hammer or round stone) to separate the fibers into something like dental floss. These fibers can be used as thread, or twisted into bigger cord. Similarly, the intestines can be cleaned out, twisted, and dried under tension to make a light-duty rope. This "gut rope" is one of the traditional cords for friction fire making among native inhabitants of the Arctic. And if you don't manage to collect the tendons and sinews, you can cut scraps of hide into strips for a strong yet flexible cordage material.

279 USE THOSE BONES

Large animal bones can come in a wide range of shapes and many of them can be used as tools and other useful things. For example, the pair of V-shaped bones in a deer's nose can be broken free and sharpened to make a great pair of fish hooks. Just drill a hole or file a notch to receive your fishing line, and hit the water. Hooks like this (and sharp splinters of broken bone) should be used as gorge hooks. Give your nibbling fish some extra line, allowing them to swallow the hook. Then gently draw them toward you and use a net or basket to land them. Many more uses abound.

MAKE TOOLS Femurs make good hide scraping tools; a shoulder blade can become a hoe or digging tool; and ribs can become part of a bow-drill for fire making.

SAW WITH A JAW Animal jaws with teeth make an interesting saw for softwood and plant fibers.

SAVE THOSE SPLINTERS Bone splinters can become needles or awls, while random chunks of bone can be used as buttons or toggles, and triangular bone chips and toe bones can be turned into arrowheads.

BUILD A FIRE KIT Many large game animal bones can be used as friction fire kit components. Larger and stronger deer ribs can be turned into bow drills. They're even flexible, just like a wooden bow. The rear ankle bones (what appear to be knees to us) can be used as hand-hold sockets for the top of the drill. They usually even have enough animal fat in them to act like pre-lubricated bearing blocks.

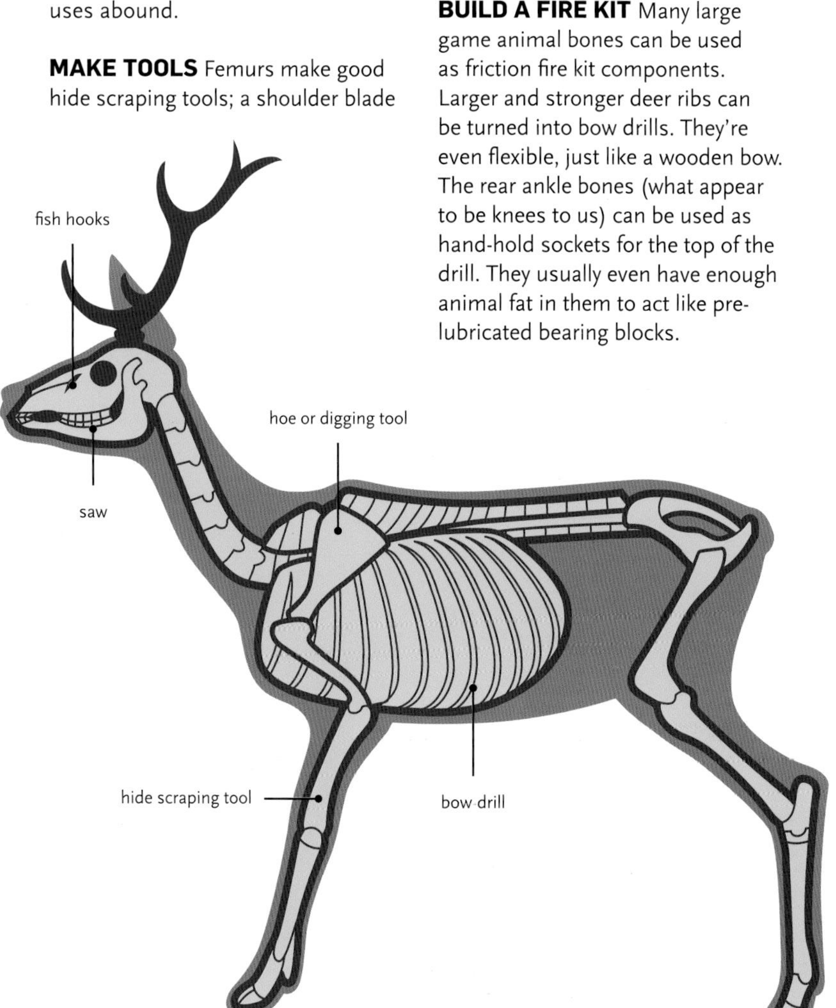

280 BREW GLUE

Hide glue can be made from scrapings or de-haired scraps of mammal skin, and many other animals and parts. Hide glue is a great natural adhesive that is great for gluing together bindings on tools and arrows for use in dry conditions. It can take any amount of heat, but if it gets wet, it will melt and let go. The fibrous proteins called collagen and elastin are extracted from the animal parts by cooking them in water. Your strongest glue can be made by simmering it at 130 to 150 °F (54–65 °C). Each cup of animal hide, called glue stock, should be simmered in 2 cups (480 mL) of water until swollen and gelatinous, which takes several hours. Replace any water that evaporates during the cooking process. When finished cooking, filter out glue stock pieces and particulates by pouring the glue through a cloth. Reduce this to glue by simmering until it has a maple syrup consistency. Then it's ready to use, or to dry for storage.

281 LIGHT 'EM UP

People have been using lights to attract fish since they could make fire. Powhatan Indians used small fires onboard their wooden dugout canoes to create a bright light to draw attract fish to the boat at night, where the animals could be speared or netted. Sometimes called "fire-fishing", the technique would be done after dark in a large wooden canoe fitted with a clay-lined hearth (to prevent lighting the watercraft on fire). Torches were occasionally used too. Eyewitness accounts vary, but a painting from 1585 by John White shows the hearth in the middle of the canoe on a stick platform. This high position would allow the light to be seen underwater. According to the onlookers, multitudes of curious fish were once caught this way. The method is now illegal, but in a survival situation, survival comes first.

282 FISH BY HAND

The crudest and simplest method of fishing is hand fishing, and it's about as primitive as fishing can get. For those with nerves of steel and quick reflexes, you actually grab the fish from the water with your bare hands (typically catfish and other large slow species, though really fast hand fishers can fling trout up onto the creek bank). To get started, use your feet to feel for structures that could harbor a fish, and then reach your hand into them. The fish will often move forward and bite your hand. Fight your natural urge to pull your hand away. Leave your hand in the fish's mouth and pull it toward you. Wrap your free arm around the fish, being careful to avoid contact with the barbs on the fish's fins. Never try this solo, go with others so that they can help you if you become injured or entangled in debris. Common injuries when practicing this form of fishing include cuts, scrapes, and scratches, which can often be avoided by wearing thin gloves that still allow you to feel.

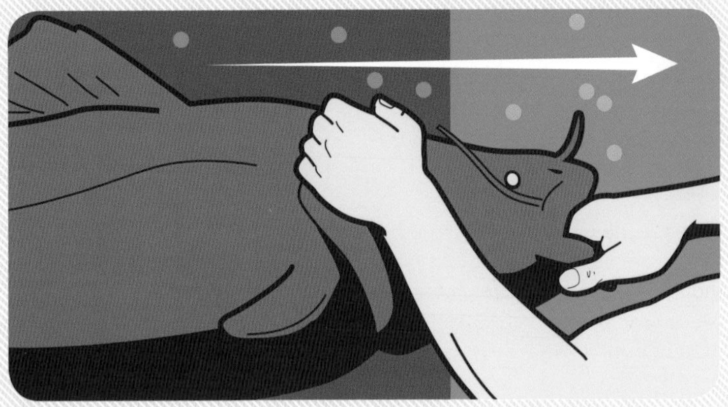

283 BLOW THEM AWAY

Dynamite fishing (also known as blast fishing) is illegal in much of the world and for good reason, though it is still practiced by tens of thousands of fishermen worldwide. Commonly seen in East Asia and the Philippines, this environmentally unfriendly fishing technique involves explosive charges detonated underwater. Blast fishermen try to target a school of fish, and the results are messy. The fish are instantly killed, but only 10 to 20 percent of them float to the surface (where they are easy to collect). This means that the rest of the dead fish sink to the bottom. This method also causes devastation to the underwater habitat (it may take a coral reef 10 years to recover from one blast). Using this method to collect fish should be a last resort after you used all your other last resorts. And you usually wouldn't have a box of dynamite lying around in your tool shed anyway. That's probably a good thing—sometimes people drop the lit stick of dynamite in the boat.

284 SHOCK SOME FISH

This method of fishing is often used by fisheries scientists to sample the fish population in smaller bodies of water, though it could be used to catch fish for eating, if the rules were out the window. This method shares the illegality of blast fishing, but it does almost no damage to the fish or the environment. It works by shooting high-voltage direct current electricity through the water, between a submerged cathode and anode. This doesn't harm the fish; it only affects their movement. Nearby fish will swim towards the anode, and become stunned by the electricity. Once stupefied, the fish are easily scooped with a dip net. Fisheries scientists use sophisticated backpack models of electrofishing devices, and larger boat-mounted units. Both of these produce an adjustable voltage, between 50 and 1,200 volts, and the stunned fish will revive in only a few minutes. To balance the scales, the users are at risk of a nasty shock themselves—water and electricity obviously don't get along well.

HACKS THROUGH HISTORY // **FISH POISON**

Although the act is illegal in most places today (and it's not very sporting), our ancestors once used plant poisons to stun fish for easy collection. Numerous nuts, roots, seeds, fruits, and leaves contain compounds that have an effect on the respiratory or nervous systems of fish, especially in still water. The stupefied fish simply float to the surface, awaiting your collection. Crushed mullein seeds have been put to use for centuries in North America as an effective fish poison. The crushed seeds release saponins, glycosides, coumarin, and rotenone into the water—compounds that can stun fish and bring them to the surface. Used in a small body of water, it can bring up fish that refuse to be caught with other methods. Again, this is illegal and unsportsmanlike, but in a dire emergency, you'll need to do what you must to feed yourself and your loved ones. Just catch and gut the fish quickly to minimize the meat's exposure to these toxins, and cook until well done. In addition to mullein, you can also use the bark and green nut husks of black walnut in North America, and a host of native-growing plants found on each of the other continents around the world.

285 BUILD A PISTON

The fire piston really is a fascinating device. The basic operation of this fire starter involves a piston slammed down into a sleeve, which generates heat and ignites some tinder imbedded at the piston's tip. This compression ignition system should sound familiar to anyone who knows the diesel engine. Legend has it that German inventor and mechanical engineer Rudolf Diesel got the idea for his famous engine by watching a fire piston in operation. Here's where all this comes home. With some skill at fabricating, you can make a fire piston from a flashlight.

GATHER PARTS Get a Mini Maglite or similar flashlight that you don't want to use anymore. You'll also need some J-B Weld or a similar epoxy, a small round (or half round) file, a tapered sink washer that fits very tightly inside the Maglite body, a dowel that fits inside the Maglite body, some tape, a little bit of lard, a small screw to attach the sink washer to the dowel, screw driver, and some char cloth.

BUILD AND TEST Fill the light's end cap with epoxy and let it cure for 24 hours. Wrap tape at the tip of your round file (to prevent scratches), and carefully file down the lip at the bulb end of the flashlight body. Screw the sink washer to the dowel and lubricate the rubber with a tiny amount of lard. Once the epoxy has hardened, screw the end cap back onto the Maglite. Once everything is assembled, give your fire piston a few tests by plunging the lubricated washer end of the dowel down into the flashlight body. If it pops back out a little, you're getting good compression.

FIRE IT UP Now you're ready to try it with the char cloth. Pack a small bit of the char cloth into the hollow of the washer, covering the screw head. Wipe a tiny bit of lard around the sides of the rubber washer, and slam it down hard into the Maglite. Pull it out quickly and see it your char is glowing orange. If so, then you did everything right. If not, try again.

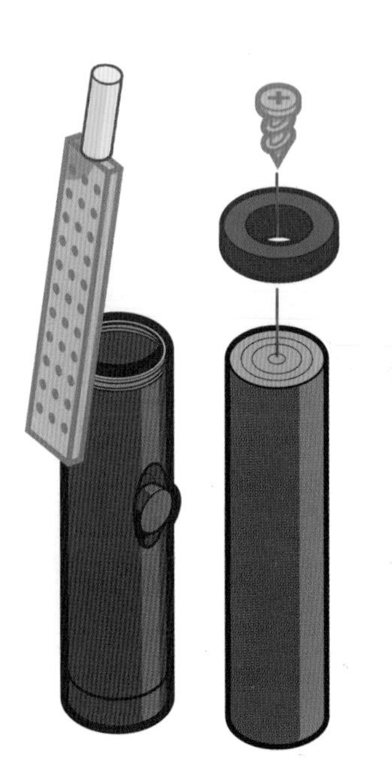

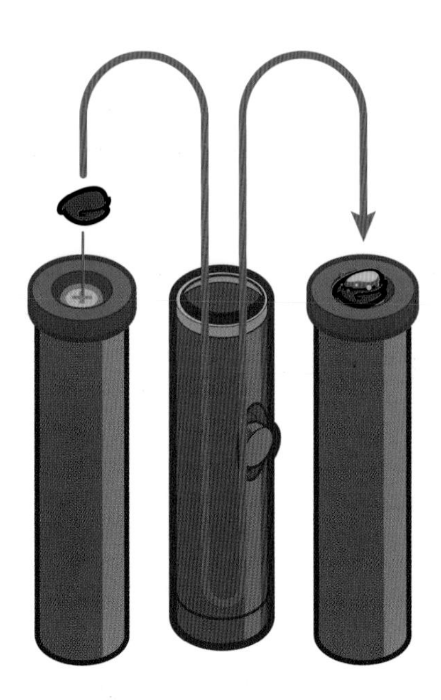

286 LIGHT A CRAYON

You've seen candles, and you've likely played with them at some point in your lifetime, so you know that wax is flammable. And you've certainly lit paper on fire before, right? So what if there was a cheap and readily available product that combines both the easy lighting of paper and the long burn time of wax? Well, there is—and it's called a crayon. The word dates back to 1644, but colored markers go back to the stone-age. Today, crayons are made of dyed paraffin wax (super flammable) wrapped in rough paper (also super flammable). To turn these colorful kid markers into fire starters, peel a bit of the paper loose at the pointy end of the crayon and light it with an open flame. The wax will begin to melt and soak into the paper, acting just like a candle. Once lit, you can maneuver this little candle around your fire lay, dripping wax as you go and lighting the structure in several spots. You can also place the lit crayon inside your fire lay and leave it to continue burning. For the longest burn and to use it like a proper candle, drip a little bit of wax onto a flat fire-proof surface. Quickly seat the flat bottom of the crayon in the hardening wax and it will stand tall and true!

287 WORK IN THE RAIN

You'll never need a fire like you need it when conditions are wet and cold. The intense energy released by burning wood seems to be the only thing that can cut through the bone-chilling cold of a raw rainy day. And even if you already light camp fires like a pro, try these tricks for your next wet weather fire.

STICK WITH STICKY STUFF Pine, fir, spruce, and most other needle-bearing trees are my first stop in wet weather because they have sticky sap in their wood. This is pitch, which is usually very flammable. Select dead twigs underneath the protection of these trees to get your fire going quickly, even when you're in damp weather.

PEEL IT OFF Bark is typically a protective structure to save the wood from a fire. Most barks aren't that flammable on their own. Tear, carve or peel the wet bark off your sticks and kindling. There's often dry wood just below the surface—especially if you got your wood from standing dead trees and bushes.

288 HIDE YOUR FIRE

Smoke is a product of incomplete combustion. And the more smoke you have, the greater the chances of being seen (or sniffed-out). When you're trying to signal for help, of course, you want all the smoke you can make. But when your smoke can draw unwanted attention, you'd better know how to make a smokeless fire. The biggest secret in this pursuit is achieving a nearly complete combustion. You'll still make a little smoke and have ashes left behind, but there are several things you can do to virtually eliminate smoke. Start by peeling the bark off your wood, just as you would do in wet weather. Next, cut or split your wood into slender strips. You'll be exposing the drier inner wood inside, and the skinnier pieces will burn more quickly. Feed the fire a little at a time and keep it small. The smaller the fire, the less smoke you'll make.

BUDGET SURVIVAL

ROAD FLARE

Road flares come in different sizes, and they're all capable of lighting a fire under adverse conditions. Simply gather the best and driest fire materials you can find, form a basic fire lay (tipi is best), and strike your flare. Aim the flames into your waiting tinder and allow the flare to work its magic. Flares aren't as fast acting as a blowtorch, but they're cheap, easy to use, and readily available in many types of stores. Keep in mind, however, that even though flares act like a long-lasting match, all the normal rules of fire making still apply. The flare won't light your fire lay if it is made with wet wood or if the pieces are too big. Build your fire materials as if you were only using one match.

Worth Every Penny

BURN GEL

This isn't a fire starter—it's the gel you apply after you've burned yourself making fire. If you make enough fires, or you're just clumsy, you're going to need this healing gel to relieve pain.

SUPER GLUE

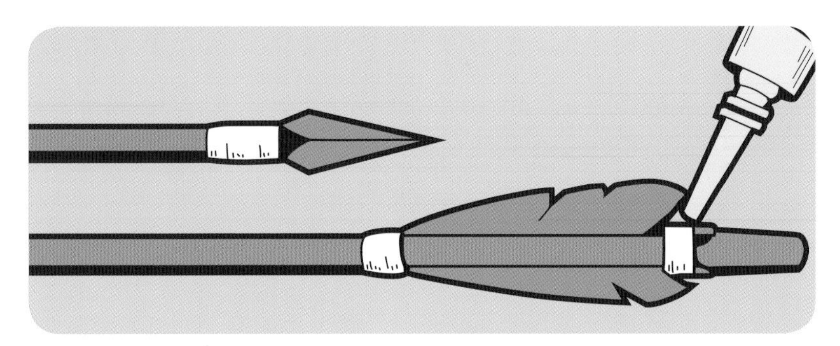

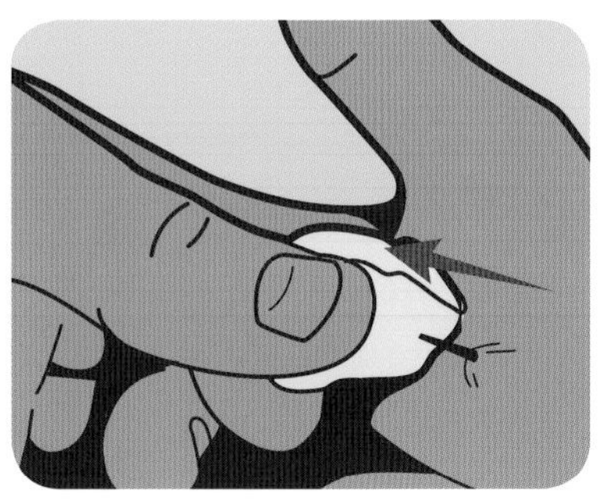

1 BUILD PROJECTILES ▲ Arrows, atlatl darts, javelins, and spears can really benefit from the adhesive powers of super glue. Some (expensive) fletching glue products are nothing more than repackaged (affordable) super glue. Use this adhesive to stick prepared feathers onto arrow shafts or to secure projectile points of any kind. Of course, thread, string, or some other thin cordage should be used in conjunction with this adhesive, particularly on notched arrowheads and natural feather fletchings. You can even use super glue to secure the knots you'll tie in that thread. Whether you're making a modern or primitive arrow, this glue is a big help.

2 MEND YOUR BOOTS ▶ In an emergency setting, you have to be able to move and travel. So, when the tread starts coming loose from the sole of your boot, or the leather starts to get a crack in it, break out the glue! Boot repair can be quick and simple with this kind of glue. Clean the damaged area thoroughly and allow it to dry. Apply glue to the necessary area and hold it still until the glue sets (less than a minute). You can even mend the aglet (that skinny tip) on your boot laces. You won't get far on a blown-out boot or if your loose outer tread is catching on every rock and vine. Take the time to repair little problems before they can grow, and your boots will continue to protect your feet.

3 FIX YOUR WEAPON Super glue was originally made for the war effort in the early part of World War II, so it shouldn't come as a surprise that the stuff can help us repair our wounded weapons. For example, if you've been shooting a wooden bow and a splinter begins to delaminate from the back of the bow, unstring the bow and apply a little super glue to the area. This will soak into the wood slightly and reduce the risk of a break in that area. And what about your firearms? Super glue isn't suitable for most metal repairs, but it's a great fit for plastics (since it's essentially a plastic itself) and it's a fine choice for wood. Fix that crack in your wooden rifle before it worsens.

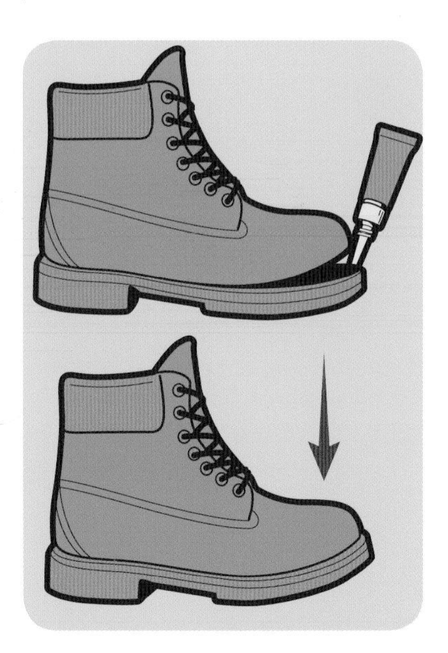

4 PULL A SPLINTER ▲ Developed in the 1940s, super glues are a family of quick-setting acrylic resin adhesives that are now used for many daily tasks, from industrial and household uses to medical applications. A sliver of wood in your finger or the tip of a thorn in your foot can be more than an annoyance during a survival situation, it can impact your ability move and to work. To use super glue for splinter removal, spread a thin layer of glue over the top of the splinter and the surrounding skin. This trick will work best if a bit of the splinter is still sticking out of your skin. Allow the super glue dry completely and then peel off the glue. If all went well, the splinter should come with it.

5 CLOSE A WOUND If you liked the splinter trick, you'll love how super glue can close up shallow cuts! This is a viable method of protecting the wound and an important option for infection prevention. Clean the cut with a disinfectant and gently squeeze the skin back together. Once the skin is in position, apply a small line of super glue just across the surface of the skin and the cut. Hold it for 30 seconds while the glue hardens, and you're done! Always use super glue sparingly and use a medical-grade glue (such as Dermabond) if you can get it. Never use super glue near the eyes or face, on jagged wounds, puncture wounds, or on wounds that contain dirt or debris. Never use it on dental work like crowns or fillings; it's poisonous!

6 PATCH A BOTTLE ▶ A crack or hole in your water bottle or hydration bladder can be a devastating problem, even when you're not in a dry climate. The ability to transport water is what lets us travel in the wild, which can mean the difference between a self-rescue and dying in the middle of nowhere. While it does smell bad and may make the water taste a little funny, super glue is a safe and effective patch for water containers once dried. For cracks on smooth surfaces, scuff the surface with a rough object such as a stone, to create scratches that the glue can grab. Then, clean that surface, dry it, and apply a thin layer of glue. For something malleable like a hydration bladder, simply apply the glue in a thicker coat and wait for it to dry before moving it. With either material, let it dry and cure for a few minutes (or hours) before adding water and testing your work.

7 FIX SOME FABRIC Your clothing is your "wearable shelter," and it plays a big role in keeping you warm and protected in the wild. Your tent and sleeping bag are also key players in any wilderness survival situation. When a tear or cut occurs in the fabric of these critical items, it can dramatically interfere with the effectiveness of your shelter. Use a few drops of super glue to patch that leaky rainfly on your tent and to keep that rip in your coat from spilling out all of the down feathers. You can also apply super glue to the cut end of rope to prevent fraying. Just make sure you don't apply super glue to natural materials such as cotton and wool. Super glue's cyanoacrylate compounds can have a surprising and very sudden exothermic reaction. The heat released can be enough to cause smoke and deliver a skin burn. Mend those ripped jeans with a needle and thread, rather than patching with glue.

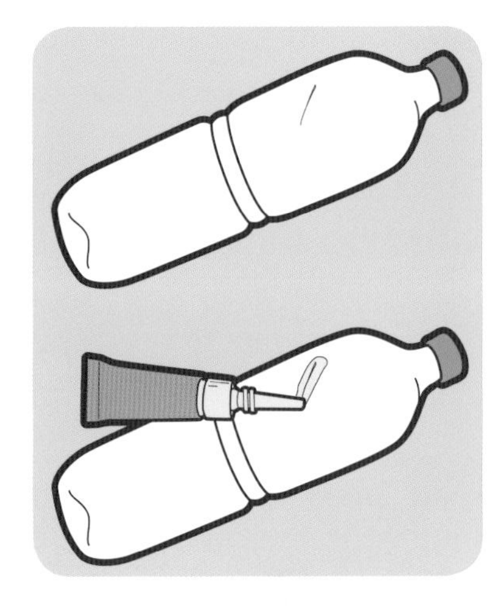

8 GO FISH ▼ Tying fishing flies is a beautiful and complex art form (with the added benefit of feeding the user), and we don't have enough room to do it any justice in just one paragraph. We can, however, remind you that even beginners can use adhesives like super glue to make improvised lures and flies for many different styles of fishing. Use a drop of glue to attach animal hairs and tiny feather fragments onto fishing hooks for wet or dry flies for fly fishing. Use odd bits of plastic and wood to build lures, plugs and poppers for other styles of fishing. Once the super glue is dry, it's perfectly fine for use in and around the water. You can even sand it down or paint over the glue.

289 FIND FRESH WATER

A lush deserted island may sound like the perfect vacation getaway, but in truth, being marooned there can quickly become the stuff of nightmares. Of all the problems you'd face, finding enough drinking water could become your most daunting challenge. If your new island residence is a flat and empty patch of sand, collecting rain may be your best hope.

WATCH THE SKIES Larger islands tend to create cloud formations above them, which can help you with spotting them at a distance. These clouds can also generate ample rainfall. Thunderstorms provide a lot of water quickly, so set out plenty of containers to collect this free fresh water.

SEARCH THE LAND You may find abundant fresh water on larger islands as well. Look for small streams or larger waterways running down to the beach, and boil the water to disinfect it. Caves may have water dripping inside them, and you could even try digging a well.

AVOID THE OCEAN Whatever you do, remember that drinking seawater will kill you. Unless you can build the equipment to desalinate it, drinking seawater will dehydrate you, as your body has to use its own water in order to rid itself of the high salt content.

290 SURVIVE BY COCONUT

Can you live off coconuts if you're stuck on a tropical island? After the 2005 tsunami, Michael Mangal survived for 25 days while stranded on an island in India's Andaman archipelago. He survived by eating and drinking coconuts before his happy rescue.

DRINK UP Green coconuts are a good source of drinkable water, holding about 12 ounces (350 mL) each. Just try not to drink too much. More than a few per day can cause diarrhea, thus losing water instead.

EAT THEM Mature brown coconuts provide about 500 calories each, due to the high fat content. The oily meat n these fuzzy brown orbs is high in potassium and many other minerals. It can be eaten raw, grated and pressed to make coconut milk, or diced up and cooked. And if you don't decide to eat them, maybe something else will try a bite. Coconut chunks can be used as trap bait on land and in the water.

BE HEALTHY Coconuts contain lauric acid, a fatty acid also found in human breast milk. This acid supports the immune system, and it's both antibacterial and antiviral. By crushing coconut oil from the meat, you can create a skin "lotion" that can help to prevent skin infections—a common ailment in situations where hygiene is poor (such as an island with no soap or a shower).

PROTECT YOUR SKIN Getting burnt? Coconuts even provide a little sunblock, which is a welcome relief in most sunny environments. Crush some of the fattier coconut meat, and apply it liberally to your exposed skin. This coconut oil residue will block roughly 20 percent of the sun's damaging rays.

MAKE FIRE Coconut shells and husks can certainly be useful as containers, but they're even more useful when you burn the dead dry husks as fuel for your fire. The husk fibers can even provide the tinder to get that fire going.

CREATE CORDAGE Many species produce hairy fibers which can be worked into cordage or fabric. These fibers can come from the coconut husk itself or from the tree trunk.

HACK HAZARDS

LOSING YOUR SANITY

For a person stranded alone, one of the hardest survival issues may be maintaining good mental health. Mental failures should not be surprising, as few humans fare well in isolation. We may crave a little solitude from time to time, but it's occasional and voluntary. A long term solo survival experience is neither. These conditions are likely to erode the mental and emotional wellbeing of the survivor, and cause them to become enormously disturbed. Aggressiveness, anxiety, paranoia, obsessive thoughts, hallucinations, and suicidal actions have been documented in cases where a person has been deprived of close social and physical contact. How can you cope with these circumstances? Survivors have had good luck maintaining some semblance of mental health by finding a higher meaning in their predicament.

Quick Tip

Ship or plane wreckage may provide you with a wealth of materials that can be used for shelters, beds, water catches, tools, and weapons. Use your imagination and let the creativity flow.

291 STAY ON TRACK

The art of tracking is an age-old skill set, providing valuable information to the tracker. From a simple series of marks on the ground, we can identify prey, stay alert to the presence of predators, and even backtrack ourselves if we become lost. But what happens when we have to track through difficult terrain? There are two things to look for when it's hard to stay on the trail.

TRANSFERENCE If you have ever tracked mud into the house, you know all about transference. Look for this type of track when material can be tracked from one surface onto another surface.

COMPRESSION In moss, leaf litter, dry sand, and powdery snow, you may not ever find a clear print—but a compression shape can help you determine who made the track. Canines leave oval compressions, cats leave round ones, and deer foot compressions are heart-shaped.

292 USE THE LIGHT

The morning and the late afternoon are some of the best times to look for tracks. With the sun at a low angle, the shadows inside the tracks will naturally be much more pronounced. This temporarily darker appearance makes the tracks stand out better on the landscape, and can even show you more detail. This is very different from midday tracking, when it's much harder to see the tracks and trails. So when you're tracking in the middle of the day (or at night), there's a way to simulate this low angle of sunlight: Shine a strong flashlight across the ground to "sidelight" the animal or human tracks. As the beam of light shines parallel to the ground, its relative absence in the track will create a shadow effect similar to morning or late afternoon sunlight. For best results, tape or tie the flashlight to the bottom of a walking stick, so that you walk upright while sidelighting the tracks. Avoid shining your side light (or other lights) down on the tracks, as the direct light will wash them out.

293 FIND SOME SIGN

Tracking isn't just the search for clear footprints. There are many more traces that are left behind. The search for these other indicators is called sign tracking, and it can be used in almost any environment. This method of tracking involves the signs, marks, disturbances, and leavings of an animal or person. Trails, beds, rubs, and chews can give a general idea of the animal species that are present. Hairs, feathers, or droppings can tell us exactly which animals are nearby. You can also look for trails, which are equivalent to the "highways" that animals use to go between feeding areas, bedding areas, cover, and water sources. You'll often find that the trails are worn down to bare dirt or rock, and filled with a variety of tracks. And for the animals that don't make nests (like deer), they will often bed down in fields and thickets, leaving an oval depression in the vegetation. It's important to learn to track by looking for these common animal signs, because in some terrains, it's all you'll have.

294 GET A COUNT

Counting plays a big role in the tracking of man and beast. By counting the toes visible in an animal track, you can then determine which animal group you are dealing with. Canines and felines will have four toes on the front feet and four toes on the rear feet, while rodents will possess four toes on the front and five in the back. You can also use a different type of counting to determine the number of people that went down a sandy or muddy trail. Choose a spot in the trail with clear prints and mark out a 1-yard (1-m) box that is the full width of the trail. Count each and every footprint (or partial footprint) in that box, rounding up by one if you have an odd number. Divide this total by two for a surprisingly accurate head count on that group. This trick works whether each person has a different boot tread or they are all the same type of boot! This works best when counting groups between five and 15 people.

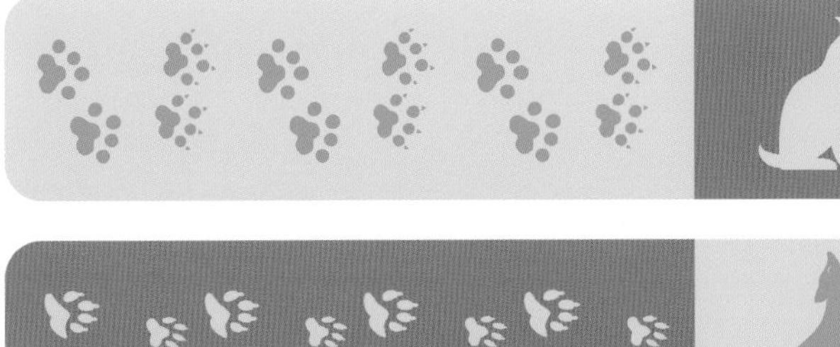

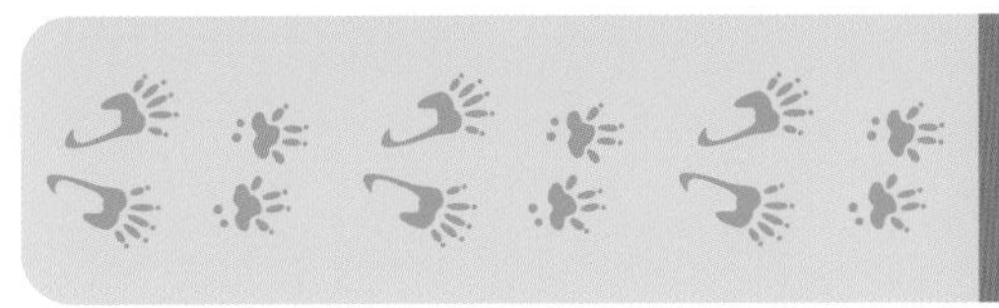

HACKS THROUGH HISTORY // MAN TRACKING

The human footprint. Is it just a shape in the soil? Or is it something more? For thousands of years, our ancestors have tracked animals by the footprints and other sign that they leave behind. And they have also tracked their fellow man. Try these tricks when following a human track.

SEEK AERIAL SPOOR In addition to footprints, we can look for aerial spoor. Classic sign, like broken branches or snapped spider webs, can tell us that something passed that way. Tracking should always include the observance of signs above the ground, and never just prints in the dirt.

LOOK FOR LITTER Intentionally discarded items (like trash) or items that have been accidentally dropped are a great indicator of someone's presence, and these items may give you clues about the person.

USE ALL YOUR SENSES Most people track by simply looking for footprints, as if their sight is the only sense they possess. Try to use more senses when tracking. Sound and even scent can be valuable. Stop and listen to the sounds of the environment periodically. You may hear your quarry moving if they are nearby. Even use your sense of smell!

DON'T FORGET THE TARGET Whether you are tracking a lost child or a trespasser on your property, don't get so focused on the tracks and trail that you forget about the "thing" at the end of the trail.

295 LINE 'EM UP

Bird counts are important, as they alert you to the presence of chicken-stealing predators like foxes, coyotes, and other local wildlife species that share your love of chicken meat and eggs. And while it's easy to count your birds when they're on the roost (they're all lined up and staying still), it's not so easy when they're running around their pen like, well, chickens with their heads cut off. So if you have more than a dozen birds, there's an easy way to count them (and feed them at the same time). Grab a bucket of their favorite grain or feed mix, and pour out a long line of grain in the chicken pen. Do this at a time when they are hungry (like early morning) and your birds will spread out along the line of grain to enjoy their meal. Once they are lined up in a row and staying relatively still, your daytime "head count" will be much easier. This technique will work with any of your birds—turkeys, chickens, ducks, and any other domesticated bird.

296 STOP EGG EATERS

For a variety of reasons, a productive laying hen can turn into an egg eating monster hell-bent on infanticide, which defeats the whole purpose of laying hens. It can be very difficult to determine which of your birds is the culprit. You can't tolerate this behavior, especially in an emergency setting. Each of those eggs provide a serving-sized dose of protein, without having to kill any of your livestock. A productive hen can lay one egg every other day or so, and the average large egg has 74 calories, 5 grams of fat, and 6 grams of protein. Stop those egg-eating hens by collecting several times a day before they have a chance to eat the eggs. You can also place a few ceramic decoy eggs in the nest boxes. The egg-eaters will peck at the rock-hard fake eggs, unable to make a dent, and they'll get discouraged in their bad behavior. You may want to mark the fake eggs somehow, as they are very realistic looking, so you can leave them in the nest when you gather.

297 STORE IT ON THE HOOF

"A chicken in every pot" was one of the campaign promises of presidential candidate Herbert Hoover in the 1928 election. This didn't exactly happen (the Great Depression started the next year), but a chicken when you need one is still a great idea. Rather than storing your chicken meat in the freezer or in canning jars, there's another way to keep your meat fresh and available, without the need for special equipment or electricity: Store the meat "on the wing" by keeping a live flock. Your birds can be dispatched as needed. This means you'll have tasty and healthy protein right outside your doorstep when you have your own chickens. Of course there are predators and human thieves, and the birds could also die from disease, age, or injury, so this isn't a risk-free approach. But in many settings, it makes sense to keep them alive rather than storing the meat.

298 KNOW THE TRICKS

More and more people are joining the backyard chicken nation, but this inexperience can have a devastating learning curve. Make use of all the information you can acquire, including these tips.

CONTROL PESTS Tick-borne diseases are awful. But lucky for bird owners, chickens are a tick's worst enemy. Sharp-eyed and quick, chickens can reduce the tick population to rock-bottom numbers in a small area, such as your yard. Your hens and roosters also eat other insect pests including spiders, ants, fleas, Japanese beetles, and other unwelcome creatures. Just keep the birds out of your garden—chickens can't resist pecking holes in your low-hanging veggies.

LEAVE EGGS AS-IS Contrary to common sense, your eggs will last far longer when you leave them dirty. Sure, it's less appealing to have chicken poop on your eggs, but underneath that or any other debris, the eggshell is coated in a cuticle, a coating that keeps them preserved for several weeks at room temperature, and much longer in cooler surroundings.

PUT OUT THE RED LIGHT Chickens don't need to sleep in total darkness. They are actually more comfortable with a light in their coop. A red bulb can provide a double benefit, as it provides light and hides the color of blood—which can keep your birds from pecking at any bleeding wounds on each other. For cold weather, your red light can even be a heat bulb, giving the birds some light and warmth.

TREAT DISEASES Take the time to learn how to diagnose and prevent the spread of diseases in your birds, before you get them. For the most part, many diseases can be prevented by keeping a clean coop that is warm at night, but you can still be at risk for common ailments that can harm your flock. Marek's Disease is a common contagious illness that can be fatal in younger chickens. It is spread by lost feathers and dust, and may manifest as labored breathing, paralysis, and weight loss. Fowl Pox is a viral disease spread by mosquitoes; it can present as a "dry" form, with warty bumps on the bird's face or legs, or "wet," creating lesions in the mouth and airways.

299 PICK A BREED

When you're trying to decide which chicken breed to get, there are almost too many breeds to choose. Many homesteaders and survivalists have their own favorite chicken breeds, and arguments over the "best" breed are very common. Your first step in choosing is determine your needs. Are you going for meat chickens, egg production, or a bit of both?

MEAT CHICKEN FAVORITES For many backyard birders, there are Brahmas, Jersey Giants, Langshams, and Cochins. These are large birds that grow very quickly.

EGG PRODUCTION Leghorns and Australorp hens can top the list when it comes to egg production, laying up to 300 per year per bird! Plymouth Rocks and Rhode Island Reds are also very popular layers, though not as productive.

Each bird breed has a lot to offer, and there's nothing stopping you from getting some of each to diversify your resources.

300 DIG DOWN

Poor soils have met their match—deep-soil preparation! Proponents of this system claim that the technique dates back to antiquity, when early farmers noticed that plants grew very large when rooted in the loose soil of a landslide. This story may be more fairytale than fact, but the results are real enough. A century ago, the French intensive gardening method popularized deeply worked soil and in more recent times, garden guru John Jeavons has carried the torch to a new generation of green thumb hopefuls. It's a fair bit of manual labor, but the technique has proven its value, time and again. To do this deep soil prep, dig a one-foot-deep trench in your garden bed, moving the dirt out of the way. Chop or loosen the bottom of the trench another foot down. Dig an adjacent trench and dump the loosened dirt into the first trench. Repeat the process until the entire bed had been worked to a depth of two feet. Add the fertilizer of your choice, and let the roots go deep!

301 SOW RIGHT

Whether you're planning a survival garden on your skyscraper balcony or at your undisclosed bug-out location, don't just grab a bunch of pretty seed packets based on their attractive marketing. You've got to do your homework. One of the biggest considerations when buying the seeds to grow a self-reliant or survival garden is the caloric value of the plants. There simply aren't enough calories in leafy veggies alone. It is worth your effort to grow some greens, but your main focus should be the higher calorie vegetables such as root crops, dry beans, and fatty seeds like soybean and sunflower. Many companies sell "survival garden" seed assortments. But be warned before you purchase that prepackaged bucket of seeds. Are there enough high-calorie plants in there, and do those vegetable plants grow well in your area? You may be better prepared by selecting your own seeds for each plant type, and taking into account the soil, weather, pests, rain fall, and frost dates of your area.

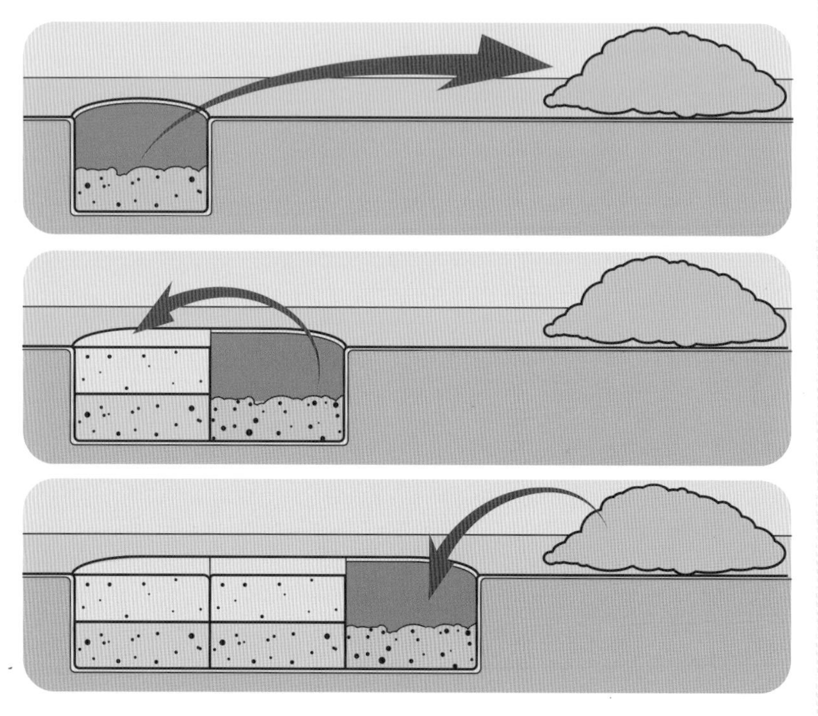

302 GROW IT ALL

Want to grow a fruit tree with vegetables on it? Many different garden plants, trees and shrubs can form a symbiotic relationship with each other, mirroring natural ecosystems by manner of skillful intercropping. A few years ago, I planted an apple tree in the north end of my garden (so that it wouldn't shade out any vegetables). After it had grown for a few years, I trained several cucumber vines to grow up into the young apple tree's branches. Not long after, I had beautiful straight green cucumbers hanging all over the lower branches, as if they belonged there. Then, a few months later, we picked our first few apples from the juvenile tree. This system of sturdy "trellis" trees and shrubs, planted with climbing fruits and vegetables, can be combined in countless ways. Grow green pole beans on into your cherry tree. Have grapes hanging from your pear tree. Train hops (for beer) to climb up a peach tree. It's all up to you.

303 GET YOUR GOAT

Goats are many things to many people, and they might become your favorite creature, once you understand that they can't resist head-butting you when you aren't looking. They can be a source of meat and dairy, and they can clear your land. Goats are relentless foragers and can eat almost any plant material, even woody vines and shrubs, if given enough time. This voracious nature, and their natural love of climbing, allows a herd of goats to become a land clearing machine. Rocky brushy terrain can't defeat a hungry goat army. One mouthful at a time, even plants that are troublesome for humans to handle (like poison ivy) go down the goat's throat to become nutrient rich goat droppings. Before you burn a brushy area, or worse, dump a bunch of poison on it, consider the goat as your partner in land reclamation. They're all too happy to help. And if you don't want to purchase your own herd, there are even companies that rent out herds of goats for land management.

304 MAKE COMPOST

You can make a mountain of free fertilizer by composting. Compost improves soil structure, provides nutrients to living plants, moderates pH and fertility problems, and stimulates beneficial organisms in the dirt. Since compost literally makes itself, all you have to do is pile up the right materials. Through the tireless toil of microorganisms, enzymes and fungi, organic matter turns into dark nutrient rich compost in as little as two weeks, under ideal conditions. For best results, you need carbon-rich to nitrogen-rich materials ratio to be approximately 25:1. High-carbon "brown" materials (like straw, wood chips, and dead leaves) and a lesser amount of high-nitrogen "green" materials (like grass clippings and kitchen scraps) can be blended and watered until they have the moisture content of a wrung-out sponge. Just mix the pile once a week to keep it oxygenated.

BUDGET SURVIVAL

DIY GREENHOUSE

For an earlier start and pest protection, build your own mini-greenhouse! Get some clear or milky plastic sheeting and several 10-foot (3-m) pieces of 3/4-inch- (2-cm-) diameter plastic PVC pipe. Over your planted garden bed, insert the ends of the pipes into the ground to make hoops, then cover them with your plastic. Shovel a good amount of dirt around the edge of the plastic to keep it in place, and leave a spot at the end that can be opened each morning, so the sun's heat doesn't cook your plants. Once you can handle regulating the heat in your greenhouse, you can use it to start your seedlings early to get a jump on spring or extend the growing season past frost!

Worth Every Penny

SOLAR POWERED FENCE

Whether you're on the grid or far away from it, a solar powered electric fence system can protect your livestock from many different predators—both day and night.

HACK HEROES 5-GALLON BUCKET

1 STORE DRY GOODS I use 5-gallon (20-L) buckets for storage of dry goods more than anything else. Either snap-on or screw-on lids are fine, provided the container is food-grade. Snap lids are fine for long-term storage, while the screw-on lids will allow you to open and close the bucket with ease. To store dry goods like white rice, flour, or beans, purchase large food-grade Mylar bags that will fit inside the bucket. Open the bag in the bucket, fill it with dry food, drop in 1500cc of oxygen absorber, and seal it up.

2 GROW FOOD ▲ You can turn a pair of buckets into a self-watering container—a great way to grow food in small spaces! Get two buckets, a small plastic takeout container, a tool to cut plastic, and a power drill with a pencil-diameter drill bit. Fit one bucket snugly inside the other, then cut a hole in the bottom of the inner bucket (just smaller than the little plastic container). Drill holes in the little container and the bottom of the inner bucket, and a small overflow hole in the outer bucket, just below the bottom of the inner bucket. Assemble the buckets by placing the takeout container in the outer bucket and sliding the inner bucket into place.

3 TRAP PESTS ▲ In a grid-down or disaster setting, you may need to kill rodents to prevent the spread of disease to humans. You'll just need a bucket with a few inches (10 cm) of water in the bottom, some bait, and a thin board, such as a paint stirring stick. Put the bucket next to something of the same height that the rodents can climb. Wipe a bit of bait (like peanut butter) on the wood and balance it on the bucket edge, resting partly on the object nearby. When the rodent "walks the plank," the stick will fall into the bucket—taking the rodent with it.

4 STORE WATER For quick storage and short term settings, just fill up your sparkling clean bucket from a bathtub or outdoor faucet, put the lid in place, and then use the water whenever you need it over the next week or so. For long term storage (months or years), fill a clean food-grade bucket with drinkable water and add unscented household bleach. Read the label to determine the strength of your bleach. If the level of sodium hypochlorite is 5-6%, add 40 drops (with an eye dropper) to your full bucket of water. If the bleach is stronger (many new formulas are 8%), only add 30 drops. Seal the lid on the bucket and store it in a cool dark place.

5 KILL A FIRE In the unlucky event that a small fire breaks out and emergency services can't respond, a group of people can take things into their own hands. Form an evenly spaced line from an open water source to the edge of the fire. Start filling buckets a little less than halfway, and pass them down the line to toss on the fire. Large, full buckets will be too heavy to carry quickly or throw. Have several quick people carrying empty buckets back to the water source for refilling.

6 RAISE CHICKENS ▼ Buckets can be turned into nesting boxes by laying them on their side and cutting away part of the side so each bucket is a little more open at the top. Secure these on a stand in your henhouse, fill them with straw, and watch the eggs pile up. You can also make an easy feeder with a bucket. Drill a few 1-inch (2.5-cm) holes in the side of the bucket, right at the bottom edge. Place the bucket in a large roasting pan to catch any spilled feed, fill the bucket with your favorite pelletized or crumbled bird feed, and add a lid; more feed will dispense as the chickens eat it.

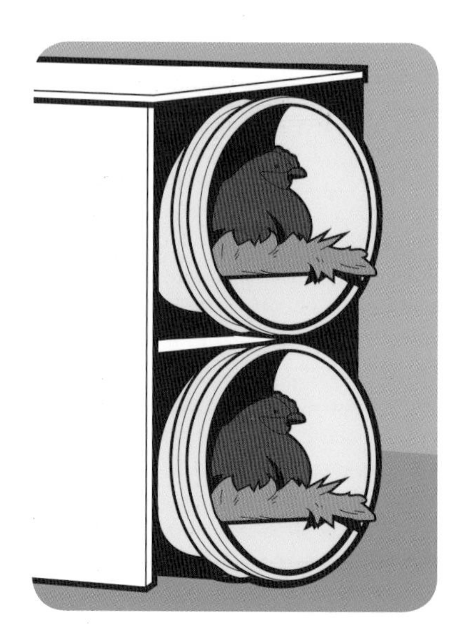

7 HAVE A WASH Ever noticed how black objects heat up in the sun? You can use this to your advantage in sunny weather to create warm water for washing, and you can even use the bucket itself as the wash basin. Grab a black plastic bucket and fill it almost to the top with water. Place it in a sunny location and wait; leave space at the top to add cool water to lower the temperature. Once it's ready, take a sponge bath, or wash clothes or dishes. For faster heating, grab a few household wall mirrors and prop them up to catch more sunlight and direct it toward the bucket. Just don't look into the mirrors or linger in their light.

8 BUILD A BOB ▲ Who says "bug out bags" have to be bags? Rugged and watertight, buckets can be loaded with food, clothing, and first aid and hygiene items. Each bucket could be a stand-alone survival kit, or your group could share items. For example, one person could have the emergency radio in their bucket while another person would have an ultralight tent. If you share items, make sure each bucket has the basics, including a flashlight with spare batteries, one or more space blankets, a rain poncho, a water vessel, water disinfection tablets, food, matches or a lighter, clothing, first aid supplies and signaling equipment.

305 BE READY

Wealth comes in more forms than just our bank statements. For most of us, our greatest wealth can be found in personal and business property—real estate. But our wealth can also be found in jewelry, vehicles, art, collectible items, gold, and of course, cash money. But what if hyperinflation stole the value of that cash? Or our stock market crashed as it did in the Great Depression? Certain items that are cheap now may be worth a king's ransom in that setting. If this scenario keeps you up at night, then consider diversifying your portfolio. Purchase long-lasting goods that will only grow in value. Things that would likely be popular include ammunition; dry goods and survival rations; liquor and other types of alcohol; tobacco; water disinfection equipment; vegetable seeds and garden tools; and useful books (such as this one).

306 BARTER BETTER

The barter system was our original ancient attempt at buying and selling, and it is still happening today through various web-based barter systems and networking organizations. You'd have to muddle through the same barter system problems that our ancestors faced, and all of this is assuming that everyone was playing nice and acting civil (which is a hell of a presupposition if we're talking about a financial collapse). Still, if a good trade works out correctly, each person walks away with something valuable and willingness to trade with that partner again, and the benefits may outweigh the risks.

CONSIDER THE BENEFITS Anything can be traded for anything, if both parties agree. A barter system works under any conditions, regardless of a failure of utilities or infrastructure. And, barter lets you trade different combinations of services, goods, and supplies for your needs.

PONDER THE PITFALLS It can be hard to determine fair trades, as supply and demand creates a heavy impact on barter situations. And some things are difficult or impossible to divide without losing value, i.e. one live chicken. Bartering requires both parties to have a desire for something the other party possesses. And the most haunting hazard is that you show others what you have when you try to barter, which could incite theft (or worse). Make sure your effort doesn't increase your problems.

HACK HAZARDS

HAGGLING

Haggling is an informal version of a business negotiation and it takes more than just charisma. First, you must be able to communicate with your potential trade partner and explain that it's in their best interest to make this trade. Second, you need to have a basis of value for your trade. Just because you really want or need something, doesn't mean you should "pay" whatever they are asking. Trades should leave each person walking away happy with the transaction. Finally, don't get emotional. If you are willing to walk away, then you are not too emotionally involved in the barter deal. This will keep the mood lighter and friendlier, which is the way you'd want it to be. With these ideas in place, you can make someone an offer, listen to their counter offer, then work back and forth until you come to an agreement. Don't be afraid to get creative.

Quick Tip

Skip the weird stuff. Nobody is going to want those sheets of copper wafers that you bought at a prepper expo, not when their family needs food or medicine. Pre-purchase goods that anyone would want.

307 STAY SHARP

Putting a keen edge back on your knife or axe is almost as important as having these tools in the first place. Follow these easy steps, and you'll be a sharpening whiz in no time.

STEP 1 Survey the damage and edge angle. Look for nicks in the edge, which take extra sharpening to remove. File away major damage.

STEP 2 Sharpen the edge on a sharpening stone using little circles, and count as you go, making the same number of strokes on each side of the blade—first medium, then fine.

STEP 3 Strop the blade against a leather belt several times to remove burs and polish the edge. Oil the metal if you plan to use it in a wet environment.

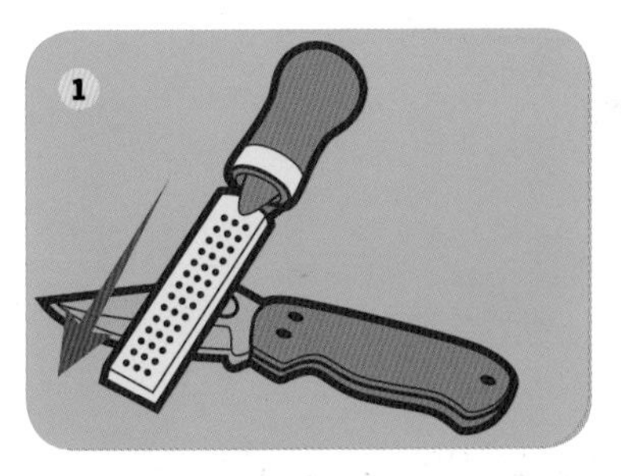

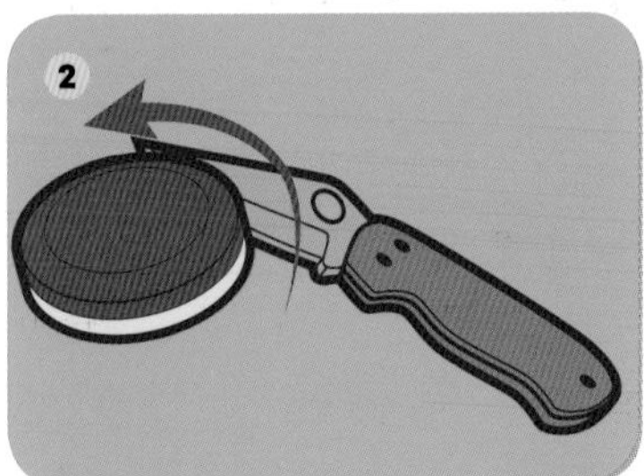

308 MAINTAIN YOUR GRIP

Tools with wooden handles, particularly axes, often take a beating. Heavy use can loosen the handle and damage the wood surface. One trick to help loose handles is a soaking in anti-freeze. Pour some in a bucket (away from pets—it's toxic) and submerge the tool head in the fluid. Leave it for a few days, and the wood will swell inside the tool and stay swollen for some time. Wipe off the excess fluid and get back to work! If an axe head becomes loose, you can try adjusting the wedges that hold it in place, but your best choice is to remove the wedge, and rework or replace the handle. For beat-up axe handles, you can clean and smooth them with a quick scouring of steel wool or fine-grit sand paper. The handle's useful life can be extended with an occasional wipe of linseed oil—just make sure you use boiled linseed oil. Raw linseed oil leaves a sticky residue that will not dry. A final handle chore involves the hafting.

309 TOUGHEN UP

It's easy for tools that have been heated to lose their hardness. When this happens on purpose, it is called tempering. It's commonly done in tool production to make a tool less brittle, but the drawback is that the tool is now softer. If you accidentally heated a tool enough to make it soft (easily dented and won't hold an edge), you can harden it again with a cycle of heating and cooling.

STEP 1 Strip down the tool by removing all burnable or non-hardening components.

STEP 2 In a forge or a campfire superheated with forced air, heat the metal until it glows orange. They'll actually become non-magnetic at these temperatures, and you can check that with a magnet on a metal rod.

STEP 3 Once your tool is hot enough, grab it with long handled tongs or pliers, held by a leather-gloved hand. Quickly submerge the tool in a metal bucket of oil, keeping your face back in case it flames up. Leave it in the oil for 30 seconds to harden.

310 USE FIRE AS A TOOL

If fire isn't one of your best tools in the wilderness, then it should be. A campfire can generate heat, boil water, and summon rescue, among many other things. Fire has the amazing ability to consume materials, and modify them too. Heat bending is very useful in bow making, especially when making recurves. For example, the heat of a fire can straighten a crooked stick, or bend a straight one. The moisture in a green wood stick, or a dry wood plank that has been soaked in water for a few days, causes the wood to become flexible after "cooking" over a fire. To do this, simply rotate the moist wood item over the fire and begin to bend it gently. The wood should begin to feel rubbery when it is heated enough. But be careful not to blacken or scorch the wood, as this will weaken the wood. Bend the wood a little beyond the point you are trying to achieve, and then hold it in that position until it has thoroughly cooled. If the bend will not stay, reheat and keep working the wood.

HACKS THROUGH HISTORY // HANGING A HEAD

With axes and sledgehammers, you'll eventually break the head off. To old-timers, the only right way to replace a handle is by "hanging" a head.

STEP 1 Clean the hole in the tool head, filing off any rough edges. Place the head near a fire while working on the handle. Heat it until it's hot to the touch, but not burning your hands.

STEP 2 Sand the end of the new handle to a very snug fit in the very warm head.

STEP 2 Hand fit the tool head on the handle, so it barely sticks on there. Hold the end of the new handle, with the barely-stuck-on tool head dangling near the ground, but not touching anything.

STEP 3 Tap the free end of the handle with a hammer, and prepare to be startled by physics: Because of the mass, the tool head tends to hang in mid-air as the wooden handle drives down into it. You'd expect the head to fall off, but it creeps up the handle a little further with each blow; hammer away until it emerges from the other side of the tool head. Drive a wedge to lock the handle in place. It's best to do this while the tool head is hot, as the metal is expanded. When it cools and shrinks, the head is even more secure.

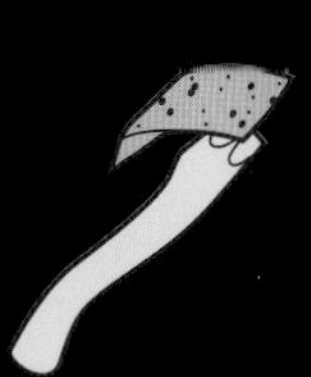

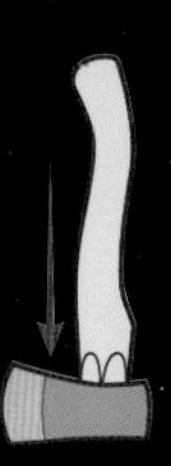

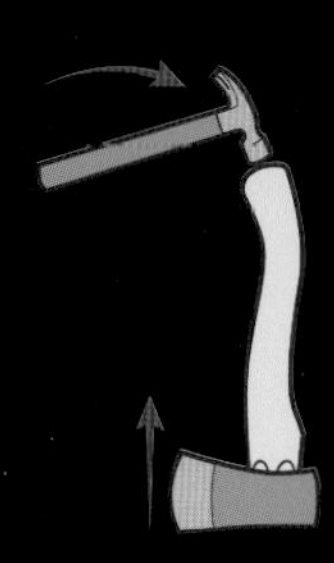

311 KNOW THE RANGE

Growing your own vegetables can be a big part of self-reliance—and the ultimate way to have a sustainable survival garden is to save your own vegetable seeds from one year to the next. This is best done when you are growing single varieties of each vegetable, to avoid the unpredictable results of cross-pollination. Let the veggies mature completely, remove the seeds, and follow the rules in this section. Two biggest players in successful storage are temperature and humidity in your storage space. An easy rule of thumb is to add the storage temperature number (in Fahrenheit) to the humidity percentage number. For example, 60 °F (18 °C)and 30 percent humidity gives you 90 points. The total of these two numbers should always be below 100 points. Lean toward the dry side in storage, and your seeds will sleep happily for years; just follow the remaining steps.

312 PICK A WINNER

If you're just starting out with seed saving, it's important to know that all seeds don't store equally. Some plants produce seeds with a very high germination rate. Other plants have seeds that almost never sprout, even under ideal germination conditions. Avoid beginner's disappointment by focusing on the easy seeds to store and replant, while skipping the seeds that are difficult to grow. Parsnips, parsley, celery, okra, New Zealand spinach, and Swiss chard regularly have low germination rates and may not be worth the bother of trying to save them. But if you do decide to save these seeds—save extra amounts of them. This will make up for the ones that don't sprout. And if you really want to make it easy on yourself, save the seeds of plants that have a high germination rate. Cucumber, squash relatives, lettuce, beans, peas, corn, and melons are very forgiving seeds to save.

313 USE THE STEPS

Since food acquisition is one of the never-ending chores in long term survival, you'll want to get every step right in this disaster preparedness strategy.

STAY DRY Seeds will go bad if they become damp. Use a watertight container and some desiccant packs to soak up the stray moisture in the seeds and packaging. Don't put oxygen absorber packs in with seeds. Each seed is a dormant living plant, and they need a little oxygen to live.

KEEP YOUR COOL Someplace cool is an ideal place to store your seeds for the long haul. Many folks use their refrigerator for this task.

GO DARK Some seeds are light sensitive, and will not last as long if they are exposed to bright light. Most storage methods for "dry and cool" will also keep them dark, but just to make sure, consider a container that will eliminate light as well as moisture.

314 FERMENT YOUR SEEDS

Dry processing is one of the most common and simple ways to prepare seeds for storage. Wet processing (fermentation) is another option for certain vegetable seeds. For vegetable seeds that are dry when fully formed (like beans, peas, the carrot family, okra, the cabbage family, grains and several others), the dry process is already done for you. Pull loose seeds right off the plant, or remove the seeds that are contained in pods, and store them for next year. Easy! For seeds that are inside a wet fruit (like tomatoes), the wet process can be a better choice. Harvest your tomatoes when they are fully ripe. Crush them in a container with a loose fitting lid. Let your mashed tomatoes mess sit at room temperature to ferment for about a few days, until bubbles stop forming. Scoop out the tomato chunks and add water. Bad seeds will float, good ones will sink. Rinse the good seeds in more water, spread them out in a thin layer to dry for 3 weeks.

315 GROW FOR CALORIES

What should you grow? If it's a survival garden you have in mind, the biggest thing to consider when buying seeds is the caloric value of the food. You can't live on salad. There simply aren't enough calories in leafy veggies to sustain a human, and the really tasty stuff isn't the answer either. Tomatoes, peppers, and similar flavorful plants are disturbingly low in calories. Instead of saving seeds for a bunch of space hogging low-cal crops, try these instead.

TRY OUT TUBERS Many root vegetables are high in carbohydrates and calories, especially rutabaga, turnips, potatoes, and sweet potatoes. Don't get too invested in carrots, though, as they're among the lowest in caloric value (not only that, but overeating carrots can lead to unhealthy amounts of Vitamin A, also known as Carotene).

LIVE ON LEGUMES Lentils, beans, peas, and more are all legumes, a variety of food packed with protein and carbohydrates. Soybeans, navy, kidney, lima, and fava beans are all counted among them, along with plenty of dry-shelling beans, black-eyed peas, and even peanuts—a food which can amount to 1,200 calories per cup (240 mL).

SUBSIST WITH SUNFLOWERS Fast-growing and easy to sprout by sowing (a couple of weeks after frost has ended), sunflowers provide Vitamins E and B1 along with many other nutrients, and can provide up 800 calories in a cup.

BUDGET SURVIVAL

SEED CONTAINERS

You don't need to buy specialized seed containers to store your treasured heirloom garden seeds. Any old bottle will do, as long as it's relatively airtight. For years, our family has used old pill bottles and medicine containers for seed storage; and there's nothing wrong with zip-top bags either. Just use a permanent marker to make sure each one is clearly labeled with the vegetable type, variety, and year it was collected. Seal up your favorite varieties of tasty vegetables and keep the containers in a seed friendly environment. Check them periodically to ensure that they are staying cool and dry, and they will sleep happily until they are needed again.

Worth Every Penny

DESICCANT PACKS

These are different from oxygen absorber packs, as these only pull moisture from the air. Repurpose the silica gel packs that come in shoe boxes and electronics, or buy new ones.

316 CONCEAL CROPS

When times get tough, even the best among us will resort to thievery to feed ourselves and our loved ones. Rather than growing a bunch of tomatoes, corn, or any other easily identifiable vegetables right in your front yard, consider growing some crops in ways that won't even look like food to the casual passerby.

HIDE IN THE OPEN One of the most effective methods of hiding a survival garden in a suburban or urban backyard is to avoid obvious food crops—and avoid planting them in a traditional garden plot. Plant your crops in flower beds, containers, and other places throughout your property so they look like ornamental plantings, rather than garden beds.

AVOID ORDERLY PLANTING Make it look random and weedy for the best camouflage. You can even scatter them on property edges so they blend in with the local weeds and brush. An added benefit to this dispersed planting strategy: The plant scent is dispersed, making it even harder for pests and thieves to find.

317 SURVIVE BY VEGGIES

Sure, tomatoes, peppers, and sweet corn taste great, but they are all low in calories and are obviously food to anyone wandering by. In a time of crisis, it would be easy for almost anyone to justify stealing the fruits of your hard labor. One great solution is to grow a secret garden of root crops. Only a savvy gardener will know what these plants look like above ground, and root crops are a relatively high calorie food that can be stored in the ground where it grew. This is a great benefit, if you feel that break-ins, robberies, and home looting are likely in your area during an emergency, as your food will be safely hidden in the ground, scattered across your property. Plant these hidden crops in places with at least 8 hours of uninterrupted sunlight each day. Water the veggies regularly if rain is scarce, and monitor them for pests.

White potatoes and sweet potatoes offer decent calories in a very filling form. Start planting your potato slips in mid-spring, once the last frost is gone. While the foliage of white potatoes is toxic to humans, the greens from sweet potatoes can be cooked and eaten.

PLANT PEANUTS In warm climates with sandy soil, the peanut is your best friend! These aren't actually "nuts" growing at the top of the plant, they're hidden underground.

GROW TURNIPS Rutabagas and their cousins the turnips are great root crops for cooler climates. But make sure you dig them before they become tough and woody.

CULTIVATE PARSNIPS Although the seeds usually have a very poor germination rate, parsnips can grow large and turn sweet after a frost. Just plant extra seeds to make up for their poor performance.

ADD COLOR Carrots and radishes are colorful root vegetables, and despite their lower calorie value, they can be good for variety. They are also quicker growing than other roots.

CHOOSE A CHOKE Also called sun chokes, the Jerusalem artichoke looks like a tall ornamental flower, though it has many edible tubers underground.

HACK HAZARDS

EAT YOUR WEEDS

Many common garden weeds can be eaten by humans, if they happen to be wild edible plants. Chickweed, purslane, lamb's quarters, dandelion, curly dock, amaranth, plantain, wild onion, and many other wild edibles pop up in my garden beds throughout the growing season each year. The weeds listed here have parts that are edible raw or cooked, and each one is packed with nutrition. When appropriately prepared, many can even be delicious. Dandelion flowers that are battered and deep-fried are one of my favorite wild treats, and they are loaded with vitamin A. Chickweed and purslane are excellent in salads and full of important minerals. You might start to wonder, why you're not just growing weeds since they are so wholesome and prolific. And once you learn to positively identify these persistent weeds, you'll see them throughout the year in your garden.

Quick Tip

Don't throw away that wrinkly old sack of potatoes! If they haven't started sprouting, they soon will. Once your spuds have sprouts growing from them, they can be cut up and planted to make a bounty of potatoes.

318 DRY FOODS

Electric-powered home dehydrators are an excellent way to preserve many foods, while cutting down on their weight and volume. But these units may be an expense that some cannot afford. Solar drying boxes are an electricity-free option, but these are very expensive to purchase and costly to build from scratch (unless you have scrap lumber and spare screen material lying around). The least expensive modern option is to make your own dehydrator from something that you probably already have: window screens. You can pop the plastic screens off your home windows, set them up on a few cinder blocks to get air flow underneath, and dehydrate many types of fruit and vegetables in dry, sunny weather. Just avoid galvanized wire and other metal wire screens, as these can leach into your food, creating "off" flavors and potentially introducing toxins (especially from the galvanized screens). Dry the thin-sliced food in the sun for a day or more, until it doesn't seem to change anymore. Store these dried plant foods in a place where they will stay dry, but also have some ventilation. You don't want them to sweat and mold in storage. For longest lifespan, don't toss them into a glass jar or plastic bag. Instead, place them in a cloth or paper sack.

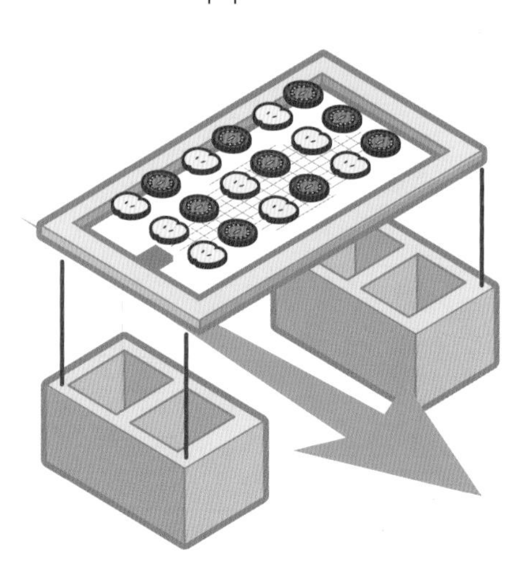

319 BRINE A PICKLE

A salty, vinegary brine can be a quick and easy way to increase the storage life of fresh vegetables. It also provides a lot of flavor to vegetables that could otherwise be considered bland. To make a simple brine, blend 1 quart (1 L) each of water and distilled vinegar together in an enameled or stainless steel pot. Bring this to a boil, then add salt or sugar to suit your taste. (I use both, but more sugar than salt.) Let the brine cool to room temperature before adding your food to it. Many vegetables can be stored by submerging them in the brine. Spices could be added as well—I am very fond of ginger, garlic, and dried red peppers in my brine. Your home-grown cucumbers become crunchy pickles this way, and wild edible greens take on a whole new flavor; fresh chickweed leaves and stems are my favorite wild veggie in this brine solution.

320 SMOKE YOUR FISH

Our ancestors only had access to smoking, drying, and brining techniques to preserve their meat and fish, and honestly, I am glad that's all they had. This gave them the opportunity to perfect these methods. There are two traditional ways to smoke fish: the hot smoking process and a cold smoking process. These can be done with the same food and the same apparatus; the big difference is the heat.

GET HOT The hot smoking technique involves a closed box to hold in the smoke and the heat from your smoke-producing materials. The fish is cooked by this heat, and permeated with a smoky flavor. Fish prepared in this manner can last for several days, up to a week, at room temperature.

GO COLD Cold smoking is done at cooler temperatures, for a longer period time. The goal in this method is long-term fish storage, which requires more of a drying process than a cooking process. Temperatures under 100° F (38° C) are ideal.

321 MAKIN' BACON

Anyone can make homemade bacon! Just gather these simple ingredients. Get 3 pounds of thick, skinless pork belly; 1/2 cup white sugar; 1 tablespoon maple syrup; 2 tablespoons coarse salt; 1 teaspoon curing salt; a 2 gallon sized freezer storage bag and some coarse crushed black pepper (to coat the bacon). Mix the wet and dry ingredients (except for the pepper) until well blended. Place the meat and the mix into the freezer bag, and massage the contents around until you have coated the pork evenly. Place the bag in the fridge, and massage the pork once daily, for the next 7 days. After a week, check the meat for soft spots. When fully cured, it will be firm to the touch everywhere. Add another sprinkle of salt and wait a few more days, if soft. Once cured, rinse and dry the meat, coat it in crushed pepper, and smoke it for the signature smoked flavor. Make sure it reaches 150°F for safety. Slice it into strips, and your bacon is complete.

HACKS THROUGH HISTORY // SAUERKRAUT

Cabbage is one of the most popular fermented vegetables in the world, often transformed into sauerkraut and kimchee. Sure, fermenting can smell pretty rank a few days into the process, but just wait, and it will soon smell "right." Cabbage naturally has the organisms on it to ferment, and these steps are all it takes.

STEP 1 Get a glazed crock or a large glass jar to use as your fermenting vessel, and pick up a package of salt without iodide. Natural sea salt or kosher salt are fine choices. Iodide can prevent fermentation, so regular table salt is not recommended for kraut making or other food fermentation.

STEP 2 Chop up your cabbage into small pieces or shred it into strips. Rinse it, then drain it for 5 minutes.

STEP 3 Place enough cabbage in the vessel to cover the bottom and sprinkle on a few grams of salt. Then use a wooden spoon, potato masher, or kraut stomper to mash the salt into the cabbage leaves for one minute. Add more layers of cabbage to the vessel, along with more salt, and repeat this stomping process. Do this until the container is full or you run out of cabbage.

STEP 4 Cover the cabbage with a weight that will keep the cabbage submerged in the liquid. Allow the 'kraut to naturally ferment for a week or two, scooping off the scum that forms periodically, then you can start eating it. Keep the container in a cool place, such as a basement.

322 LEARN TO BREW

Breweries and wineries are often large businesses, full of specialized machinery and huge vessels for fermentation. Touring these places can be very intimidating to someone who wants to start making wine and beer, but don't worry! Home brewing is easier than you think. In the simplest terms, brewing happens when you add live yeast cells to a sugar-water solution. The hungry little yeasts are going to gobble up most of the sugar, reproducing prolifically along the way. This booming population of fungal organisms will spend their days floating around in the sweet liquid you have provided. As they consume the sugar, they produce carbon dioxide and alcohol. This is the process of fermentation, which will last about a month. During this time, you'll want to have a special airlock cap in place to let the CO_2 bubble out of the container while keeping oxygen from entering the brewing jug. If all goes right, the yeast will drop to the bottom and your sugar water will transform into alcohol.

323 STEP IT UP

It's fun (and tasty) to make your own hard cider from apples and other fruits. You'll just need to buy or borrow a cider press, or get creative and make one.

STEP 1 Squeeze the chopped and mashed fruit in the press to extract the sugar-rich juice; you can feed the solids to your livestock if you have any. Pour your juice into a large enamel or stainless pot.

STEP 2 Heat the juice to boiling for 30 minutes to kill any stray wild yeast or bacteria, then let it cool to room temperature.

STEP 3 Add a packet of cider yeast or wine yeast to the cool juice, and stir with a sanitized spoon. Pour the juice into a large sanitized glass jug. Add a water-filled airlock on top.

STEP 4 Let it bubble for 45 days, then pour the cider off the top (leaving the sediment) and enjoy the fruits of your labor: a tasty adult beverage you made for yourself!

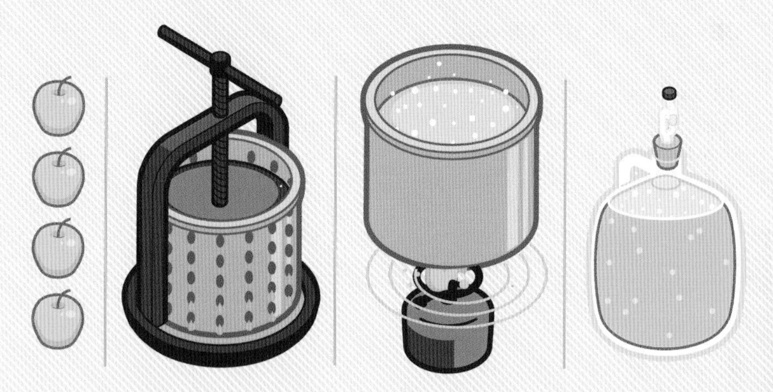

324 LOCK IT DOWN

Airlocks are a necessary cap on any fermentation jug or vessel. Store-bought versions commonly feature an S-shaped water trap, just like you have under your sink. The CO_2-rich air can bubble out through the water in the lock, but the oxygen-rich air can't get back inside (to sour your brew). I also like to use a vinyl tube going into a glass of water for an airlock when brewing foamy beer. The foam would push the water out of a normal airlock, but dissolves into the glass of water instead. You can even use a balloon with a pinhole pierced into it for an air lock. Stretch the mouth of the balloon over the jug opening and secure it with a few rubber bands. As the CO_2 builds inside the balloon, it swells up. Once enough pressure is achieved, the pinhole will allow some of it to hiss out. Once the pressure drops again, the hole closes. Again, just make sure you have secured the balloon so it cannot pop off the top, exposing and spoiling your fermenting brew.

325 EMBRACE OPTIONS

There are so many options when it comes to brewing recipes, equipment, and useful supplies that anybody should be able to throw a brewing kit together.

COLLECT YOUR SUPPLIES You'll need a 1-gallon (4-L) glass jug, yeast, a sugar source (such as honey, malt, table sugar, or molasses), clean water, and a wine lock cap for the jug. One other item of note is a sanitizer; a quick fix is cheap vodka. The wine lock is the only part that may need to be improvised (if you don't pick one up where you buy your yeast).

BE SWEET To brew beer that tastes like beer, you'll need malt. This can be found as a canned product with hops already added or as a powdered extract. For old school brewing, sprout some barley, then toast and grind it. Simmer the ground grain in water for an hour, and filter out the malt-rich water, which then boils with the hops for another hour. If you're making wine, you can use a mix of fruit and table sugar. For mead, all you need is honey and water (plus wine yeast).

GET CARBONATED To make your beer bubble or your champagne fizz, you will need to carbonate it after fermentation. This can be done by adding more sugar to the brew and sealing it in a pressure-safe vessel. The dormant yeast will wake up to produce a little more CO_2, carbonating the beverage. Add an ounce (28 g) of table sugar or corn sugar to each gallon of brew, and seal it in bottles. Clean soda bottles and self-capping ones will work fine. Let it sit for one week, then chill and enjoy.

326 BE FRUGAL

"Waste not, want not"—this little saying from the 1700s essentially means that if you do not waste anything, you will always have enough. Being frugal can be tricky, but there are some easy ways to save money, time, and resources when you brew. For example, you could sprout your own barley and other grains to create homemade malt. This building block for beer is cheap, and once you've pulled the sugar out for brewing, you can feed the leftover grain to your livestock. And let's say you didn't have enough fruit or berry juice to do an all-juice batch of wine. Don't worry; you can use table sugar to make your wine stronger. Mix two pounds (1 kg) each of sugar and fruit juice with enough water to make one gallon (4 L) of wine. But what if you run out of yeast packets? Most stores don't carry wine and beer yeast, just bread yeast (which doesn't produce as much alcohol). But fruit skins carry yeast, and we can just toss a few chalky-looking raw fruits into the cooled-down batch of boiled brew to provide some wild yeast. It's a gamble to the risk the flavor this way, as certain strains can produce some strange flavors; the wrong one can leave your brew tasting like Band-Aids. On the other hand, your concoction might taste like butterscotch with the right strain.

327 BUILD A STILL

Stills aren't just for moonshine, though they can make that too. They can also be used to purify water, distill essential oils, and even make fuel! If you're good at metal work and soldering, you can make a full-sized traditional still for many different applications.

GET A KETTLE First, build or improvise your kettle. This is the big pot (typically copper) that holds your undistilled material, and it's where the heat will be.

FIRE UP Your kettle could be heated by wood fire, propane burners, even solar power if you are particularly creative.

KEEP YOUR HEAD Atop the kettle, you'll have your still head. This is tightly fitted so that no vapor can escape, and it is tapered to connect the kettle to the condensation coil (worm).

STAY SEALED If the still isn't portable, all of the metal joints can be soldered to make them airtight. Otherwise, they can be caulked with a flour-and-water paste.

COOL AND COLLECT From the still head, the worm then spirals down into a container of cold water, where the vapor is then condensed into a liquid. Whatever you are distilling is collected at the end of that line.

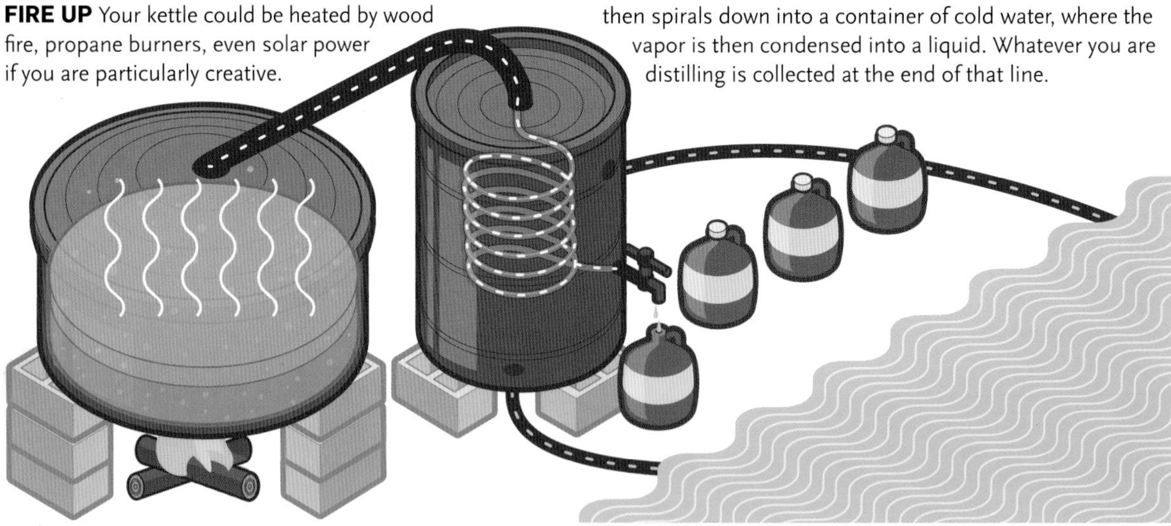

328 CONVERT A CANNER

You can make a small water purification still from a pressure canner and 4 feet (1.3m) of ¼-inch (6-mm) copper line. Set up your canner pot on your stove top, over a camping stove or over an improvised cinder block fireplace outdoors. Fill your canner pot two-thirds with questionable water and screw on the canner lid. This can be salt water, muddy water—virtually any water except that tainted by fuels (which evaporate at low temps). Make the coil, also known as the "worm" from the copper line coiled in a downward spiral. Use a stick or some other support for the coil, to avoid stress on the joint at the canner's steam vent. Ream out one end of the copper tubing and force it down over the steam fitting on top of the canner lid if it's smaller than the steam vent. Compress the line if it is bigger than the vent. Adjust the heat for best results. It you run it too hot, you'll just blow steam out the coil; too cool, and nothing will happen. If just right, the surrounding air will naturally cool the copper and condense steam into distilled water.

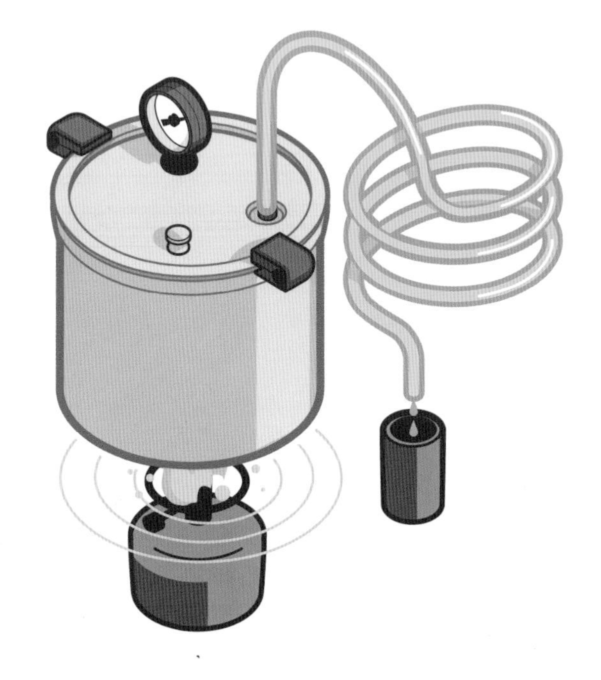

329 DISTILL OILS

Ever wonder where essential oils come from? Producers use a still to make these medicinal and healthful oils. But please note: Once you've used a still for this, you don't want to use it for anything else (unless your rosemary-infused moonshine becomes the next hipster trend). Here's the process: Add fresh plant material, and enough water to cover it, to your still kettle. (It's best if it's packed tight.) Add the still head and connect the condensation coil. Turn on your heat source, and then the cooling water, once the coil has started to warm. When liquid starts to trickle from the coil, adjust the cooling water flow to keep the distillate lukewarm. When you have distilled about 80% of the liquid that you used in the still, turn off the heat. Let your watery distillate sit for several hours, so the oil can separate. Nearly all oils are lighter than water and will float. Skim the oil off the top when the water has cleared, and bottle your essential oils in small, well-labeled, dark glass containers.

330 ICE YOUR DRINK

Most of the methods that separate alcohol from water involve heat, but there is one curious method better suited for the cold. It's called freeze distillation, and it works in the exact way you'd imagine: Chill your alcoholic liquid so far below freezing that the water in it begins to freeze into ice crystals (despite the antifreeze qualities of the blended alcohol). Pour the icy slush through a fine strainer and the liquid alcohol will run right through (while the water ice gets caught in the strainer). This isn't a perfect system, as plenty of alcohol gets caught in the ice. But it does represent a very different approach—one that requires a lot less equipment! If you're on the grid or you have your own power supply, you can even do this trick outside of winter, set your bucket of hooch in a deep freezer for several hours, then strain.

331 CATCH THE STEAM

What if you don't have any metal to work with, or the tools to work metal? There's a very primitive method to distill water and other non-flammable liquids, and all it requires is a wide boiling vessel, a heat source and an absorbent piece of cloth just a little larger than boiling vessel. Start by heating up your water to boiling, and while that takes place, pierce two small holes on each side of the cloth. Tie a short length of cord on each side of the cloth, so they can act like handles. Pull the cloth tight over the vessel and steam will begin to collect in the cloth. Once saturated, move the hot wet cloth through the air to cool it, and wring it out into a clean container. Repeat until you have enough water. This method is slow and likely to burn your fingers a little, but it will separate mud, salt, mercury, lead, and many other chemicals and compounds; it will even separate radioactive fallout.

BUDGET SURVIVAL

HYDROMETER

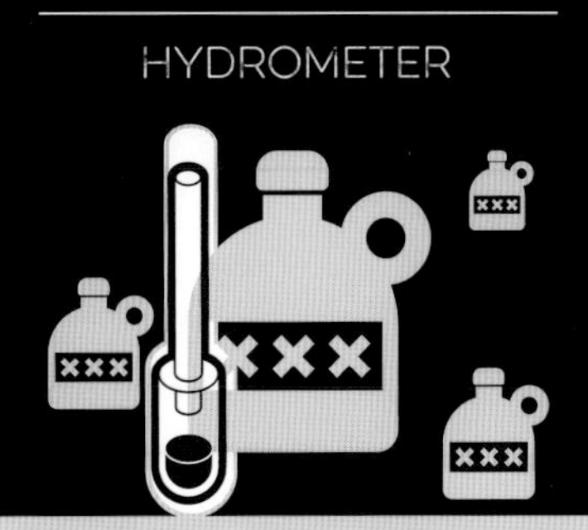

The modern distiller has an easier (and safer) time measuring the "proof" of their alcohol then our predecessors who proofed with gunpowder. A small glass float called a hydrometer can be dropped into a tall cylinder of alcohol, and it will settle at different depths for higher- or lower-proof hooch. The float has a scale inside its clear glass body that can give you the exact percentage of alcohol by volume. This strange tool works best with a tall and slender cylinder to hold the liquid. And it works even better if your brew temperature is exactly 60 °F (18 °C). Most of these floats are based on that heat level, although you can correct your reading with a little math or a hydrometer chart.

Worth Every Penny

COPPER TUBING

Copper is a little expensive, but it's still the perfect metal to build a still. It's malleable without being flimsy; easy to cut and solder back together; and it doesn't add off flavors.

HACK HEROES | COTTON BALLS

1 CREATE TINDER ▲ Typically used in the home to remove makeup and nail polish, these fluffy little bundles of cotton fiber can perform many tasks in a survival situation. The thing I use them for the most is tinder. Dry cotton balls right out of the bag can be torn apart a little and used as tinder for ferrocerium rods and any other ignition source. These don't last long when dry, but if you add an additional fuel, you may get a four or five minute burn. This extra fuel could be petroleum jelly, cooking oil, melted wax, bacon fat, or some other oily or waxy substance.

2 APPLY YOUR MEDS Cotton balls are great at soaking up blood, but they can also dispense liquids. Load a cotton ball up with a needed medicinal liquid and strap it over the affected spot with a band aid or gauze for a long slow delivery of medicinal goodness. This is a great way to deliver tannic acid to an ingrown toenail or boil. It's also handy when keeping medicines on rashes and infections. Add a few drops of clove oil to a small piece of cotton and place it in a dental cavity, or next to your gum line for a toothache. You can also use a mass of wet cotton balls in a plastic bag to create a cooling compress after exposing the bag to the cold.

3 MAKE A TORCH ▼ Ever wonder how they make those cool torches you see in movies? This isn't it, but it works just the same. Cut a 3-foot (1-m) stick from live green wood (since it won't light on fire itself), ideally with a fork at the end. Use a bit of thin wire to wind a fistful of cotton balls onto the forked end of the stick. Spread them around and secure them tightly, so that the wad of white fiber looks like a giant Q-tip. Soak the cotton head in cooking oil for 30 seconds, allow it to drain for the same amount of time, and then light it with an open flame. The torch will begin to burn, and you'll have enough light to read in the dark.

4 FILTER WATER Getting sediment or debris out of your water can make a big difference in water disinfection. Particulates will mercilessly clog commercially available water filters and absorb disinfection chemicals before they can do their job, leaving the water unsafe to drink. Thankfully, cotton balls can come to the rescue here. Cut the bottom out of a small water bottle and take the cap off. Pack the cavity with cotton balls, and pour your dirty water in the larger end. The cotton fibers will grab some of the filth, and cleaner water will emerge from the other side, although it will not be as safe to drink as more properly filtered water.

5 HOLD A SCENT ▶ Scent can be a powerful tool in nature, and can lure or repel. You could drip bug-repelling oils into some cotton balls and hang them around your vegetable plants with small paper clips. You could add an enticing scent to cotton balls and use them to lure game animals into a trap. You can even affix them to your electric fence and drip vanilla extract on them. When deer and other garden destroyers come to sniff the interesting aroma, they get zapped right on the nose by the fence wire. However you use cotton balls to hold and convey scent, keep in mind that scent wears off, and you'll need to reapply after a rain, or every few days in drier weather.

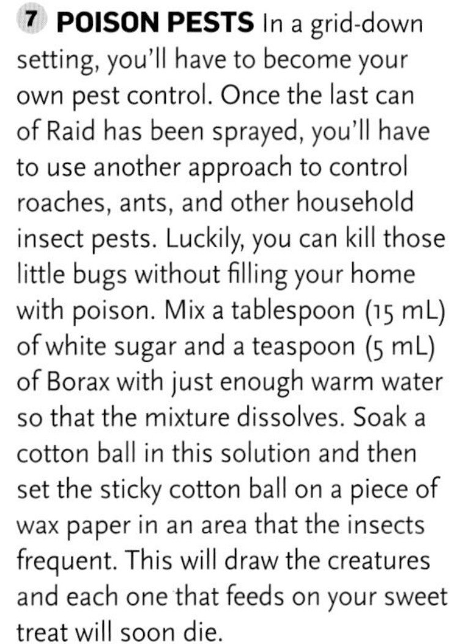

7 POISON PESTS In a grid-down setting, you'll have to become your own pest control. Once the last can of Raid has been sprayed, you'll have to use another approach to control roaches, ants, and other household insect pests. Luckily, you can kill those little bugs without filling your home with poison. Mix a tablespoon (15 mL) of white sugar and a teaspoon (5 mL) of Borax with just enough warm water so that the mixture dissolves. Soak a cotton ball in this solution and then set the sticky cotton ball on a piece of wax paper in an area that the insects frequent. This will draw the creatures and each one that feeds on your sweet treat will soon die.

6 BUILD BLOW DARTS ▼ The darts for your blowgun can be made from a variety of materials; hardwoods are best for the shafts, but whatever shaft type you choose, you'll need a fletching at the end. This stabilizes the darts' flight, and acts as a gasket to make a seal for air to propel the dart. Thistledown and rabbit fur are traditional choices, but cotton balls work too. Using a floss-diameter thread, you'll tie a knot around your dart about 2 inches (5 cm) from the end of the shaft. Begin spinning the dart and stuffing shredded cotton ball material under the thread wrappings, then tie or glue the end. There is a lot of technique involved in this skill, so be patient.

8 FORM A WICK The fluffy off-white seed down from cattail plants was once used a lamp wick material by a cave-dwelling remote ancestors. We can borrow this idea and use a more contemporary material: the cotton ball. In a dish of oil (edible or not), place one or more cotton balls so that they are partially submerged in the oil. Light the top of the greasy cotton ball with an open flame and it will begin to burn like a candle wick. Going a step further, you can roll and twist a cotton ball until it becomes elongated and resembles a fat piece of cordage material. Use this as an oil-lamp wick or in a container of melted lard.

332 SMITH SAFELY

Blacksmithing is an amazing skillset that uses heat and tools to hammer, bend, cut, and shape metals like iron and steel—an activity inherently dangerous to many parts of your body! Your lungs, skin, eyes, and ear drums (and more) are at risk. Use all due caution, always wear protective gear, and work in a well-ventilated area. Making cool things out of metal isn't worth permanent bodily harm.

ARMOR UP Burns are inevitable, so wear leather boots, leather gloves, and a leather apron while you're working. You'll also need to wear cotton, wool, or other natural-fiber clothing under your protective gear (synthetics are too flammable). Wear eye protection and ear protection too.

BREATHE SAFELY Inhaling coal smoke has been proven to be dangerous. Worse yet, fumes from galvanized and zinc-coated metals are very toxic, even lethal, and they can contaminate your equipment, so be very careful if you decide to work unknown scrap metal.

333 GATHER TOOLS

Before you build a forge, you'll need to assemble the tools and materials you'll use. For simple projects, ordinary mild steel is a very forgiving material to work. It's available at most home-improvement stores in the form of round rods, square stock, and flat bars. Ordinary hammers and pliers can be used instead of expensive and specialized blacksmith hammers and tongs. The gloves and leather aprons used by welders are affordable protective equipment. The anvil, however, takes some work to find or improvise. Old anvils (and new ones) are in high demand these days, as popular television shows have put smithing in the public eye. You can use a chunk of railroad track if you know someone in the industry who can get you a scrap piece. A short section of I-beam can work, if you know someone in the steel-building arena. You might even find a real anvil at a scrap yard. Whatever you get, just make sure it sits securely on a stump or base, with no danger of falling over.

334 BUILD YOUR FORGE

You can have all the hammers, anvils, and steel in the world, but they won't do you any good without a forge. Many people make forges from vehicle brake drums by brazing some legs onto the sides, adding an old hand crank forge blower. But if you can't score these junkyard treasures, you can make a forge with the materials you have at hand. Grab a small hamburger grill and some local rocks that you have tested to be fire-safe. (Get these rocks from a dry location, and test them in a campfire from a distance to make sure they don't explode. Never use rocks collected by a waterway.) As for your forge blower, an ordinary hair dryer works great; it even has variable speeds! Tape the hair dryer to a steel pipe butted up against the air intake at the bottom of the grill. Line the grill with stones, fill it with charcoal, and light it up. Turn on the hair drier and start forging!

335 HAMMER A HOOK

Metal hooks are a handy fixture of camp life, and learning how to make them is a great way to learn blacksmithing. You can choose to make hooks from thicker or thinner material. The smaller stock has the benefit of heating up quickly, however, it also cools down quickly. Larger stock such as 1/2, 5/8, or 3/4 inch (1.25, 1.5, or 2 cm) takes a little longer to heat up, but it holds the heat much longer than small stock. Get started on a basic S-hook by drawing out a point on both ends of a rod. Create the hook shape by bending each end to make opposing curves. This "pointed" hook will hang pots over the fire, or suspend hunks of meat over a fire for roasting (essentially, it's a meat hook). For something a little fancier, add a scroll tip to each end of the pointed stock, before you take it from straight to S-shaped. The scrolls can be carefully hammered into shape, or bent with scrolling tongs or needle-nose pliers. Rub beeswax on the piece while it is still very warm for a rust-resistant coating.

HACKS THROUGH HISTORY // FORGING A KNIFE

There are plenty of projects you can do with a blacksmith's forge and tools, but one of the most useful ones—and a good traditional way to get some practice—is making a simple knife. You'll need your forge hot, your tools assembled, and a good piece of steel (like an old file, a railroad spike, or a bit of leaf spring from a vehicle suspension). You could also use lesser steels, like mild steel, though they won't harden as well.

STEP 1 Fire up your forge, and heat the steel in the coals until it is glowing orange.

STEP 2 Pick the metal up with tongs, and hammer it on the anvil to flatten it and begin making one side of the knife's edge.

STEP 3 Reheat as needed, and work on both sides to prevent distorting the steel. Save a good chunk of metal at one end for a handle.

STEP 4 Continue forging the blade's point by hammering to shape the metal, and then give the opposite side a bevel by hammering near the point. Shape the tang (where the handle will go) as desired.

STEP 5 Grind or file the blade into shape and rough sharpen.

STEP 6 Heat the blade until very hot as in Step 1, then dip into a pan of oil to harden the steel. Do a final sharpening, clean off any oils, and epoxy some handle scales onto the tang.

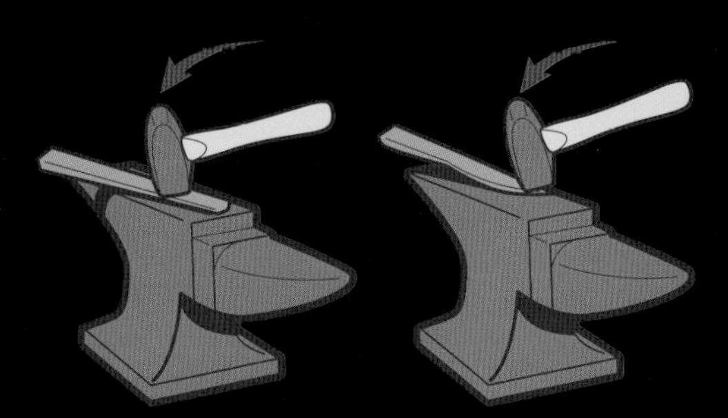

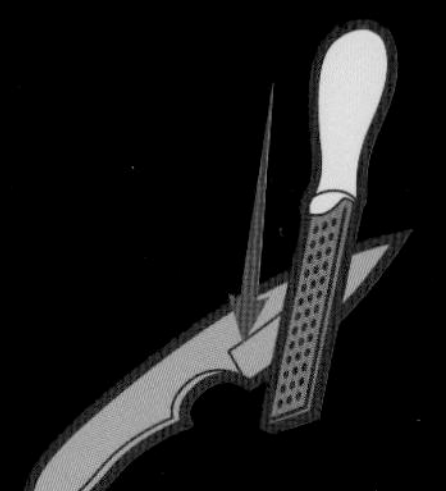

336 DEVELOP STRENGTH

Whether you're in lockup because you deserve it, or you were falsely accused of a crime you didn't commit, you're in a different kind of jungle now—this is truly a place with its own unique set of rules. In there, your own weakness can be your worst enemy (that, and the guy who's been eyeing you like a hungry wolf). One of the most valuable survival assets you can cultivate for this situation is mental toughness. This can be a tall order to fill in lockup, as the lack of sound sleep and the emotional stress can wear away at your fortitude. And to be clear, we're not talking about physical toughness, such as stamina, calluses, pain tolerance, or how many face tattoos you possess (though that last one doesn't hurt). No, this refers to the strength of your will, and the resilience of your mind. It's the ability to tolerate the intolerable and suffer your way through the insufferable.

337 SURVIVE IN THE CAGE

In the jail house, the more people skills and useful talents you possess, the more value you have.

DON'T SNITCH There are very few things of value that a person can possess in the prison, and chief among them is the value of your word. If you can be trusted to keep information to yourself, you are valuable. And if you can't . . . well, there's a reason for the phrase, "snitches get stitches."

EAT HEARTY In recent years, some prison systems have reduced the food volume going to the average inmate. This cost-cutting measure has left prisoners hungry and unable to gain muscle. Don't turn your nose up at any food. Chew it very thoroughly too, to digest every last calorie from it.

FIND SOLACE IN SOLITARY Getting picked on a lot? Maybe it's time for a time-out. Acting up a little can get you thrown in solitary confinement. This can be a living hell for people who aren't wired up for it. But it can also be a break for those who are. Having someone to talk with can save your sanity, so talk to any guards outside the cell (even when they're not there).

SING THE BLUES You probably have more reasons to sing the blues while you're incarcerated than any other time in your life. If you are musically inclined, find an outlet for it. This can pass the time and perhaps even help you to make some friends.

BREW SOME PRUNO There are many colorful names for this "fragrant" prison hooch—but not nearly as many as there are possible ingredients. Mix a yeast source (like raisins or bread) with a sugar-water solution in a tied-up plastic bag. Place the bag in a warm spot and "burp" it periodically as the CO_2 builds up so the bag doesn't explode. Once it stops bubbling, strain and drink—carefully.

LEARN A CRAFT Prison tattooing, toilet-paper sculpture, hair braiding, and other fine crafts can be cultivated in lockup. Pick something you're good at to pass the time.

HACK HAZARDS

KIESTERING

Even the most simpleminded human usually knows they are a person—not a kangaroo. But despite this realization, plenty of people still try to improvise a bodily pouch for storage. Known in some circles as kiestering, this is the risky act of storing items such as drugs, contraband, and even weapons in your rectum (aka "prison wallet"). The hazard here is multipronged. First, anyone engaging in such an act is at risk for bodily injury in a very tender area, leading to infection and even death. Second, handling objects that have been stored this way can transmit diseases from person to person—including cholera, HIV, herpes, and other pathogens. Finally, those with prohibited items always seem to get caught. Whether your fellow inmates catch you or the prison guards, your secret stash can get you in all kinds of trouble.

Quick Tip

Wearing a one-piece jumpsuit? That can be a trip hazard. Make sure you take one leg completely out of your suit when you sit on the toilet. If you get jumped, you can fight without waddling around like a penguin.

338 HIJACK A CART

Whether you're preparing a feast to celebrate your survival after a major disaster, or you're just trying to eat up all your refrigerated food before it goes bad after a power outage, you'll want it to taste good. It's hard to "eat, drink, and be merry" in the face of destruction without something good to eat. Before those frozen steaks, sausages, and burgers thaw out and start to rot, create the grill to end all grills with an old metal shopping cart. You can burn firewood underneath the cart and use the bottom of the basket as the grill. You could also flip the cart on its side and burn a larger fire in the cart while using the side as a grill. Wipe down your improvised grill to clean it off similar to a standard barbecue. Keep some water nearby for fire safety, and use a shovel to move coals and burning chunks of wood in and out of the cart. Once it's ready, set food on the grill of the cart and start cooking. Try not to fuss with your food too much, especially the burgers. Don't flip them until they "release."

339 STEP INTO THE LIGHT

No fire or fuel is needed with a solar oven. Just place your food in the oven, close the door, align the box into the right orientation with the sun, and let the light do the rest.

STEP 1 Place a dark-colored container of food inside the oven and close the door. Adjust the tilt of the oven, and orient it so that the reflectors are facing directly into the sun. Some units come with a "shadow" sighting attachment for perfect alignment.

STEP 2 Turn the oven once every 30 minutes to track the sun through the sky.

STEP 3 As the sun rises higher into the sky and then drops, raise or lower the zenith adjustment to match.

STEP 4 Allow the food to cook. It will usually take about four hours to bake bread. Tender roasts and baked apples will cook in about five hours. Savory soups and stews cook in about six hours.

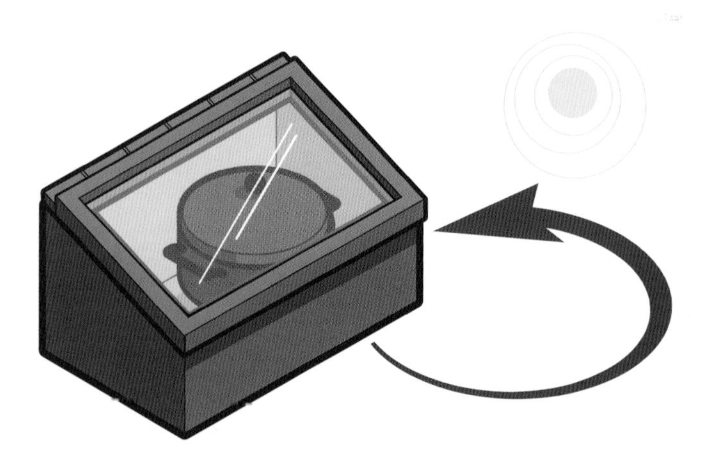

340 FORCE AIR FLOW

When your firewood materials are damp or otherwise slow to burn, a little forced air can be just the thing to stir up the flames. You don't want to start blowing too early. When you just have small flames, you can blow them out (like a candle), but once a small batch of embers are present, you can blow them to life with a little forced air. A drinking straw or a section of telescoping radio antenna can act as a blowpipe to force air. One of those little battery-powered fans that you see people cooling themselves with in the summer will get a fire to roar when aimed at the base of your fledgling blaze. And if you don't have anything that can direct or move air, there's still one more trick left. Put your thumb and forefinger together on each hand, then touch those four digit tips together. This will make a small diamond-shaped opening that you can place against your lips and blow though. This restricts your breath and creates a jet of air. Once you learn to aim this jet, use it to reinvigorate an ailing fire.

341 SPICE IT UP

Variety is a wonderful thing, especially on a "survival" diet. And lucky for us preparedness types, there is a great variety of seasonings and flavors that will last indefinitely. While most of our beloved plant-based spices lose their flavor quickly (especially after being ground up), these are the flavorings that can stand the test of time.

SALT This is one of the most common seasoning items. It never goes bad and it provides necessary nutrition. No desiccant packs or oxygen absorbers are needed to store it, as it preserves itself. Store iodized salt for food seasoning, jerky production, and certain other food-preservation techniques. Keep sea salt for fermentation.

SOY SAUCE This age-old condiment is a great seasoning for many different dishes. And with its insanely high sodium levels, this briny brew will never decompose. Soy sauce can be used as a table condiment, a recipe ingredient, and as a jerky marinade which assists in preservation.

SUGAR Not that white table sugar is particularly nutritious, but it does make a great staple due to its calories and its indefinite shelf life. Add sugar to anything for a sweet upgrade and calorie enhancement.

EXTRACTS Vanilla, rum, mint, and more—there are plenty of different extracts that can turn your bland food into something tastier, and they generally last years or decades.

HONEY Make amazing marinades and sweet sauces with this hive-made product. This blend of natural sugars has an indefinite shelf life and bacteriostatic properties.

VINEGAR This acerbic liquid has an extremely long shelf life, and can be a surprise hit in sauces, dressings, and other flavorful creations. Apple cider vinegar is loved for its complex flavor, and distilled vinegar is used for its clean and simple sour taste.

342 BUILD A FIRE IN A HOLE

The Dakota fire hole is a brilliant Native American fireplace style which limits the fire hazard you'd face in dry, grassy terrain that's buffeted by constant wind. In fact, this type of fireplace burns best with steady wind. Start off by selecting a place where you can dig into soft soil with few roots or rocks. Dig a hole about a foot (30 cm) deep with an opening that is less than a foot wide. Now, dig a second hole of the same depth in line with the wind, then dig a tunnel that connects the bottoms of the two holes together. The upwind hole acts as a wind funnel, catching the breeze and feeding fresh air into the bottom of the other hole, which will be used as a fire pit. The upwind hole can go straight down, and connect to the first hole in a U-shaped fashion, or the upwind hole can simply be funnel-like.

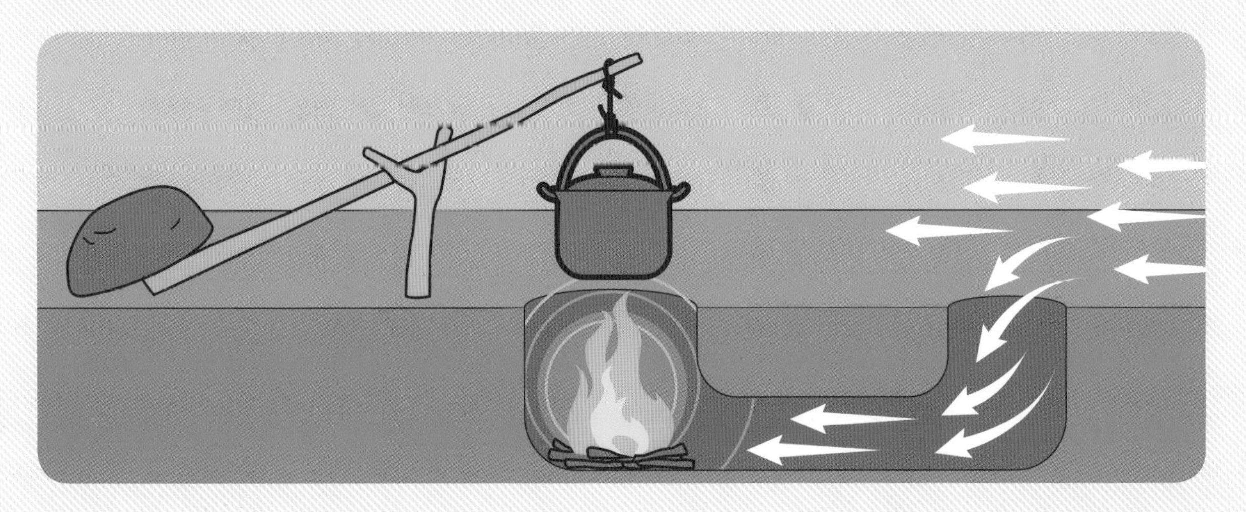

343 JUMP START IT

A dead battery is a common issue that leaves people stranded. A set of jumper cables can bring a car back to life and remedy the situation, if you have another vehicle present that's running. But to be as self-reliant as possible, consider carrying a jump box: a portable battery jump-starter in your vehicle. These battery packs can deliver 400 to 1,700 amps of engine-cranking power with integrated jumper cables that can connect to your dead vehicle battery—and you won't need another running vehicle! Some jump box models have extra features, such as air compressors, battery power level gauges, built-in lights to illuminate your work area, and 12-volt DC charging sockets which can power and recharge devices such as cell phones. Don't forget that you can also push-start a manual-transmission vehicle by getting it rolling and then popping the clutch.

344 SIGNAL FOR AID

The statistics clearly show that people who stay with the car in an emergency are more likely to survive. Your vehicle makes a shelter from the elements, and it offers protection from dangerous animals too. And from an aircraft, it's a lot easier to spot a vehicle than a person. If that wasn't enough, your vehicle provides many materials that can be used for distress signals. Try tearing off a side-view mirror for signaling with sunlight. You can also flash the lights and honk the horn, as long as your battery lasts. You can also light a fire with most car fluids. Engine oil, and fluids for the transmission, and braking and power-steering systems, are all flammable and make dark-colored smoke. Drain these fluids and pour them on a campfire. Release the air from a tire and cut into the sidewall for a pressure release. Roll the tire into a large fire for a huge smoke cloud.

345 GET GOING

After a disaster, or in the middle of nowhere, it may fall on you to patch up your damaged vehicle. In addition to some hand tools and basic survival supplies, you should carry some specialized tools and materials to be more self-reliant and get the job done. This is where a little forethought and education can make all the difference.

UNSTICK IT As a simple example, if your battery is good but your engine won't turn over, it might be your starter. If the starter isn't even clicking, it may be stuck. A few swift taps with a hammer may free it and allow the engine to start.

FILL IT UP What about a dry radiator when you have no water available to pour in? Disconnect the line leading to your windshield sprayers and place it in the radiator reservoir. Hit the button to wash the windshield and it will pump the alcohol-and-water mix into your vehicle's coolant reservoir. This can be enough to get you back on the road until you can do better.

346 CRAFT A FLOP WINCH

The flop winch, often accredited to bushcraft genius Mors Kochanski, is an ingenious way to free a stuck vehicle. You only need a pair of strong 8-foot (2.5-m) poles, and a static rope to do it.

BUILD YOUR WINCH Tie one end of your rope to the vehicle frame or axle. Secure the other end to a solid anchor, such as a sturdy tree, leaving a little slack in the rope. Place the two strong poles together, making an "X" with two short legs. It helps to carve a flat spot on each pole, right where they touch, so the lever pole doesn't slip.

FREE YOURSELF Wrap the rope around the poles as shown, with the pulley pole on your right. Flop the pulley pole over to your left to tighten the rope and then start flopping the lever to begin spooling the rope around the pulley pole. With the mechanical magic of leverage, the poles will wind up the rope and slowly draw the vehicle out of the quagmire you have driven into. If you can, enlist a buddy to help you move the flop lever and keep the rope spooling evenly around the pole.

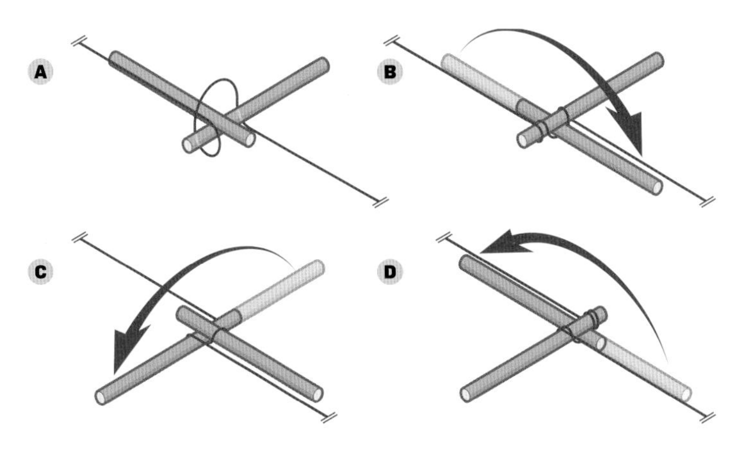

347 PLUG A TIRE

We all get flat tires from time to time, often at the worst possible moment. That's why it's handy to carry the gear to plug a hole in a tire, namely, a tire plug set and a portable air compressor. These two items can repair gaping holes in tires and refill the lost air. The plug set consists of rubber cement, and compatible rubber plugs. You'll also have a tool to shove the plugs into the hole in the tire. The compressor can also provide a little necessary inflation, even when you don't have a flat tire. These air pumps are easy to use; just plug one into your cigarette lighter or a 12-volt power outlet. They are capable of inflating tires on cars, SUVs, and light trucks, and will provide plenty of air compressing power, but it may take several minutes to fully inflate larger tires. Extras can include an in-line tire pressure gauge, long air hoses, and various nozzles.

BUDGET SURVIVAL

GAS JUG AND SIPHON

Sometimes, the only thing wrong with a vehicle is an empty gas tank. You may have to do whatever it takes in an emergency, and siphon from any available gas tank. By carrying a small empty gas jug and a siphon pump, you now have the ability to pull fuel from abandoned vehicles and motorized equipment. Keep in mind that many vehicles have anti-siphon features, and never mix diesel and gasoline. You may also want to carry full gas jugs when traveling thru places with few gas stations. It's better to have the siphon equipment and some gas jugs, and deal with the stinky fumes, than to have no supplies and a serious need for them. Preparation is the key to survival and success.

Worth Every Penny

GAS TANK PATCH

It's surprisingly easy to patch a hole in the fuel tank, by using a super-sticky patch. Purchase a few of these at auto parts stores, and keep them on hand inside your vehicle.

348 CREATE A COMPASS

The earth is essentially a giant magnet with a large magnetic field around it. When a magnetized needle can spin freely, it will align itself with this magnetic field. But what if you've lost your compass, or you just didn't bring one? Don't give up; you might still have the materials to make your own. Improvising a compass can be especially important if you're dealing with overcast weather, thick forests, or other conditions which hamper most direction-finding techniques. And if you think you can't do it, think again. Our ancestors have been making navigational tools for ages, with less refined materials than we have today.

STEP 1 Take a needle or a bit of steel wire, and rub a magnet repeatedly against the needle, going only in one direction. Rub the magnet twenty to thirty times against your prospective compass needle.

STEP 2 Set the needle in a curved leaf in a water-filled container (or larger leaf filled with water).

STEP 3 Block it from the wind completely, and if everything went right, the needle should swing into a north/south alignment. Now you just have to figure out which is which . . .

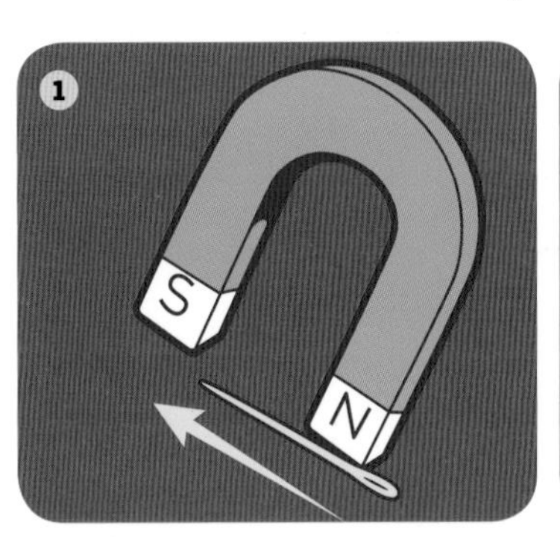

349 USE THE SMALL STUFF

There are plenty of little pathfinding tricks you can use, in the wild and even in an urban setting. You just have to learn to use the ones that are legitimate and ignore the tips you have heard that are wrong.

CARRY COMPASS AND MAP Nothing beats the real thing. Bring a local map and a proper compass, and you'll have the tools to find your way there, and home again.

USE A SATELLITE Most satellite dishes will point the same way in urban and suburban locations. In the northern hemisphere, they often point in a southerly direction.

GET GOOSED Yes, Canadian geese fly south in autumn to spend the winter in a warmer climate, and then they travel north again in the spring. But they also fly to bodies of water and feeding grounds along the way, making their flight path less than reliable. Since you can't read the goose's mind, you have no idea where it's heading.

IGNORE THE MOSS Moss on the north side of the tree? Not in my region. Don't trust algae or moss for directions. Depending on the species and the habitat, it can grow on any side of a tree or rock, and will lead you astray.

STUDY THE STORMS Prevailing winds and bad storms usually come from the same direction over and over. Learn what that is for your area, and you've got a good chance of using that to point the way.

MAKE A SUN COMPASS Around midday, poke a stick into the ground and place a rock where the end of the shadow falls. Wait an hour or two, and mark the tip of the shadow again with another rock. The line between these two rocks is an east-west line. The stick is in the south, the first rock you set is in the west, and the second rock is in the east. These contraptions can't fit in your pocket or travel with you, but they can be set up in different places at midday to keep you on track as you travel through the wild.

Quick Tip

Learn the local landmarks. Do the valleys and rivers all run a certain way in your area? Where is that huge mountain peak located in relation to the area you'll hike? Learning the land can prevent getting lost.

HACKS THROUGH HISTORY // LUNAR NAVIGATION

For thousands of years, our ancestors have observed that the moon moves from east to west, just like the sun. Due to the moon running on a different schedule than the sun, it may not rise or set at a convenient time to assist your navigation, but it at least follows a similar path. And that's not the only way that the moon can give directions. The crescent moon is a shape recognized around the world, but few people realize what the "horns" of the moon are telling us. When the crescent moon is high in the night sky, use a straight stick (or just your imagination) to make a line that touches each tip of the "horns" and extends down to the horizon. This spot on the horizon will be roughly south (for those in the Northern Hemisphere). If you're trying this below the equator, the line passing by the horns and extending to the ground will show a rough northerly position. This trick also works when the moon is in other phases (except full and new).

INDEX

D

E

F

INDEX

INDEX

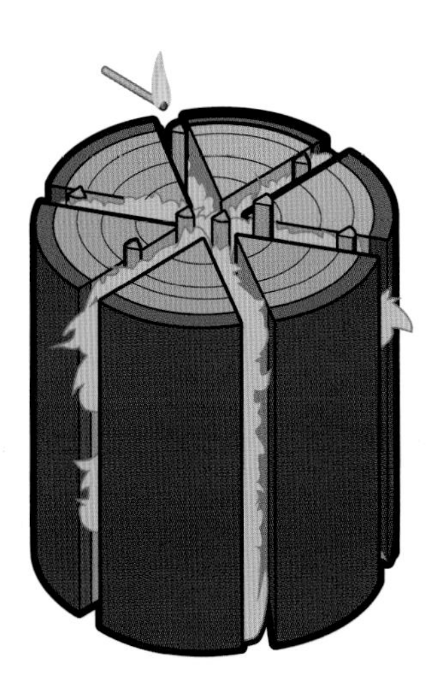

ABOUT TIM MACWELCH

This is the seventh *Outdoor Life* survival manual from Tim MacWelch. His love of the outdoors started at a young age, growing up on a farm in the rolling hills of Virginia. Tim became interested in survival skills and woodcraft as an offshoot of backpacking as a teen—while out in remote areas, it seemed like a smart plan to learn some skills. The majority of his training over the years has involved testing survival skills and devising new ones, but the biggest leaps forward came from his experience as a teacher. He has worked with Boy Scouts, youth groups, summer camps, and adults in all walks of life, as well as providing outdoor skills training for numerous personnel in law enforcement, search and rescue organizations, all branches of the United States Armed Forces, the State Department, and Department of Justice agencies. Tim and his wilderness school have been featured on *Good Morning America* and several *National Geographic* programs, and featured in many publications including *Conde Nast Traveler,* the *Washington Post,* and *American Survival Guide.* Tim is also the resident survivalist for the Outdoor Channel's hit hunting and fishing radio show, *The Revolution,* with Jim and Trav Ferguson. Since late 2010, Tim has written hundreds of pieces for *Outdoor Life* and many other publications. Tim's current and past articles and galleries can be found at outdoorlife.com. Tim has been an active practitioner of survival skills for over 3 decades, and a teacher of outdoor skills for more than 20 years.

ABOUT OUTDOOR LIFE

Since it was founded in 1898, *Outdoor Life* has provided survival tips, wilderness skills, gear reports, and other essential information for hands-on outdoor enthusiasts. Each issue delivers the best advice in sportsmanship—as well as thrilling true-life tales, gear reviews, insider hunting, shooting, and fishing hints, and more—to more than 1 million readers. Its survival-themed web site also covers disaster preparedness and the skills to thrive anywhere from the backcountry to the urban jungles.

ABOUT ADVANCED SURVIVAL TRAINING

When you were a kid and you saw the other kids riding a bike, was just watching them enough to be able to do it yourself? Of course not!

The same is true when learning survival skills. You can learn a certain amount from books and videos, but you have to actually do the skills to gain the experience for yourself. And there's no better place to gain that experience than under the watchful eye of Tim MacWelch himself—owner and head instructor at Advanced Survival Training. Acquire the skills you've always wanted—without the painful learning curve of struggling on your own! Come and take a class. You can learn more about these hands-on classes, held in Virginia, USA, by visiting the survival school at www.AdvancedSurvivalTraining.com.

ACKNOWLEDGMENTS

I would like to thank my family for their encouragement and patience as I took time away from them to write another book. I'd also like to thank all of my teammates at Weldon Owen Publishing, especially Mariah Bear and Allister Fein—thank you for all your hard work and your confidence in me. And to Conor Buckley, I'm very appreciative of your fun, colorful and detailed illustrations. Thank you also to my friends at *Outdoor Life* magazine. It is my honor and privilege to continue writing for you. Finally, to my students – you keep me inspired; you teach me new tricks; you provide me with great company and conversations; and I am ever grateful for the kindness and support you have shown me.

CREDITS

PHOTOGRAPHY All photos are from Shutterstock except: Patty Brookes: (Author Introduction); JRPInternational (www.jrpproducts.com): 134; Morakniv: 157; SteriPen: 055; Walt Sturgeon: Hacks Through History: Cracked Cap Polypore; Waterbob: 061; Western Frontier: 070.

ILLUSTRATION All illustration by Conor Buckley except: Hayden Foell 143, 145, 162; Vic Kulihin Hacks Through History: Sand Pit, 271, 342.

A NOTE TO READERS

While every skill in this book has been fact-checked and field-tested, the publisher makes no warranty, express or implied, that the information is appropriate for every individual, situation, or purpose, and assumes no responsibility for errors or omissions.

The information in this book is presented for entertainment value only, for an adult audience. Before attempting any new activity, make sure you are aware of your own limitations and have adequately researched all applicable risks; this book is not intended to replace professional advice from an experienced outdoor guide.

Always follow all manufacturer instructions when using the equipment featured in this book. If the manufacturer of your equipment does not recommend use of the equipment in the fashion depicted, you should comply with the manufacturer's recommendations.

You assume the risk and full responsibility for all of your actions, and the publishers will not be held responsible for any loss or damage of any sort, whether consequential, incidental, special, or otherwise that may result from the information presented.

weldon**owen**

PRESIDENT & PUBLISHER Roger Shaw
SVP, SALES & MARKETING Amy Kaneko
ASSOCIATE PUBLISHER Mariah Bear
ASSOCIATE EDITOR Ian Cannon
CREATIVE DIRECTOR Kelly Booth
ART DIRECTOR Allister Fein
PRODUCTION DIRECTOR Michelle Duggan
IMAGING MANAGER Don Hill

Weldon Owen would like to thank Kevin Broccoli of BIM for the index.

Weldon Owen
1045 Sansome Street, Suite 100
San Francisco, CA 94111
www.weldonowen.com

ISBN 978-168188-424-0
10 9 8 7 6 5 4 3 2 1
2018 2019 2020 2021 2022
Printed in China

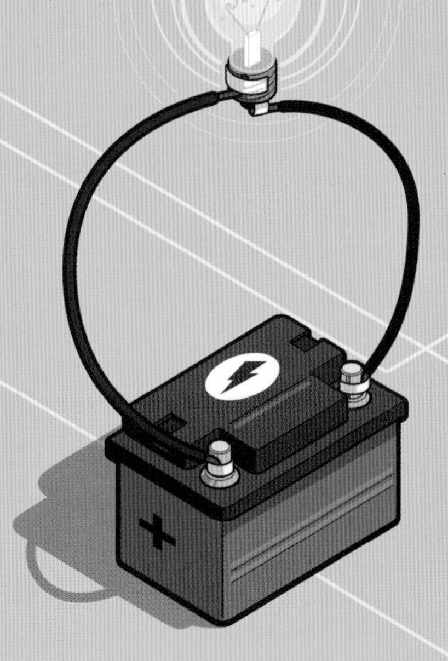

OUTDOOR LIFE

GROUP EDITORIAL DIRECTOR Anthony Licata
GROUP CREATIVE DIRECTOR Sean Johnston
EXECUTIVE EDITOR Alex Robinson
SENIOR EDITOR Natalie Krebs
DEPUTY EDITOR Gerry Bethge
FISHING EDITOR Joe Cermele
HUNTING EDITOR Will Brantley
SHOOTING EDITOR John B. Snow
GROUP MANAGING EDITOR Jean McKenna
MANAGING EDITOR Margaret M. Nussey
PRODUCTION MANAGER Judith Weber
COPY CHIEF Cindy Martin
CREATIVE DIRECTOR Pete Sucheski
ASSOCIATE ART DIRECTOR Russ Smith
PHOTOGRAPHY DIRECTOR John Toolan
DIGITAL DIRECTOR Nate Matthews

2 Park Avenue
New York, NY 10016
www.outdoorlife.com